The Old English Sheep Dog

Joan McDonald Brearley

Title page: Champion Tamara's Qubic, owned by Mary Anne and Robert Brocious of Livonia, Michigan.

Distributed in the UNITED STATES by T.F.H. Publications, Inc., One T.F.H. Plaza, Neptune City, NJ 07753; in CANADA to the Pet Trade by H & L Pet Supplies Inc., 27 Kingston Crescent, Kitchener, Ontario N2B 2T6; Rolf C. Hagen Ltd., 3225 Sartelon Street, Montreal 382 Quebec; in CANADA to the Book Trade by Macmillan of Canada (A Division of Canada Publishing Corporation), 164 Commander Boulevard, Agincourt, Ontario M1S 3C7; in ENGLAND by T.F.H. Publications Limited, Cliveden House/Priors Way/Bray, Maidenhead, Berkshire SL6 2HP, England; in AUSTRALIA AND THE SOUTH PACIFIC by T.F.H. (Australia) Pty. Ltd., Box 149, Brookvale 2100 N.S.W., Australia; in NEW ZEALAND by Ross Haines & Son, Ltd., 18 Monmouth Street, Grey Lynn, Auckland 2, New Zealand; in SINGAPORE AND MALAYSIA by MPH Distributors (S) Pte., Ltd., 601 Sims Drive, #03/07/21, Singapore 1438; in the PHILIPPINES by Bio-Research, 5 Lippay Street, San Lorenzo Village, Makati Rizal; in SOUTH AFRICA by Multipet Pty. Ltd., 30 Turners Avenue, Durban 4001. Published by T.F.H. Publications, Inc. Manufactured in the United States of America by T.F.H. Publications, Inc.

CONTENTS

How to Feed the Newborn Puppies . . . Feeding the Adult Dog . . .
The All-Meat Diet Controversy . . . Obesity . . . Gastric Torsion

Acknowledgments

Much time and many people are involved before a book is finally published. All those who have contributed so generously to help make this book a lasting tribute to a magnificent breed have my sincerest thanks for giving so willingly of their knowledge, memorabilia, and photographs. I appreciated the efforts of Diane Rau, secretary of the parent club; June Soderstrom and Joanne Sewell of Australia; Miss Chieko of Japan; Robert R. Shomer, V.M.D., for veterinary counsel over the years; and to my parents, Stephen and Lillian McDonald, who helped care for and have enjoyed my dogs and who instilled in me my great love for all of God's creatures.

Joan Brearley
Sea Bright, New Jersey

Preface

It is not the purpose of this book to name each and every Old English Sheepdog, breeder, owner, or exhibitor that ever lived, nor is it to chronicle a complete history of the breed since its beginning. There are other books which have striven to accomplish this and there are enough other things to be said about the breed without resorting to any such repetition or competition. Neither is it the intention of this book to educate or instruct those of us who have been familiar with the breed for these many years. We have learned through experience the gentle art of doing our best to improve and perpetuate the Old English Sheepdog.

It *is* the purpose of this book to reach those who are drawn to the breed as it exists today and who wish to know the highlights of its history and background in the dog world; it is, as well, an update for the book I wrote with Marlene Anderson, published in 1974, entitled *This is the Old English Sheepdog.* Our Old English Sheepdogs have remained so beloved, so admired, that anything new or old that is said or written about them can be of value if it adds to our knowledge regarding their care and place in our lives.

We would like to think that this book is another entry in our Old English Sheepdog mutual admiration society and that all who read it and enjoy our Bobtails will regard it as the meaningful tribute to this wonderful breed that the author meant it to be.

About the Author

Joan Brearley is the first to admit that animals in general—and dogs in particular—are a most important part of her life. Since childhood there has been a steady stream of dogs, cats, birds, fish, rabbits, snakes, alligators, turtles, etc., for her own personal menagerie. Over the years she has owned over 30 breeds of purebred dogs, as well as countless mixtures, since the door was never closed to a needy or homeless animal.

A graduate of the American Academy of Dramatic Arts, where she studied acting and directing, Joan started her career as an actress, dancer, and writer for movie magazines. She studied ballet at the Agnes DeMille Studios and was with an Oriental dance company which performed at the Carnegie Recital Hall. She studied journalism and creative writing at Columbia University and has written for radio, television, and magazines; she was a copywriter for some of the major New York advertising agencies, working on the accounts of Metro-Goldwyn-Mayer movie studios, Burlington Mills, *Cosmopolitan* magazine, White Owl Cigars, and *World-Telegram* and *Sun* newspapers.

While a television producer-director for a major network, Joan worked on "Nick Carter, Master Detective"; "Did Justice Triumph"; and news and special feature programs. Joan has written, cast, directed, produced and, on occasion, starred in television commercials. She has written special material or programs for such personalities as Dick Van Dyke, Amy Vanderbilt, William B. Williams, Gene Rayburn, Bill Stern, and many other people prominent in the entertainment world. She has appeared as a guest on several of the nation's most popular talk shows, including Mike Douglas, Joe Franklin, Cleveland Amory, David Susskind, and the "Today Show," to name just a few. Joan was selected for inclusion in the *Directory of the Foremost Women in Communications* in 1969 and the book *Two Thousand Women of Achievement* in 1971.

Her accomplishments in the dog fancy include being a breeder and exhibitor of top show dogs, a writer and columnist for various magazines, and an author of over 30 books on dogs and cats. She is a contributor to *World Book Encyclopedia* and *Funk and Wagnalls Encyclopedia* as well. For five years she was Executive Vice President of the Popular Dogs Publishing Company and editor of *Popular Dogs* magazine, the national prestige publication for the fancy at that time. Her editorials on the status and welfare of animals have been reproduced as educational pamphlets by dog clubs and organizations in many countries of the world.

Joan is almost as active in the cat fancy and in almost as many capacities. The same year her Afghan Hound, Champion Sahadi Shikari, won the Ken-L Ration Award as Top Hound of the Year, one of her Siamese cats won the comparable honor in the cat fancy. She has owned and/or bred almost every breed of cat. Many of her cats and dogs are Best in Show winners and have appeared in magazines and on television. For several years she was editor of the annual *Cat Fanciers' Association Yearbook*, and her book *All About Himalayan Cats* was published in 1976.

In addition to breeding and showing dogs since 1955, Joan has been active as a member and on the Board of Directors of the Kennel Club of Northern New Jersey, the Afghan Hound Club of America, the Stewards Club of America, and the Dog Fanciers Club. She has been an American Kennel Club approved judge since 1961. She has appeared as a guest speaker at many dog clubs and humane organizations, crusading for humane legislation, and has won several awards and citations for her work in this field. She is one of the best-known and most knowledgeable people in the animal world. Joan is proud of the fact that her Champion Sahadi Shikari was top-winning Afghan Hound in the history of the breed for several years and remains in the top three even today. No other breeder to date can claim to have bred a Westminster Group winner in her first homebred litter. She has also bred champion Yorkshire Terriers.

Joan is a former Trustee and is still an active member of the Morris Animal Foundation, does free-lance publicity and public relations work, is a Daughter of the American Revolution and member of the New York Genealogical Society. In her "spare" time she exhibits her needlework (for which she has also won prizes), haunts the art and auction galleries, is a graduate auctioneer with the full title of Colonel, and is a Realtor Associate. At the same time she is working toward her degree in Criminal Justice and Law at Brookdale Community College.

This impressive list of activities doesn't include all of her accomplishments, since she has never been content to have just one interest at a time, managing to dovetail several occupations and avocations to make for a fascinating career.

Joan lives with her dogs, cats, hamsters, guinea pigs, and over 20 tropical birds in a townhouse on the oceanfront in Sea Bright, New Jersey, where she also serves as Councilwoman, Secretary and active member of the First Aid Squad, and Trustee of both the Sea Bright Village Association and the Sea Bright Partnership. On the county level she is a Director, Assistant Recording Secretary, and Publicity Chairwoman of the Monmouth County Federation of Republican Women and has been appointed to the Monmouth County Heritage Committee by the Board of Chosen Freeholders.

Circa 1947   the Reverend William Buchanan with an Old English Sheepdog owned by Mrs. Edward P. Renner of Great Barrington, Massachusetts.

10

Chapter 1

Early Canine History

Many millions of years ago dinosaurs and other strange-looking creatures roamed the earth. As "recently" as 60 million years ago a mammal existed, which resembled a civet cat, and it is believed to have been the common ancestor of dogs, cats, wolves, and coyotes. This animal was the long-extinct Miacis (pronounced *My-a-kiss*). The Miacis were long-bodied, long-tailed, short-legged beasts that stalked and chased their prey; grasped it in their long, powerful, fanged jaws; and gnashed their food with their teeth. Just 15 million years ago the Tomarctus evolved from the earlier Miacis and provided an even truer genetic basis for the more highly intelligent prototype of the domesticated dog.

It has been only 15 to 20 thousand years since the first attempts were made to domesticate these ferocious, tree-climbing animals. Archaeologists have uncovered the skeletal remains of dogs that date back to the age of the cavemen and that co-existed with them as members of their families in several ancient civilizations.

There are several schools of thought among scholars and scientists as to the exact location of the very first creatures to live with man. Some contend that the continent of Africa was the original locale. Ancient remains unearthed near Lake Baikal date back to 9000 B.C. Recent diggings in nearby Iraq that are said to date back 12,000 years have produced evidence of what is called the Palegawra dog. Siberian remains are said to date back 20,000 years. The Jaguar Cave Dogs of North America have been dated circa 8400 B.C. Others say Asia and claim the Chinese wolf to be the ancestor of the dog.

Advocates of the Chinese wolf theory point out that the language barrier was responsible for this animal not being known or acknowledged in earlier comparisons. When scientists could not translate Chinese writing, they could not study or authenticate the early Oriental findings. Their theory is also based on the presence of the overhanging bone found in the jawbone of both the Chinese wolf and the dog. This is believed to be significant in the change from their being strictly carnivorous creatures to creatures that eventually became omnivorous carnivores.

The general consensus among scientists dealing with prehistoric and archaelogical studies seems to settle on the likelihood that dogs were being domesticated in many parts of the world at approximately the same period of time. Since dogs were to become so essential to man's very existence, they were naturally absorbed into family life wherever and whenever they were found. Climate, geography, and other environmental conditions all played a part in the evolution of the dog; and much later in the individual types, sizes, and breeds of dogs. The three most primitive types originated in three parts of the globe. While all bore certain very exact characteristics, the wolf-type seemed to evolve in southern Asia and Australia, the pariahs in Asia Minor and Japan, and the Basenjis in Africa.

The dingo found its way north to Russia and Alaska, across what is now the Bering Straits, into North America. The pariahs moved far north, learned to pull sleds, and developed into the various northern breeds in the arctic regions. The Basenjis and Greyhounds coursed the desert sands and hunted in the jungles of Africa when they weren't guarding royal palaces in Egypt. As dogs found their way across Europe, they served as guard dogs in the castles, rescue dogs in the Alps, barge dogs on the canals, and hunting dogs in the forests. The smaller dogs were bred down even smaller and became companions and pets for the aristocracy. Kings and queens of the world have always maintained their own personal kennels for their favorite breeds.

BREED DEVELOPMENT

While the caveman used the dog primarily as a hunter to help provide meat and to provide meat themselves, he also made use of the fur as clothing and used the warmth from the dogs' bodies when sleeping. Dogs were to become even more functional as time went by, according to the dictates of the climates and geographical regions. Definite physical changes were taking place which eventually would distinguish one dog from another even within the same area. Ears ranged in size from the little flaps that we see on terriers to the large upright ears on the Ibizan Hounds. Noses either flattened greatly, as they did with the Pekingese, or they grew to amazing lengths, as we see in the Borzoi. Tails grew to be long and plumelike, such as those we see on the Siberian Husky, or doubled up into a curl, such as those we see on the Pug. Legs grew long and thin for coursing Greyhounds or were short and bent for the digging breeds such as the Dachshunds and Basset Hounds. Sizes went from one extreme to the other, ranging from the tiniest Chihuahua all the way up to the biggest of all breeds, the Irish Wolfhound. Coat lengths became longer or shorter. There were thick, woolly coats for the northern breeds and smooth, short coats for the dogs that worked in warmer climates.

SENSORY PERCEPTION

As the dogs changed in physical appearance, their instincts and sensory perceptions also developed. Their sense of smell is said to be 30 million times keener than that of their human counterparts, allowing them to pick up and follow the scents of other animals miles in the distance. Their eyes developed to such a sharpness that they could spot moving prey on the horizon far across desert sands. Their hearing became so acute that they were able to pick up the sounds and vibrations of the smallest creatures rustling in the leaves across an open field or in a dense forest.

All things considered, it becomes easy to comprehend why man and dog became such successful partners in survival and why their attraction and affection for each other is such a wondrous thing.

YOUR DOG'S ZOOLOGICAL CHART

In the scheme of things, namely your dog's place in the world of living things, the correct line of descent is as follows: Kingdom: Animalia; Phylum: Chordata; Class: Mammalia; Order: Carnivora; Family: Canidae; Genus: Canis; Species: familiaris.

International, English and American Champion Prospect Blue Rodger, owned and shown throughout his remarkable show ring career by Mona Berkowitz of Thousand Oaks, California.

14

Chapter 2

The Breed in Great Britain

The British have always been known as dog lovers. Dogs, no matter what size or for what purpose they may have been created, have always been prominent in the lives of the people. Dogs have worked and played with the peasants and with royalty, and everything in between, ever since earliest times. Little wonder then that the marvelous working dog we have come to know as the Old English Sheepdog was to make a mark for itself over the years until it has gained the place it enjoys today—first in the field, and now in the field and the show and obedience rings. And just as night follows day, there soon came to be a governing body to administer to the fancy to protect and propagate the good and welfare of our beloved dogs.

THE KENNEL CLUB

The Kennel Club in England was founded in 1873 and held its premiere dog show that very first year at the Crystal Palace. Shortly thereafter came the publication of a stud book and their publication, *The Kennel Gazette*, used to announce the registrations and to publicize all other matters concerning pedigreed dogs.

The enormity of the sport of dogs in Britain continues to impress us when we avidly follow the results of Crufts competition, for instance. Crufts is not only the largest dog show in England, but in the world, with entries exceeding 10,000 dogs . . . and it's growing still! Each year England has many large shows with entries in the thousands.

The British allow dogs in all public places, on transportation vehicles, and at private parties—canines truly are members of the family. There is no denying it, the British adore their dogs.

FIRST CLASSES AT THE SHOWS

1873 marked the first of the separate classes for Old English Sheepdogs. This was at the Curzon Hall Show in Birmingham, England. There was an entry of three, but at least the breed had gained recognition. By 1888, at this same show, there were two classes for an entry of 20, and by 1899 there were 50 entries at the Kennel Club show.

Around this period of time and at the turn of the century, those who contributed greatly to the breed were Dr. Edwardes-Ker, Mrs. Fare Fosse, F. Freeman Lloyd, and J. Thomas. Then there was Sir Humphrey de Trafford, founder of the first Old English Sheepdog Club, serving as its first president until 1911. He was perhaps best known for his bitch, Ch. Dame Barbara. Other prominent breeders were W. G. Weager, Parry Thomas, Dr. W. Bott, F. H. Travis, H. Dickson, Dr. Stork (a baby doctor, perhaps?), Messrs. Tilley, F. W. Wilmott, Aubrey Hopwood, G. F. Wilkinson, and E. Y. Butterworth, Dr. Lock, R. Abbot, and Messrs. Thickett and Shaw.

According to *Hutchinson's Popular and Illustrated Dog Encyclopedia*, one of the earliest dogs of record was Ch. Sir Cavendish, whelped in May 1887 and sired by Sir Caradoe ex Dame Ruth. He was bred by Dr. Edwardes-Ker, owned by Dr. Lock, and was shown from 1888 to 1894. It is acknowledged that he was behind many of the pedigrees at the time and it was on his name that the "Watch" prefix line was established. Ch. Young Watch, owned by Messrs. Thickett and Shaw, was himself the sire of many good dogs, including Ch. Stylish Boy, Ch. Victor Cavendish, and Ch. Bouncing Lass, purchased as a puppy by the Tilley brothers for over £200 . . . a considerable sum in those days. This dog later went to America. Young Watch's sire, Ch. Watch Boy, is credited with making a major contribution to the breed.

WALL-EYED BOB

One of the first and surely most famous of the early "greats" was a dog named Wall-eyed Bob. Born about 1883, he never made the grade in the show rings, and thus never had the champion title before his name, but he surely left his mark on the breed.

One of his famous get was Jack's Delight and he was the grandsire of Harkaway, a dog specially renowned for correct coat. He was also the grandsire of Sir James, the sire of Ch. Rough Weather, whelped in 1900, and Ch. Fair Weather, whelped in 1898. Fair Weather had Wall-eyed Bob as her grandsire on her dam's side, and she was later stuffed and resided at the Natural History Museum. It should be remembered that it was Mrs. Fare Fosse who bred these two famous "Weather" dogs, as well as Ch. Tip Top Weather, Glorious Weather, and Moonshine Weather, to mention just a few. She also was the first female president of the club in 1913.

Wall-eyed Bob was exhibited at the 1898 Botanic Show when he was at least 15 years of age and still a prime specimen. He died shortly thereafter, but present-day championship requirements would have made him a champion even then. He was responsible for a bitch named Wall-eyed Flo; and it was this "wall-eyed" characteristic, handed down to some of our modern-day dogs, that was much desired by the farmers of the time, who believed that wall-eyed dogs maintained their remarkable eyesight.

EARLY BRITISH WINNERS

The first two Old English Sheepdogs to gain fame were named Sir Cavendish and Ch. Sir Ethelwolf, owned by Dr. Edwardes-Ker. Another was Wall-eyed Bob, reportedly sold for 20 shillings at a public house. This dog was later owned by Mr. J. Thomas, who was known for bringing some of the first purebred dogs from England to encourage breeding programs in the United States. Bob was later owned by Mrs. Fare Fosse. Thought to be a qualified specimen, Bob was not at all like the type of dog depicted in Taplin's book published in 1803.

In 1890, Watch Boy was born and was a better specimen with a coat which more or less resembled that which we see today. This dog was followed by Harkaway, Ch. Fairweather (bred by Mrs. Fosse), and winner of over 50 first prizes and innumerable trophies at shows.

At the turn of the century and in the years before World War I, the most important dog in the breed was named Shepton Laddie, owned by Mr. J. J. Oakman. Mrs. A. E. Phillips showed her Home Farm Shepherdess, and Mrs. S. Charter her Brentwood dogs, most notable of which were Brentwood Hero and Brentwood Merry Widow. In the years following the war, plaudits were going to Mrs. K. M. Beard's Elkington Squire and Mrs. E. Brakespear's Faithful Tramp. Mrs. Fosse continued her interest in the breed and brought out her Matchless Weather and Glorious Weather. Darkest of All, owned by Mr. W. N. Tod, was competing with Mrs. M. F. Sheffield's dog, Blue Blossom. These are just a few of the champions that were competing during these early years in Great Britain.

Mr. E. Y. Butterworth made a remarkable contribution to the breed which extended over the turn of the century. His Champion Bouncing Lass, born June 18, 1899, was sired by Young Watch ex Peggy Primrose. Peggy was a direct descendant of Watch Boy and made history, as did Dairymaid, one of the best bitches in the breed. She won her first three Challenge Certificates at Hinchley in 1901 and at Manchester and Aquarium in 1902.

When sold to Mr. Tilley, she added championships at the Crystal Palace, Birmingham, Liverpool, Birkenhead, Crufts, Leamington, and Richmond to her list as well. These were all prestige shows then, and she went on to win the Brewers and Lord Mayor's Cup at Birmingham in 1902. In just 12 months she captured nine cups, 11 medals, and over 100 first prizes. In that same year she took two firsts, a championship, and the Vanderbilt Cup in New York. She did a repeat performance in 1904.

JUDGE LANE AND CHAMPION CUPID'S DART

In 1900 Charles Henry Lane, a breeder, exhibitor and judge in England, published a book he had written entitled, *All About Dogs—A Book for Doggy People*, in which he revealed some of his own personal experiences with Sheepdogs at the turn of the century. His account of his experience with the Bobtail is so charming that we included it here, noting that the chapter title is "Dogs Used in Work," and the listing for the breed is called "Bobtail Sheep Dogs."

Another very favourite breed with many is the Old English, also called the Short-tailed, more commonly known as "Bobtailed" Sheep Dogs, and, except for being rather large and carrying a heavy coat, both of which are objections in a house, they are very agreeable companions as they are very warm, in fact devoted, in their affections; capital guards; quick to learn and carry out their owner's wishes; well able to take care of themselves in any difference with any other breed of dog; and so marvelously active and muscular that I have seen a "Bobtail" win prizes in open jumping competition with all other breeds. To look at them no one would have the slightest idea of their lively and active character. I have had a great deal to do with them, having kept and bred them for many years, and almost my earliest remembrance of any kind of dog is connected with a shaggy old customer of this breed called "Billie," belonging to a very old friend of mine, at a Somersetshire farm, with whom I was on the closest terms of friendship and whose companionship used to impart a strong "doggy" odour to my garments on the occasions of my visiting him. I am very pleased to say that this breed, which had been much neglected on account of the influx of Scotch Collies and was even in danger of becoming almost extinct, has been very much taken up the last few years; and even in London you now often see very decent specimens accompanying fashionable ladies and carriages. It may not be generally known, but I have proved it by actual practice with a great many of my own specimens, that a "Bobtail" is a capital dog to follow carriage, trap, or a rider on horseback. I have come many miles, on the darkest nights across country roads and lanes with a couple following me, and never knew an instance where they missed me or failed to turn up at the end of the journey, and the same in the crowded streets of a large city I often visit. It is supposed to be one of the oldest breeds of dog we have; and in one of Shakespeare's old English comedies, which was lately mounted in unusually first-class style and with many novel realistic effects by a popular and well-known manager at a West End theatre, a quaint old shepherd appeared on the stage, accompanied by a rugged

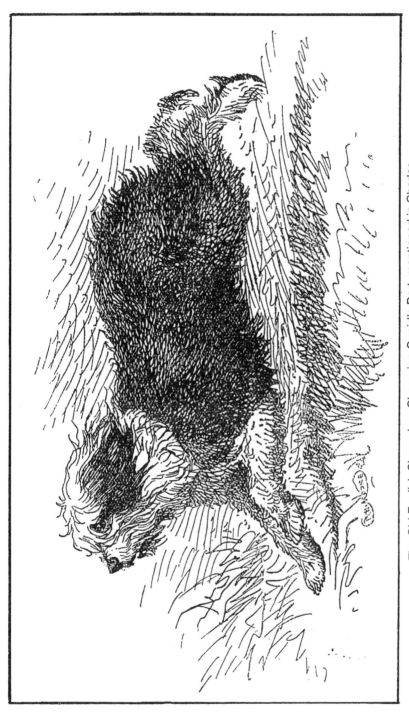

The Old Old English Sheepdog, Champion Cupid's Dart, mentioned in Charles Henry Lane's book, *All About Dogs*. Mr. Lane, a breeder, exhibitor and judge, published his book in 1900 and writes about this dog, owned by F. Wilmot.

Bobtail who made herself quite at home in her novel surroundings, and gave a great finish to the scene. The Bobtail in question was lent by me, and is the sister of a well-known "Champion" belonging to one of the most successful exhibitors and spirited buyers of Sheepdogs in the United Kingdom. The points of this breed, as show specimens, are: Head square and large, eyes rather small and dark, but wall or marble eyes are considered an advantage when obtainable, particularly in light-coloured specimens; body should be large and powerful, without coarseness, sloping rather to front; legs straight, very strong and muscular, well covered with hair down to toes; hindquarters high and heavy; ears small for size of animal, neatly set on side of head, densely coated with a harsh, straight and broken coat of weather-resisting character; colours very various, but shades of blue, mixed with white, especially on head, chest and forelegs, most desired; weight 45 to 55 pounds. Champion Cupids Dart . . . is one of the best of the breed at present before the public.

I think this excerpt from Mr. Lane's book gives a marvelous insight into the breed at the turn of the century and an intriguing comparison of the Standard for the breed at that time. The drawing of Champion Cupids Dart, which was included in the book, is in my private collection.

IMPORTANT OPINIONS
Two of the most respected men in the breed in early days were Mr. H. A. Tilley and Aubrey Hopwood. Being breeders of note, they quite naturally had their opinions on just what the Old English Sheepdog should stand for.

Mr. Tilley wrote in part, ". . . built on lines of a light, heavyweight hunter. First and foremost, good legs and feet . . . ." Surprisingly, when writing on color he said, "The general colour is blue or grey-and-white, sometimes black-and-white or occasionally all white." He further stated, "It is highly intelligent, and as a working dog has no superior. It will retrieve, watch, herd and tend cattle and sheep, can run rabbit or rat; takes readily to water; is generally good-tempered and does not fight or seek a quarrel with other dogs, but can hold its own when occasion arises." Do we hear any arguments?

Aubrey Hopwood stated his opinion a little differently. "He is an ideal companion. His common sense, his hardihood, and his innate good manners mark him out as a canine 'pal.' He is devoted to his master, an excellent guard and house dog, and he is endowed with a gentlemanly instinct for moving about a room with the least possible noise and fuss. Give him his food at regular hours, all the exercise you can manage, and he will thrive—even in London . . . In his quaint, unobtrusive way he will make himself at home in a drawing-room, a railway carriage, a hansom cab, or the show bench. Wherever you take him, he is ready to adapt himself to his surroundings; sensible, even-tempered, picturesque, and never ridiculous."

While the English Club was founded in 1888 and had a very small entry for their first show, by 1914 the entry for their "Specialty" reached an amazing 111 Old English Sheepdogs! Unfortunately, with the onset of World War I, not only dog shows but the very dogs themselves suffered severe and tragic setbacks. Large dogs were hard to feed if you could get meat at all, and many a top-quality breeding stud or brood bitch was put down because of the inability to maintain them. This applied to all breeds of dogs, of course, and tragically, there were even reports of dogs being sacrificed for food. Knowing how the British revere their dogs, we can only imagine what a supreme sacrifice this meant to them and how it almost destroyed their long-range breeding programs.

POST-WORLD WAR I

The decade of the 1920s represented another start. It meant picking up the pieces with the few dogs they managed to save and to begin once again. In 1925, Mrs. Breakspear's Ch. Faithful Tramp was the sire of Ch. Tommy Tittlemouse, a winner in 1928 and owned by Miss Tireman. By 1929 Mrs. Tod was showing Ch. Wall-eyed Bill, the sire of another of her 1929 winners, namely Ch. Tamara. In 1924 Miss Flint made a champion of her Newcote Blossom, sired by Mrs. Sheffield's Ch. Blue Coat. In 1927 Mr. Sander's Ch. Lucky Prince was sire of Mr. A. Howard's Ch. Blue Stocking and Mrs. Sheffield's Ch. Blue Knight was the sire of her Ch. Hillgarth Blue Boy, also known in the rings in 1927.

In April 1926, Champion Aristocrat was whelped. He was sired by another well-known dog, Sergeant Murphy, a son of Ch. Night Raider. In 1928, Aristocrat won four prizes, in 1929 two prizes, and in 1930 four Challenge Certificates and his championship. Oddly enough, he never won a Kennel Club championship show. Such is the way of fame . . . .

Around the time Tommy Tittlemouse was being shown Miss A. Tireman, a leading breeder, was also showing International Champion Pastorale Bopeep. Formerly named Montford Lucy, the dog was shown under its new name and enjoyed great success, once acquired by Miss Tireman. The Pastorale name was known during the period with Wadhurst Bobby Pastorale, sire of Ragtag of Pickhurst, bred and owned by Mr. T. E. T. Shanks.

Certainly a contender for the "most unusual name" title was Ch. Robbery In Broad Daylight, bred by Miss V. Croft. A kennel mate runs a close second, however, as Ch. Highroad Robbery. In this pedigree were dogs such as Ch. Armistice Sunshine, Ch. Night Raider, and Ch. Tip Top Weather. Also in the late 1920s was Mrs. M. E. Bradford's homebred, Colin of Gayton. Sired by Careful Jim, his sire and dam, the well-known Blue Coat and Blue Blossom, were both champions.

THE 1930s

Ch. Stoneybroke, owned by Mrs. Keith Gibson, was the 1933 winner at Crufts. He was sired by Mrs. Tod's Happy-go-Lucky, who in turn was out of another prominent sire at the time, named Old Henry. Mrs. James, who was also showing at Crufts this same year, had her photo taken carrying her exhibit into the show hall and it made the Wide World news services—publicity for the breed to be sure.

Another photo picked up by the Wide World service featured Miss Leefe and three of her dogs making their way into the Crystal Palace for the October show and showed a "bobby" holding up traffic for her. Both of these charming photographs are included in the Hutchinson's Encyclopedia. Mrs. Bradford was another breeder who exhibited several of her dogs at the Crystal Palace shows.

EARLY BRACE

Perhaps the very first brace in the breed were Miss McTurk's Sergeant Murphy and Blinker Bill. Miss McTurk will also be remembered as the club's second female president, a term she served in 1922.

Another famous International Champion was Dolly Grey. Dolly was bred by Mr. F. H. Travis and owned by the Tilley brothers. She was sired by Stylish Boy. Whelped in 1901, by 1904 she had done more than her share of winning, including the Crufts International Bowl for the Best Non-Sporting dog in the show. Her total record included over 130 first prizes, 200 special prizes, and seven cups. On nine occasions she was awarded a special prize for the best exhibit in the show.

EDWARD C. ASH

Another famous dog man in Great Britain was Edward C. Ash who had a few words to say about the Old English Sheepdog in his book, *The Practical Dog Book*, published in 1930. He says in part, "In olden days the word Sheep-dog described any dog, whatever be its type, its colour, or its size, discovered helping the shepherd here and in other parts of the world. Now and again naturalists attempted to suggest a distinct variety of Sheep-dog, and we find in 1792, in a Natural History, the following description: 'The Sheep-dog: It has erect ears, and the tail is woolly underneath.'

"In 1847 a dog fancier named Richardson compared the breed as a type of Collie that appeared to be a cross with the Great Rough Water Dog, without a tail. In 1878, Walsh, in his *Dogs of the British Isles*, suggests that the shepherds of the day thought this tailless dog could run faster because it had no tail! Also, Mr. D. J. Thomas Grey referred to it as 'the hairy moued Collie' and described it as 'a tousy-looking tyke, with a coat like a doormat.' "

It is ironic then that Mr. Ash himself, after relating all these rather outlandish descriptions of the Old English, should himself say in his book, writing about the Lhasa Apso, or Lhasa Terriers as they were called at that time, "It is difficult to know where to place these dogs. In type they resemble the Old English Sheepdog, so I am placing them here, merely on such superficial resemblance."

He lists as the faults in the breed at the time . . . "long backs, light eyes, heavy fronts, leggy appearance, weak hindquarters with cow-hocks, the last two being very noticeable in many dogs of today." He also mentioned the tendency of breeders to increase the size of the breed and warned against sacrificing type. He went on to describe the ideal dog as ". . . stands well off the ground, but somewhat stocky in appearance, rather narrow in front and very broad in the hindquarters, which are distinctly higher than the shoulder."

A. S. L. WALLIS ON THE BREED

Another dog man of the 1940s also wrote on our breed. While he admitted believing it was an "old" breed, he said that he felt, according to paintings he had seen, that the breed dated back at least to the 15th century, for van Eyck, Gainesborough, and Dürer rendered portraits with likenesses of the breed in them. He also pointed out that in these portraits the tail was not docked. He noted too that in the original Standard for the breed, it stated specifically ". . . free of all Poodle or Deerhound character." This bears evidence that at that time there was apparently a crossing with these two breeds. He himself believed that if crosses were made, it was more than likely they would be to the Russian Owtchar, which had been reported as being imported to the area from the Baltic countries around that time.

He also cautions that the Old English Sheepdog is not a breed for everyone unless one is a "fanatic for hard physical exercise." He pointed out that it was a breed in need of considerable physical exercise and one that required much grooming attention. He stated, "A knotted and matted coat is a disgrace to the dog's owner, and there is nothing more ugly than a badly-kept Bobtail, just as there is nothing more beautiful than a well-kept one."

EARLY SHEEPDOG TRIALS

In Brian Vesey-Fitzgerald's book, *The Book of the Dog*, published in England circa 1948, he includes an article on Sheepdog trials contributed by J. A. Reid. According to Mr. Reid's contribution to the book, Sheepdog trials were begun on October 9, 1873 in Wales by Mr. J. Lloyd Price. Ten dogs competed at this first event with the win going to a Scottish-bred dog whose name was not recorded. Trials were held elsewhere the following year and apparently met with a bit of success. In 1875, in Bala, a cup was offered to the winner among the 30-odd dogs competing. After their inception, these trials were held annually except for the war years 1915–1918 and 1939–1945.

The trials were said to have reached the pinnacle of success in 1889 when Queen Victoria and her royal entourage attended a private exhibition which made the event an established practice. From Wales, the sport spread to England in 1876 and to Scotland at about the same time. In fact, it wasn't long before such trials were being held all over the world. Needless to say, most of the original competitors were Collies, but it was not long before Sheepdogs of all varieties were gaining recognition in these competitions.

A Society for the running of the events soon followed the initial events and the development of national and international rules and regulations for championship were not far behind. Classes, categories, trophies, point systems, etc., became technical and specific and the trials were a formidable success.

JILL A. KEELING

Early in the 1960s, Jill A. Keeling had published a little book on the breed. She had been breeding and rearing Old English Sheepdogs for many years and wrote for all admirers of the breed this little book on Sheepdog husbandry. Her own Amberford Kennels in Chesterfield, Derbyshire are well known, and her list of kennels and their prefixes give a good general picture of the leading kennels of the day in England. Alphabetically they are: *Beanville*, owned by her sister, Miss V. Keeling; *Beckington*, Mrs. K. Gibson; *Bewkes*, Misses Smailes and Knight Bruce; *Bleakdown*, Lt. Col. M. D. Lister; *Bluecote*, Mr. W. J. Calvey; *Bluewave*, Mrs. E. Rollo; *Blumark*, Mr. A. J. Baker; *Bobbycroft*, Miss C. F. Workman; *Boldwood*, Mrs. W. Grillet; *Broadwell*, Mr. J. Wasley; *Cemaes*, Mrs. J. D. James; *Dalcroy*, Miss A. Lloyd; *Danum*, Mr. F. Brocklesby; *Daphnis*, Mr. E. J. J. Minett; *Duroya*, Mrs. A. E. Woodiwiss; *Ellinghurst*, Mrs. J. C. R. Chapman; *Fairacres*, Mrs. E. M. Bloor; *Farleydene*, Mr. G. Gooch; *Fernville*, Mr. N. W. R. Harrison, *Gordale*, Mr. C. D. St. J. Stacey; *Grendonfell*, Mrs. I. F. Cooke; *Greystoke*, Miss J. M. Back; *Hornash*, Mr. and Mrs. R. F. Mathews; *Keandor*, Mr. and Mrs. A. R. Wood; *Knockanyln*, Mr. J. A. Muirhead; *Lanseer*, Mr. and Mrs. W. Ashley; *Linnifold*, Mr. and Mrs. J. S. Mason; *Litteparc*, Mrs.

E. Jackson; *Marlay*, Mrs. H. Booth; *Pastelblue*, Miss I. Webster; *Pearlstone*, Miss P. M. Peart; *Pinehurst*, Mrs. W. Heyward; *Reculver*, Mr. and Mrs. A. G. Wilkinson; *Rollingsea*, Mrs. J. R. Gould; *Shepton*, Miss F. Tilley; *Squarefore*, Mrs. I. C. Nichol; *Talmora*, Mrs. S. M. Talbot; *Tansley*, Mrs. E. Goodwin; *Watchers*, Miss Tucker; *Weirwood*, Mrs. C. Barclay; *Yasabel*, Mrs. M. Murray; and *Yeldhams*, Mr. and Mrs. H. Linsell-Clark.

While a mere listing for those active in the breed during the decade of the 1950s is hardly a true picture of their dedication and accomplishments in the breed, it is still worthy of note the number of names we can call to mind in our United States pedigrees from the dogs produced at these kennels. Many of our important imports carry these kennel names that helped cement the breed in this country as well as in their own.

BRITISH CLUBS

In addition to the original Old English Sheepdog Club founded in 1888 in Middlesex, there are the Northwestern Old English Sheepdog Club, founded in 1923 and located in Sheffield, and the Southeastern Old English Sheepdog Club in Kent. The current secretaries and addresses for these can be obtained by addressing The Kennel Club, 1–5 Clarges Street, Piccadilly, London, W1Y 8AB England.

There is also an Old English Sheepdog Club of Scotland and an Old English Sheepdog Club of Ireland. Addresses for both of these might also be obtained by writing to The Kennel Club (of Great Britain).

THE SHEPTON CENTENNIAL CELEBRATION

We have read with interest about the achievements of the Messrs. Tilley in developing and establishing the quality of the breed with their Shepton bloodlines. It was with great pleasure that the Chairman of the Old English Sheepdog Club in England, I. E. Thick, commemorated 100 years of breeding within the Tilley family by presenting Miss F. Tilley, currently president of the club, with a trophy to mark the occasion. Miss Tilley, a direct descendant of the Messrs. Tilley, served as club president from 1966 to 1981. It will be remembered that H. A. Tilley was the president in 1926 and both brothers were instrumental in starting the parent club in the United States. The presentation was made by Mr. Thick at the July 25, 1981 Royal Bath and West Show on behalf of the parent and regional clubs.

Anne Weisse's 10-week-old "Junior." This darling puppy grew up to be American and Canadian Champion Greyfriar's Lord Fauntleroy. Junior was 10½ years old in 1970.

Chapter 3

The Breed Comes to America

The first Old English Sheepdog came to America around 1888, which marked the breed's first attention from the dog lovers in this country. This can be greatly attributed to the very enterprising Mr. William Wade of Hulton, Pennsylvania and his friend, the philanthropist Andrew Carnegie. These two dog lovers were intent on establishing the breed in the United States and there was no stopping them from pursuing this goal.

Through his friendship with Mr. Freeman Lloyd, an internationally known judge—perhaps one of the greatest authorities on working dogs at the time—Mr. Wade managed to have published in an 1889 issue of *Turf, Field, and Farm* a monograph entitled "The Old English Sheepdog." *Turf, Field, and Farm* was a sports magazine for which Mr. Lloyd reported, and he himself later authored the monograph, introducing the breed to the American dog fancy.

The monograph was of great influence, and this was partly responsible for the breed's getting further coverage in the press. Also, Mr. Wade had the habit of depositing bobtail puppies on the doorsteps of his friends, who could not resist the woolly bears once they had made their acquaintance. Ironically, it was at about this time that interest in the breed in England began to wane, and it didn't pick up again until after the breed was well entrenched and highly regarded in this country.

It was by 1903, when Freeman Lloyd judged the first class of Old English Sheepdogs at the Westminster Kennel Club show, that a large group of them showed up in the ring. Mr. Henry Arthur Tilley, who was to later found the parent club of Shepton Mallet, England, brought out an imported team of Old English especially for competition at this show, and they stirred a lot of interest in the breed. In fact, it was many of the fine dogs shown at this show that led to the purchase of other Sheepdogs by prominent people in the fancy, who can be said to have done much to help establish the breed in this country.

Most notable among them, it might be said, were the well-known theatrical producer Charles Dillingham and the war correspondent Richard Harding Davis. It was Mr. Dillingham's stock, which was later sold to the very wealthy Reginald Vanderbilt (of the Newport, Rhode Island Vanderbilts), that produced and established the white-headed, blue-bodied bobtails which did all the winning during the 1930s, which included Ch. Sandy Boy Raap.

Unquestionably, however, the major contributor to establishing the breed was the very dedicated Mrs. Edward Renner. Mrs. Renner, whose Merriedip prefix is still revered in the breed in this country, gave the necessary prestige, fame, and popularity to the Old English Sheepdog. It was at this time that Mrs. Renner (then Mrs. Lewis Roesler) imported some great dogs, and the bobtail was off and running at the U.S. dog shows. Much gratitude is due her famous Pastorale and her Ch. Downderry Vanquisher, with which she won three Bests in Show!

From 1905 until 1920, Old English Sheepdog show dogs became "the vogue" and did a lot of winning. Some of the more famous ones were Stylish Boy, Midnight Slumber, Ch. Brentwood Hero, and the two famous British imports, Dolly Grey and Tip Top Weather.

Several well-known exhibitors made names for themselves and their kennels at this time also. The early 1920s introduced the breeding of Mr. and Mrs. Tyler Morse of the Beaver Brook Kennels; Mr. Morris Kenney of the Kennelon Kennels; Mr. William A. Jamison of Willinez Weather Kennels; Mrs. Joseph Urban of

Yonkers; Mrs. Rumpf of Buckingham, Pennsylvania; Mrs. Laura A. Dohring of Cliffwood Kennels; Miss Edith N. Buckingham and her Cloeftaegel Kennels; Mrs. W. K. Hitchcock and Mrs. Roland M. Bakers of Woodland Farm Kennels; Mr. P. Hamilton Goodsell and son, Percy, of Tenacre Kennels; Judge and Mrs. Wilbur Kirby Hitchcock; Mrs. Doris M. Briggs of the Cartref Kennels; Fred LaCrosse and the Waltons of the Royal Kennels; Marjorie and Helen Cluff of Clearbrook; Mrs. Mary Schloss of Bovla Kennels; Mrs. V. Cline; and Mrs. Rosalind Crafts of Rosmoore. There were others, of course, who also gave of their time and energies to help establish the breed during those early days after the turn of the century and beyond.

The first Old English Sheepdog shown in the United States was a dog named Hempstead Bob, bred by Dr. Lock of England and imported and owned by the Hempstead Farms. He was exhibited at the Westminster Kennel Club show in New York in 1893.

The Old English Sheepdog was exhibited extensively, by Mrs. George Thomas, even before there were specific classes provided for the bobtails. Mrs. Tyler Morse also made valuable strides in the show ring by winning the Spratt's Trophy for Best Brace, all breeds, at the Garden in 1908 and 1909. She imported many of England's best Old English Sheepdogs in her efforts to get the breed started in America.

Mrs. Wilbur K. Hitchcock was the well-known secretary of the Old English Sheepdog Club, starting in 1923 and for many years thereafter. P. Hamilton Goodsall was another known name who served as president of the club from 1919 and for many years after. He was also recognized as a canine authority, judge, legislator, and breeder of Old English Sheepdogs. Miss E. P. Palmer and Dr. William Bott were enthusiasts, Dr. Bott being a judge of the breed as well. It was Dr. Bott who waged a vigorous campaign to maintain the excellence of the Old English Sheepdog; he advocated to keep the size down and insisted on strict adherence to type and quality.

It was this guarded Standard of excellence that brought several of the show dogs into the limelight at the time, among them the International Champion Weather; Ch. Kennelon Halloween; Ch. Beau Brummel; Ch. Clovelly Weather; Ch. Lassie of the Farm; and Ch. Montfor Marksman, to name the most prominent.

THE PARENT CLUB

In 1905, Mr. Henry Arthur Tilley of England encouraged the founding of the Old English Sheepdog Club of America. They held their first Specialty show in 1921, and it brought out an entry of 42 dogs. After two years the entry was up to 52 dogs, and the club was firmly established and dedicated to the breed.

Mrs. Wilbur K. Hitchcock was the well-known Secretary of the club, from 1923 until many years thereafter. P. Hamilton Goodsall was President of the club, from 1919, for many years, and was a recognized canine authority, judge, legislator and breeder of Old English Sheepdogs. Miss E. P. Palmer is another famous past president who also offered financial support to the parent club and other organizations that related to the good and welfare of the bobtail.

By 1930, just a quarter of a century after the breed club had been founded in this country, the club held its Specialty in conjunction with the North Westchester Kennel Club and drew an entry of 61 dogs. A reasonably successful show the following year made the parent club realize that, while firmly entrenched in the dog show world, the tendency for the breed to gain in popularity, and therefore, entries at shows, was fast coming to a halt.

Fortunately, now, the parent club is enjoying a tremendous membership of over 1000 and is most active in all phases of the fancy. It is so large that the country has been divided into regions, and they are supervising the various clubs which are mushrooming all over the country.

KENNELON

There is no doubt that one of the most outstanding kennels for our breed in the 1920s was the famous Kennelon Kennels near Butler, New Jersey, owned by Morris Kenney. Kennelon were acknowledged to have bred some of the finest "bear dogs" at the time, and all of them thrived in their year 'round, outdoor, individual kennels that contributed to their luxurious coats and general good health and condition.

The property devoted to the dogs had runs divided into two sizes, with yet another run of extra large size for several uses. The five larger yards were 15 × 70 feet, each with a large "house" for the dog, or dogs, since some were penned in pairs. Fourteen other runs were 6 × 40, usually for single dogs. All led to a large kennel building where the dogs received special attention and grooming. The main kennel was 30 × 100 feet for isolation or whelping.

While the emphasis was never 100% on the show ring, perhaps the pride of Kennelon was Mr. Kenney's famous Ch. Kennelon Tower. He was regarded as one of the leading stud dogs in his day and a dog that worked with sheep and cattle in the fields as well. He was called the prize specimen by Mr. Kenney's kennelman, Rudolph Dalstrom. Mr. Dalstrom was the one who brought Tower back from Mr. Kenney's father's farm in Iowa to try his luck in the show ring. The rest is history.

There were other "greats" at Kennelon—a bitch named Minikin, a British import, loved swimming *under* water. Other bitch imports were Ch. Milkmaid, who did her share of winning in England before being imported to this country and her place at Kennelon, and Ch. Elusive Tramp, who won a championship in England before winning another one in this country. Another top stud dog at Kennelon was Ch. Tip Top Weather, sire of Ch. Kennelon Selection. Ch. Night Rider, Tower's sire, was yet another. Ch. Brentwood Hero, by Night Rider, and Ch. Shepton Hero, by Ch. Lord Cedric, were all imported to this country after gaining fame in England.

MERRIEDIP

The death of Mrs. Edward P. Renner in December 1965 signified the end of an era in Old English Sheepdogs and Pembroke Welsh Corgis. Her legacy to both breeds remains one of the most important contributions we can look back on today when reviewing pedigrees of some of the best bobtails over many decades.

In 1933 Mrs. Helen Lewis was in Europe on a judging assignment and looking for additional breeding stock for her Sheepdog lines when she fell in love with the Corgis; these she added to her kennel. Some of her famous Sheepdogs were, of course, Ch. Merriedip Master Pantaloons; International Ch. Mistress Petticoats of Pastorale; Ch. Mistress Merrie O'Merriedip; Ch. M. Silverday; Ch. Downderry Volunteer; and her imported, farm-trained Shepton Marguerite of Merriedip, Merriedip David, and Ch. Merriedip of Pastorale.

Her Voyager finished for her championship in 1931, after starting an excellent show career in 1928, and was retired after being bred to American and Canadian Ch. Downderry Irresistable.

From this breeding came the excellent bitch Ch. Merriedip Ethel Ann. When Ethel Ann was bred to Ch. Derrydown Volunteer, they produced Ch. Merriedip Ethelyn, dam of Ch. Merriedip Master Pantaloons.

Pantaloons was considered the very best of Helen's breeding; his show record at Westminster is well known. The only bobtail to beat his record was his sire, Volunteer, whose show record was also fabulous over a five-year stint in the show rings. Helen's Ch. Mistress Patience of Pastorale, another import, finished for her championship in 1934 and was the dam of Ch. Merriedip Silverdale, who was later owned by Mrs. D. M. Briggs. Patience was Best of Breed at the 1935 Westminster show and at Morris and Essex in 1936. Another dog of note was Ch. Merriedip Vindex, who finished in 1937. He took a Breed and Fourth in the Group at the big Trenton club event that same year.

Merriedip quality also spread to Canada. Although he was bred in Canada out of a litter by Snow Lady, Ch. Walleyed Snow Bobs O'Merriedip was a credit to Mrs. Lewis when he finished his title in 1935.

During the years 1938 and 1939, Mrs. Lewis is reported to have travelled approximately 18,000 miles from her kennel in Great Barrington, Massachusetts to see that her dogs got their share of the wins. She also made several trips to England where she judged many times.

THE OLD ENGLISH SHEEPDOG CLUB

By 1930, just a quarter of a century after the Old English Sheepdog Club had been founded in this country, the club held a Specialty show and other clubs began to consider starting their own in various areas of the Eastern seaboard. This was despite the fact that the parent club activities slowed down a bit, as the breed began to "spread out." The Old English Sheepdog Club of New England was one of the first, and it excelled beyond the parent club for almost two decades (until 1950, to be exact) when both clubs became aware of the influx of new members and their interest; the breed once again took a foothold up and down the Eastern seaboard.

It was during the 1940s and the 1950s that the New England Club really came into its own under the guiding lights of Mmes. Crafts, Roesler, Baker, and Buckingham. The Merriedip Kennels gained considerable fame and brought great honor to the breed with Vanquisher's three Bests in Show, and Canadian Champion Snowflake was campaigned to record wins by Marjorie and Helen Cluff of the Canadian Clearbrook Kennels. Mrs. Rosalind Crafts, in her late sixties at the time, won a Best in Show award with her Ch. Rosmoore Sinney when the dog was just 15 months of age; and she scored a spectacular win, the Bobtail Best in Show, at Morris and Essex in 1938 with Ch. Ideal Weather.

In a 1941 *National Geographic* article devoted to "Working Dogs of the World," written by Freeman Lloyd, Mr. Lloyd had the following to say about our breed: "What the Collie is to Scotland, the Old English Sheepdog is to England, though he is not generally distributed over his homeland.

"The Old English Sheepdog is commonly known as the Bobtail, since his tail is bobbed or cut off close to the rump. This dog carries an enormous coat, and a long hairy tail would gather so much mud as to impede the free movement of a hardworking farm dog. Many are born tailless or with short bobs. For the last fifty years, to my own knowledge, this breed has been producing long-tailed, short-tailed, and tailless puppies, often in the same litter.

"The Bobtail was and is popular for driving sheep and cattle from fair to fair or other points for disposal or slaughter. His voice is sharp and loud—a valuable asset, since 'noise' helps in keeping livestock on the move.

"Shaggy and compactly built, the Bobtail frequently brings forth the remark, 'Look, there's a dog like a bear.' He is very sagacious and makes a nice dog for play as well as work. Among the best-in-the-bench show dogs of the day, an Old English Sheepdog is often acclaimed as the winner, and that highest of all exhibition attainments should say much for the position that the Bobtail holds in the U.S."

Additional remarks and descriptions of this dog are also interesting enough to bear repeating. "The outer hair should be long and free from curl, and the under coat of a lintlike or pile description." Further along in the same article we find, "Bobtails have thick, rainproof coats, mostly of pigeon-blue color with white markings. Their bark is loud, their skull well formed and 'brainy.' " And then the most glowing comment of all the bobtail fanciers can most relate to was the comment, "Through hair that all but hides their eyes they peer at the world with an air of dignity and wisdom."

WORLD WAR II

Dog shows were greatly curtailed, or cancelled entirely, during the early 1940s because of World War II gas rationing; but still the devoted bobtail breeders managed to persevere. Mrs. Renner, for one, went on campaigning her dogs whenever and wherever possible, and was still winning at the shows with the renowned Ch. Master Pantaloons, Ch. Merriedip Mr. Personality, Ch. King's Messenger, Ch. Black Baron, and Ch. Royal Victor, among others.

KINGS ROW

Needless to say that with Anne Weisse being involved with bobtails since 1948, she has a rich, rare history in the breed. Her Kings Row Kennels were well known over the years, though she never had a large operation or bred more than two litters in all this time. Anne's dogs are very important in her life and she has many stories to tell about their experiences, especially in the shows and in her travels.

Anne's interest in the breed began in Germany and then in this country. She has managed to finish five champions: four Canadian and American titlists, and one in America only. She has been a member of the parent club since 1955 and belonged to three different breed clubs over the years. Anne has also taught conformation classes for eight years. While Anne admits to being in her seventies, she will soon tell you that she has owned and loved dogs since she was four. Her dogs have appeared on various TV programs and in the media, and she and her dogs both have been a credit to the breed.

MONA AND MOMARV

After World War II, perhaps the greatest dog in the breed to that date, Ch. Merriedip Duke George, emerged from Mrs. Renner's famous kennel—owned and handled by Mrs. Mona Kucker Berkowitz. George was perhaps the most famous of all bobtails during the 1950s and was followed by the great show dog and sire, Ch. Fezziwig Ceiling Zero, owned by the Hendrik Van Renssel-

The famous Mona Berkowitz, owner-handler of her equally famous Bobtail Champion Merriedip Duke George winning a Group at the 1957 26th Annual dog show at Morris and Essex Kennel Club. Judge was Joseph C. Quirk. Evelyn Shafer photograph.

aers. This magnificent dog won 15 Bests in Show. Around this time we were seeing winnings in the rings by a lovely Canadian dog, Ch. Blue Admiral of Box. Other United States winners were Ch. Shepton Surprise; Ch. Tarawoods Blue Baron, winner of nine Bests in Show; and Ch. B. and H.'s Holiday Showcase . . . all strong contenders in the show rings and on the rating charts.

In 1964 Ch. Fezziwig Raggedy Andy set records with 13 Bests in Show and ranked second of all Working Dogs that year, according to *Popular Dogs* magazine's famous Phillips System ratings of the top show dogs in the nation. Ch. Tarawood's Blue Baron ranked third right below him. In 1965 Ch. Fezziwig Raggedy Andy was back to top his 1964 record by being top Old English Sheepdog in the country and fifth ranking dog of *all* breeds in the nation. In 1966 he ranked number one!

Champion Prince Andrew of Sherline was warming up on the sidelines around this time and later came into prominence as top Old English Sheepdog, breaking more records. Ch. Rivermist Hollyhock, sired by the Barry Goodmans' magnificent import, International Champion Unesta Pim, became one of the few undefeated bobtail bitches in the show ring. Mona Berkowitz introduced from her famous Momarv Kennels many top contenders for the winner's circle. And today Mona Berkowitz, the Van Rensselaers, and Barry Goodman are still among those remembered as some of the top breeders of the time.

Other leading kennels of the 1970s were Morrows, Bear Creek, Knightcap, Windfield, Droverdale, Silvershag, Beau Cheval, Ticklebee, Sunnybrae, St. Trinian, Bahlambs, Silvermist, Tamara, Greyfriar, Waterfall, Ambelon, Double JJ, Tatters, Happy Town, Ivyridge, Tarawoods, Jendowers, Robinswood, Bufferton, Shaggybar, Rosecliffs, Misty Isles, Beaverbrooks, Loyalblu, Windswept, Shiler, Gigglewyck, Windjammer, Downeyland, Echoe Valley, Lillibrad, Crofton, Orchards, Ragbear, Bobmar, and many others.

As the 1980s come to a close, we can see represented in this book photographs of the leading dogs from the leading kennels of this decade and can rejoice in the quality of the breed as we know it today. The bobtail remains as beautiful and as beloved as ever and is holding its own in popularity.

THE WESTMINSTER WINNERS

Perhaps the most coveted and prestigious of all Best in Show awards is the Westminster rosette and the fabulous silver trophies that go with it. The first Best in Show award was given in 1907. Group judging, with the alignment of breeds as we know them today, only dates back to 1930. With this in mind, we present herewith the winners of these awards:

Best In Show

1914 was the first year that a bobtail went "all the way" to the top at Westminster. The dog was Ch. Slumber, owned by Mrs. Tyler Morse. In 1975, another Old English won the Best in Show. This was a Canadian dog named Ch. Sir Lancelot of Barvan, owned by Barbara Vanword, another breeder-owner-exhibitor whose name has been synonymous with the breed for many years.

Group Winners

Several other dogs have managed to capture Working Group Firsts since they began in 1930. F. T. James' Snowman was the first. His win was in 1932, followed in 1934 by Snowflake, owned by the Clearbrook Kennels. In 1942 Mrs. Helen Lewis's Ch. Merriedip Master Pantaloons won the Group. More than two decades passed before another Old English won a Westminster Group. It was in 1966 that Hendrik and Serena Van Rensselaer's Ch. Fezziwig Raggedy Andy took the Group, followed by Mr. and Mrs. Howard Sherline's Ch. Prince Andrew of Sherline in 1969. The next was in 1975 with Sir Lancelot, who did the breed so proud by going on to Best in Show.

Other Westminster Group Placings

Several other bobtails won Group placements after 1930. Another Canadian dog, Ch. Ideal Weather, took second in the Group at Westminster in 1937 and again in 1938. In 1939, Ch. Merriedip Master Pantaloons was second in the Working Group before winning it in 1942. In 1941, Merriedip Bob-A-Long took a Group Second and in 1944, Ch. King's Messenger captured a Group Third.

In the 1950s, Second place wins went to yet another Merriedip dog, this time to Ch. Merriedip Duke George in 1957 and 1958, and in the following year he took a Group Third.

In 1961, Ch. Lillibrad Prince Charming was second, and in 1963 and 1964 Ch. Fezziwig Ceiling Zero won the Second Place rosette.

Ch. Lillibrad Prince Charming, circa 1960's, owned by Mr. A. V. Gustafson of Chicago, and handled for him by Jack Funk.

Chapter 4

Leading American Kennels

We have just received an early history of the breed and have cited the major leaders in establishing the Old English Sheepdog in America, those people who were also responsible for the resurgence of interest in the Bobtail in its own country by our enthusiasm and support. While there is no doubt that there were a few outstanding, large kennel enterprises, during the time since the 1920s and 30s there have been other kennels, working diligently in the background and in the show rings, that helped to maintain the steady growth and interest in the breed that brought it to its present popularity.

Here, then, is a sampling of some of the other American kennels that helped lead the way to continued success in all phases of the dog fancy.

DOUBLE JJ

James and Joyce Anderson own the Double JJ Farm in Bigelow, Minnesota where they have had Bobtails since 1959. The Andersons started showing dogs in 1960, having finished 12 champions and two obedience titlists. They have belonged to the parent club since 1960, as well as other Old English and all-breed kennel clubs, and Joyce has taught 4-H obedience for 16 years. Their first

dog was Ch. Greyfriar's Double JJ Penny, C.D. which they purchased as a puppy in 1958.

AMBELON
Anne M. Raker of Lincoln, Massachusetts is the owner of the
Ambelon Kennels. Since that day in 1960 when she established
her kennels, she has finished 19 champions and one U.D. dog.
She also runs a large welfare adoption program for the breed in
her area. In 1972, Shih Tzu joined the kennel as well. She started
showing and breeding in 1960 and got involved with obedience in
1961.

BOBMAR BOBTAILS
Marilyn Mayfield, of Burbank, California, started showing Bobtails in 1964 and breeding them in 1966. Since that time she has
finished 30 champions and five obedience titlists. She has been a
member of the parent club since 1971 and is their Health and Research Chairman. She is also a member of the Malibu Kennel
Club and the San Fernando Kennel Club. A real dog lover, Marilyn has also had a Tibetan Terrier since 1984.

TAMARA
Tamara Old English Sheepdogs came into existence when
Tammy and Marvin Smith brought home their "Patches." Ch. Tamara's Patches of Perse became the dam of nine champions and
was a devoted companion in the Smith household for 10 years.
The second addition to the Tamara effort was an imported male
from England; and with the aid of Mr. Eric Minet, an English
judge, "Harvey" came to the United States. Ch. Tempest of Dalcroy is the sire of 21 champions, nine of which were from the successful breedings with Patches. Dalcroy was a Top Ten Producer
in the breed.
Since 1965, when this all began, the Smiths have finished 40
champions. They have belonged to the parent club since 1966 and
also, while living in the area, were members of the Livingston
County Kennel Club. While they purchased their first Bobtail in
1962, they didn't have their first litter until 1964 and didn't start
showing until 1965. The Smiths retired from breeding in 1981 and
now reside in Ocala, Florida. Those of us who love the breed will

always remember their wonderful motto which still adorns their stationery: "Very Special Dogs for Very Special People."

BELLEWOOD FARMS

While the Larry Dugans were involved in Sporting dogs as early as 1958, it was 1968 before Old English Sheepdogs came into their lives. Since that time they have finished 14 champions and eight obedience dogs. They have been members of the parent club since 1966 and since 1976 have had Labs and English Cockers.

Larry and Melinda, of Roanoke, Texas, are both AKC-approved conformation and obedience judges and belong to other Old English Sheepdog and all-breed clubs. Ch. Squarecote Rollicking Rumba was their first Bobtail and they take great pride in the fact that their Ch. Bellewood Farms Blue Tango, C.D. lived to be 14½ years old.

STONYCOMBE

Ed Johansen of West Redding, Connecticut has been showing Old English Sheepdogs since 1968 and breeding them since 1969. In that time he has finished eight champions, and uses Stonycombe as his kennel prefix. He is a member of the parent club, the Old English Sheepdog Club of Greater New York, the Ox Ridge all-breed club and the Newtown Kennel Club.

Mr. Johansen is also very active in the fancy in other capacities as well. He is a delegate to the American Kennel Club, and a judge and columnist for the *American Kennel Gazette*. While his only breed is the Bobtail, he is approved to judge them and four other breeds as well.

RAMBLING ACRES

1969 was the year that Dick and Linda Kender established their Rambling Acres Old English Sheepdog kennels in Windsor, Ohio. They started showing in 1970 and had bred a litter in 1969. They have finished two champions to date: American and Canadian Ch. Rambling Acres Casey Blue and American and Canadian Champion Rambling Acres Grey Surge. Both Casey and Spike lived to ripe old ages, 16 and 13, respectively.

A litter in 1984 produced three show males, Webster, Thatcher, and Pip, and Molly and Heather on the distaff side.

They have been members of the parent club since 1972 and the year before that had joined the Western Reserve Old English Sheepdog Club.

HI BOBGEN

Eugene and Barbara McGuirk of Cold Spring, New York, started with Shelties in 1969 and in 1970 added Bobtails to their Hi Bobgen program. They started showing in conformation in 1983 but have been members of the parent club since 1970 and are also active in clubs in their area. They intend to start breeding in the near future, and showing as well.

DOLLHOUSE

1969 was the year that Helen E. Dollinger of Ft. Lauderdale, Florida, started her Dollhouse Old English Sheepdog Kennels. She began showing in both obedience and conformation classes and to date has bred three Best in Show dogs and 30 champions. She has also earned two Old English Sheepdog obedience titles and also put one on a Kerry Blue Terrier. She started breeding Bobtails in 1974.

Helen Dollinger has been a member of the parent club since 1970 and is also a board member of the Ft. Lauderdale Dog Club. She is proud of all her dogs and their accomplishments but perhaps her best known is Ch. Dollhouse Bill Bailey. She has also co-bred some litters with Carla Dollinger.

WINNOBY

Brian and Judy House Still have been in the breed since 1969 and now maintain their Winnoby Kennels in Milford, Michigan. As handlers of dogs, both their own and other people's, they have owned many other breeds as well. In fact, Brian began handling dogs in 1969 and Judy began in 1981.

Over the years they have finished 12 champions and 10 obedience titlists, though it is Judy's mother, Carolyn House, who does the training. They have also given lectures on handling, showing, and caring for dogs, and explaining the Old English Sheepdog Standard to newcomers in the breed.

They joined the parent club in 1970 and also belong to the Dog Owners Association and the Old English Sheepdog Club of Greater Detroit.

Their most recent accomplishments are breeding the No. 1 Old English Sheepdog in the nation for 1984, American and Canadian Champion Winnoby's Dictator of Talisman, R.O.M., co-owned by Carolyn House and Neil and Barbara Feola, and the No. 1 Old English Sheepdog Obedience dog for 1984, American Canadian Ch. Winnoby's Much Ado, R.O.M., also trained by Carolyn House.

THE DECADE OF THE SEVENTIES

The 1970s initiated a new surge in the popularity of the breed with both show entries and breed registrations on the increase. Shortly after the first half of the decade one of the breed fanciers with a penchant for statistics came up with an impressive listing of kennels and the number of champions finished from 1971 through 1975.

A record was kept of all of the kennel names and included by years the number of champions finished by each of them. The report was made by collecting the last five-year totals for each kennel and recorded how many times in the last five-year period that kennel had produced champions. Kennels which produced one champion in the five-year period were not individually listed but were recorded for following years. The second number beside the kennel name is the number of years the kennel had been producing champions during the five-year period.

It is interesting to note how many of the kennels are no longer in existence at the time of this writing, but how very many of them are in the pedigrees of our great dogs of today.

Trystin Tyrrell of Mingo, owned by Laura Scott of Columbus, Ohio. The sire was Tamara's Impresario X Tamara's Ms. Mischievousness. Tristy was photographed here in December 1979.

We list here this very interesting study.

5-YEAR STUDY ON KENNEL NAMES
AND NUMBER OF CHAMPIONS FINISHED
1971–1975 INCLUSIVE

Kennel	Chs.–Yrs.	Kennel	Chs.–Yrs.
Tamara	16–5	Ellenglaze	3–4
Jendower	15–5	Heritage	3–5
Greyfriar	14–5	Knightcap	3–5
Windfield	11–5	Lillibrad	3–5
Double JJ	10–5	Limey Lane	3–5
Knottingham	10–4	Mitepa	3–3
Loyalblu	10–4	Momarv	3–5
Ambelon	8–5	Pawprint	3–3
Bahlambs	8–5	Pickwick	3–5
Barnstorm	7–5	Sleepy Hollow	3–4
Moptop	7–1	Sunnybrae	3–5
Rolling Gait	7–5	Bearwood	2–1
Shaggiluv	7–4	Bellewood Farms	2–5
Some Buddy	7–5	Blindbluff	2–3
Droverdale	6–5	Blue Panda	2–5
Merryrogue	6–5	Blu-Myst	2–5
Morrow	6–5	Bobtail	2–5
Ragbear	6–5	Bobtail Acres	2–5
Rivermist	6–5	Chatelaine	2–1
Banbury	5–4	Cricket	2–4
Barrelroll	5–5	Echo Valley	2–5
Dandalion	5–4	Eilean	2–5
Fezziwig	5–5	Fogbound	2–5
Aragorn	4–4	Giggleswyck	2–5
Bobmar	4–5	Graceland	2–5
Cheerio	4–4	Ha'Penny	2–3
Cricketshire	4–4	Haystack	2–5
Feliciana	4–5	Heart G	2–5
Pinafore	4–3	Hydecrest	2–5
Stonehenge	4–2	Ivyridge	2–4
The Hermitage	4–5	Lake Shore	2-5
Leach	2–4	London	2–1

Other well-known and actively exhibiting kennels during the 1970s were the Barvan Kennels of Mrs. Barbara Vanword in Ontario, Canada, and the Dandalion Bobtails of Ron and Janice McClary of Los Angeles, whose Ch. Dandalion's Lord Tanker was No. 2 Old English Sheepdog in 1974, always owner-handled. Another was Dick and Lorry Boerner's Loyalblu Kennels. Their Ch. Loyalblu Hendihap won the Northern California Specialty show in 1975. He was bred by Dr. and Mrs. Hugh Jordan and shown by Linda Jordan. There were Kenneth and Paul Leach, Deborah Rasmussen and John D. Cook, and Robert Arble, Cassandra Moulton and David Shepper whose Ch. Vidmars Visibility Zero took a National Specialty in 1975.

Russell and Jane Shaw were active in the 1970s, as were Captain and Mrs. F. E. Rich, Arthur P. Donahue, Jacqueline Malick, T. M. McGinty, Dr. and Terry Carter, Jerome and Jane Lemkin, Anne Raker, Karen Murdock, Arliss and Charles Nygard, Mrs. Jackie Trevarthen, Pauline Davis, Marion Brown Donald and Barbara Krumpe, Cliff and Caryl Gheen who also had show winners.

Dr. and Mrs. W. J. Schlitt III were breeding out of their Pendragon Kennels in Salt Lake City, and were doing some importing.

We also heard from Dan and Carol Jones and their Hallmark dogs, Nancy Olson and Poppycock, the James Andersons and the Double JJ Farm, Mary Garvin and her Swedish and American Champion Holymans Adamson, C.A.C.I.B.

There were Roger and Nancy Smith and their Pinafore line, and Dick and Kathy Sewell and their Champaigne Powder Kennels. Susan Mogan was breeding under her Bluecote line.

There were also Richard and Ruby Bahner and Gingerly Ways, Joe and Susan Cunningham and Braeshire, Bill and Doris Hall with Wag'N'Bottom Kennels, Dave and Denny Ulrich, Dr. and Mrs. Michael Jacobs and Weatherby, Cheryl Whiteaker and Pembridge Bobtails, the Silvermoon Kennels, Rob and Cindy Bowe and their Shannonbo Kennel which produced the No. 1 Old English Sheepdog in the Midwest, No. 8 in the U.S. according to the Kennel Review System, and No. 6 Dispatch System. This was their Ch. Shannonbo's Jumpin' Jack Flash, C.D.

East Gate was the name used by Skip and Margaret Boothe and the marvelous MopTops, bred, owned, and handled by Woody Nelson.

SCALAWAGG

Pat and Mike Bolen of Encinitas, California, got into the breed in 1970 and joined the parent club in 1972 when they started their breeding program. Since their start they have finished 12 to 14 champions with more on the way.

The Bolens also run a boarding and grooming kennel and have recently gotten into Sealyham Terriers. In the past Mike has served as President and Treasurer of the National Club and they are also members of two other California Old English Sheepdog clubs.

SHAGGYPANTS

Margaret LaMorte of Glenwood, Illinois, started her Shaggypants Kennel in 1970 with the acquisition of Ch. My Shaggy Clown Pants, and quite obviously from which she derived her now famous kennel name.

In the years since 1970, at which time she also joined the parent club, she has finished 12 champions since starting to breed in 1972. When one inquires as to her other dog activities, her reply is, "Brushing, brushing, brushing, brushing and brushing."

JEN-KRIS

While the Jen-Kris Kennels are now located in Columbus, Ohio, they were originally started in Connecticut back in 1970. Laura Martin, a past vice president of the Old English Sheepdog Club of Greater New Haven is a former teacher, and is now thoroughly devoted to this breed in both show and obedience work. Since its inception, Jen-Kris has finished 11 champions and two obedience titlists. At present the Martins belong to the parent club and are most proud of their daughter Jennifer being named Top Junior Handler for 1984 by the Old English Sheepdog Club of America. They also bred the Top Producing Bitch for 1984, a tie, and plan to continue their winning ways.

Jen-Kris have sent dogs to Japan and the U.S.S.R. as well, and are proud of the fact that so many of their dogs are the foundation stock of other important kennels.

SHERWOOD SHAGGIES

Back in 1970, Julie LaBore of St. Paul, Minnesota began her Sherwood Shaggies Kennel. Since that time she has been active in both the show and obedience rings and to date has finished six U.S. and six Canadian champions and five U.S. and three Canadian titles, which include degrees from C.D. to U.D.

Julie spends her time as a professional groomer and uses her dogs in demonstrations at various nursing homes, etc.

QUBIC

1970 was the year that Mary Anne Brocious-Ninnis and Robert A. Brocious of Livonia, Michigan, began showing and breeding Old English Sheepdogs. They have finished 15 champions to date and Robert has belonged to the parent club since 1971. They also belong to the Ann Arbor all-breed club.

They use the name Qubic for their kennel and have also had Shih Tzu in their kennels. They have also been associated with Leader Dogs for the Blind and other dog organizations.

ERR-TAILS

Jerry and Bernice Ertel got into dogs in the 1970s. In 1976 they had Chocolate Cockers for awhile but started showing Old English in May of 1970. In 1977 they started breeding and have been active in the breed ever since. They are members of the parent club since 1978 as well as other clubs in which they have served in several capacities. They helped start the Greater Cincinnati Old English Sheepdog Club, and Bernice was President for four years. Their Err-Tails Kennels is one that has bred the natural born Bobtails.

HUG

Paula Coffman has been active in the breed since 1970, and since then has finished seven American champions and three Canadian champions. In obedience her record is equally impressive. She has finished three American C.D., two Canadian C.D.s and has one dog with the first leg on a C.D.X. She has also won a Dog World award.

Paula joined the parent club in 1972, has been a member of the Old English Sheepdog Club of Greater Cincinnati since 1980, and of White Water Valley Obedience Club since 1971. Needless to say, she chose her Hug Kennel name because she finds this breed so huggable! Her kennel is located in Liberty, Indiana.

PIROSKA

Irma Fertl of Houston, Texas, started showing dogs in 1971. Her breeding started in 1973 and to date she has finished six champions. She trained one of her dogs in obedience in 1975. She belongs to the parent and other Old English Sheepdog clubs and also has Persian show cats.

MYLUV

Mrs. Ellana L. Clarke of Stoutsville, Ohio, has been active in the breed since 1971, when she established her Myluv line. She joined the parent club at that time, and had her first litter in 1972. She is also in the grooming and boarding business and used to write a monthly column for *Dog World* magazine. She also has had Chinese Shar-Pei since 1982.

LOVE'N STUFF

Kristi and Marilyn Marshall are the owners of the Love'n Stuff Kennels in Sepulveda, California, where, since 1972, they have been showing and breeding Old English Sheepdogs. Since that time they have finished nine champions and one obedience titlist. They are members of the parent club since 1972. Kristi is show chairman for the Southern California Specialty show and Assistant Show Chairman for the Los Encinos Kennel Club. She is also on the Board of Directors for the Old English Sheepdog Club of Southern California and 1st V.P. for Los Encinos.

These two sisters will tell you their kennel is a wonderful hobby even though they take their dogs very seriously. They intend to do more in obedience, and they belong to the Valley Hills Obedience Club with this in mind.

SNIFLIK

The Sniflik name has been associated with Old English Sheepdogs since 1972 when Bob and Linda Burns first started showing and breeding in Green Valley, Missouri.

Members of the parent club, they have also finished many champions over the years and are still active in breeding Bobtails. Their most recent pride and joy bears the name Ch. Aphrodite Snow Sniflik, who was in the all-time Top Ten Producing stud dogs in 1983 and was Top Producing Stud Dog in 1981 and 1982. "Shadow" has produced 29 champion offspring to date, including two National Specialty winners.

JUBILEE

Bobbie Malott of the Jubilee Kennels in Warrenton, Virginia, started showing Old English Sheepdogs in 1972. While she is active in the show ring, and a member of the Bull Run Old English Sheepdog Club as well as the parent club, she does not consider herself a breeder. She admits to having bred one litter which she considered a "disaster" and since then has left the breeding problems to others. However, now that her husband is out of the Armed Service, they will perhaps be better able to show dogs a little more extensively. Meanwhile, she enjoys her 13-year-old "Anna" and Jubilee Jessica, along with Limey Lane Jubilee Jennifer.

AMIABLE

Warren and Carol Cooke of Chesapeake, Virginia, started showing Bobtails in 1973 and became active in obedience in 1977. Since then they have finished four champions and three obedience titlists to date. They have been members of the parent club since 1974 and Carol has been treasurer of the parent club since 1980. They are also active in the New England Club, the Old English Sheepdog Club of Rhode Island, Tidewater Kennel Club, Hampton Roads Obedience Training Club, Chesapeake Dog Fanciers Association, and the owner-handler association. Their littermates, Ch. Amiable's Star Warrior and Ch. Amiable's No Tails To Tell both finished for their C.D. titles at the same show on the same day.

LUVTYM

Janice Peterson of Grafton, Wisconsin got into the breed in 1974 when she began breeding Bobtails. She started showing them in 1975 and has finished five champions in the meantime. In 1979 she added English Cocker Spaniels to her Luvtym Kennels. In 1972 she joined the parent club and is also active in the Old English Sheepdog Club of Southeastern Wisconsin.

WHIMSEY OLD ENGLISH

Mr. and Mrs. William F. Brown of Winfield, West Virginia, have chosen "Whimsey" as their kennel name and have an impressive coat-of-arms to go with it. They joined the parent club in 1974 and to date have finished four champions. They are also members of the Magic Valley Kennel Club and have taught classes at Southern West Virginia Community College. In addition, they have also had Tibetan Terriers since 1977. Brenda Brown is also active in welfare rescue of dogs, and reports that, unfortunately, some are Old English Sheepdogs, which she frequently manages to place in proper homes.

FAMILYTREE

John and Danna Bankovskis of Beavercreek, Ohio, joined the parent club in 1974. Since their interest in our breed grew, they soon joined the Dayton Kennel Club in their area. They began showing   May 6, 1975, but they didn't begin breeding until January 1982. They have since finished a champion with several others pointed and on the way to gaining their titles. Danna has also illustrated for the national club magazine and for a local Old English Sheepdog club calendar.

MIDSOMER

Mrs. Sally Shawfrank of Jacksonville, Florida, has used Midsomer as her kennel prefix since breeding in 1976. She has been showing Bobtails since 1974 and has finished seven champions to date. She has been a member of the parent club since 1974 and has done limited judging.

Her Ch. Whisperwood Midsomer Snow was the No. 1 Old English Sheepdog bitch, No. 10 Old English Sheepdog in 1983, and also No. 3 Old English Sheepdog bitch and No. 6 Old English Sheepdog in 1984. Snow has 18 Groups, 20 Group Seconds, eight Group Thirds and eight Group Fourths. Whelped in 1982, she was the winner of the Canadian National Specialty show from the classes, and winner of the Chicago Old English Sheepdog Spe-

Champion Whimsey's Piece of the Rock, owned by William F. Brown of Winfield, West Virginia, pictured finishing for champioship with handler Bobby Barlow. The sire was Champion Jendower's Paddy X Brown's Lady Blue Feathers.

cialty from the 9–12 Puppy Class. She was a Group Winner at 12 months of age and is always owner-handled.

MERRIWEATHER
Clare Switzer started showing Old English Sheepdogs in April 1975. Her kennel name is Merriweather, and it is located in Mt. Carmel, Pennsylvania. She started breeding in 1981, and in 1976 joined the parent club. She is also a member of the Mid-Susquehanna Valley Kennel Club.

Her kennel consists of about five Old English. Needless to say, the fact that she is a professional dog groomer helps with this long-haired breed!

WXICOF
Don and Coreen Eaton started showing Old English Sheepdogs in 1975 and haven't stopped since. They have been active in both the conformation and the obedience rings and belong to the parent club as well as to a local specialty club in St. Louis.

To date they have finished one American and two Canadian champions in both the show ring and in the obedience rings. Not only do they show dogs at dog shows, but Coreen usually has a booth at the show where she sells gift items and books. She describes her shop as being a unique shop specializing in "Pet-Pourri."

Their kennel name is pronounced "walks off," is an aviation term.

HAIRLOOM
Lyle and Helen McDonell of Kansas City, Missouri, got into Old English Sheepdogs in the mid 1970s. They have finished two champions and have been breeding since 1980.

They are members of the parent club and concentrate only on this one favorite breed. Some of their top dogs are Ch. Warwyck Stanley Steamer, which they co-own with Melvin and Vinita Smith, and their Ch. Hairlooms April Showers.

GALAXIE
Mike and Nancy Fournier of Lewiston, Maine, have the Galaxie kennels since they got into the breed in 1976. They are members

of the New England Old English Sheepdog Club and while they only started breeding in 1983, they are known for having one of the top winning dogs in the breed.

Their American and Canadian Champion Whisperwood Winslow was owner-handled to both of his championships and later by Bob Forsyth to a record of five Bests in Show, a Specialty, 82 Bests of Breed, 17 Group Firsts and 26 other Group Placements.

Troy was retired from the ring at Westminster Kennel Club in 1979 after winning the breed under Dee Mattern and then on to a Group Third. Mike and Nancy attribute a lot of his success to Joyce Wetzler and acknowledge his sire Ch. Bahlambs Brazen Bandit and his dam Ch. Rivermist Morning Glory. Troy was Top Old English Sheepdog in 1978 and is still one of the all-time greats in the breed.

COBBYSTOCK

Lorraine Gipson of the Cobbystock Old English Sheepdog line is located in Firth, Idaho. Lorraine and her daughter, Patricia, have been busy in the breed since 1976 and have literally made history with their various activities and achievements.

Lorraine taught in the 4-H program for over nine years while Pat was also a junior leader with them for nine years. In fact, Patricia won a trip to the National Congress in 1984 for a dog project she put together. Both of them judge at local 4-H fun matches. To date they have finished three conformation champions, five C.D. titles and two C.D.X.s.

Perhaps their most outstanding accomplishment to date is Pat and her record with Gipson's Big Moses, C.D.X. Not only did she pick him out at birth as a very special dog, but started training him when she was eight years old. Since then they have won 108 trophies, two consecutive trips to compete at Westminster, and another trip to Chicago International and the National 4-H Congress. Pat was Top Junior Handler for the parent club in 1979 and 1980, and Idaho's Top Junior handler for the same years. She was also the first from that state to qualify for Westminster, and was in the Showmanship finals at Westminster in 1980 and 1981. Moses has appeared on the stage in musicals in 1983 and 1984. Pat is currently training him for U.D. title.

She has also shown other Old English Sheepdogs to both obedience and show titles winning three majors in three days and a

C.D. title in three consecutive shows with scores in the 190s, with her Ch. Pembridge Doing My Thing, C.D.

Their first Best in Show dog was Ch. Cobbystock Lord Chumly, C.D. who was born on St. Patrick's Day in 1982. His record to date is two Group Firsts, three Group Seconds, one Group Third, the aforementioned Best in Show and 15 Bests of Breed. He finished as No. 13 Old English Sheepdog in the nation for 1984 and qualified for Showdog of the Year that same year.

To date Doing My Thing is the dam of two champions and a C.D.X. titlist. Truly a story to be proud of.

NOB-LEE

Since 1976, when Barry L. Deist of Carnegie, Pennsylvania, started breeding and showing Bobtails, he has finished five champions. He is a member of the parent club since 1984 and the all-breed Columbiana Kennel Club as well as other Old English Sheepdog clubs. He handles and co-owns several top dogs that are winning in the show rings.

POOH BEAR

1976 was the year that Robert and Kathie Dhuey of Mantua, Ohio, started their Pooh Bear's Country Kennel. They started showing Bobtails that summer and began their breeding program July 4th of the same year. Since then they have finished eight champions.

They belong to the parent club and on July 4, 1985 celebrated Ch. Pooh Bear's Pinball Wizard's ninth birthday. Some of his get that they are especially proud of are Ch. Pooh Bear's Special Edition, The Magic of Talisman, Gandalf the Grey and Australian Champion Royal Salute.

CARDWELL

Charilyn Cardwell resides, along with her dogs, in Palmer, Alaska, where she is a member of the Old English Sheepdog Club of Alaska. She is also a member of the Old English Sheepdog Club of America and has been both in the breed and a member of the clubs since 1976, when she started showing.

Her first champion to date is Marimoor Regal Sir Ruggles.

JOJO'S

In 1977, Jo Ellen Spaeth of West Bend, Wisconsin, started showing and obedience training her Old English Sheepdogs. Since then she has finished one champion with another on the way and three Old English. She also has Shelties and she has put three titles on her Shelties. As a matter of fact, she has been teaching obedience training since 1977. At this time her children are also actively involved in dogs, making JoJo's a family affair.

IT'S MAGIC

Ann Marie Levin of Reseda, California, is interested in both showing and obedience training. While she started in conformation classes in 1977, 1985 was the year that she says she got into obedience work. Her ex-husband finished their Landy Pandy of Lorne, and the first litter that carried her It's Magic kennel prefix was whelped in 1982.

Ann is a member of the parent club since 1976 and also the Golden State, and Southern California clubs as well.

BOCKENOD

Joan Murphy started showing "Chip," otherwise known as Tamara's Great Expectations, in 1977. She has also shown in the obedience ring and did some of the research for the obedience training book, *Companion, Competitors and Clowns* by B. Foster. Unfortunately, while Chip is pointed in both the U.S. and Canada, Joan was unable to complete his championship.

SNOWHITE

Adrienne and Ralph Schneeweiss of Pembroke Pines, Florida, started showing dogs in 1977 and have branched out in the breed since then. They and their dogs are members of both the parent club and the Ft. Lauderdale Dog Club, have been in obedience since 1984, and have had the pleasure of seeing their dogs in advertisements for many major products.

Their first Old English was a British import that was also their first champion, and it sold them on the breed. Their second champion was Ch. Moptop's Show 'n Tell, who also did his share of winning.

The Schneeweisses had their first litter in 1983. They have chosen Snowhite as their kennel prefix and Adrienne declares she would like to become a judge at some time in the future.

WHIRLWIND
Dave and Suzy Bethards own the Whirlwind Kennels in Cleburne, Texas. In 1978, Suzy was eight years old and began showing dogs and loved it, as she states. The heartbreak came when one of their dogs was killed tragically after Suzy had already put two legs toward title on the dog.

Suzy also has a Pet Show for grooming supplies and is a professional dog groomer. The Bethards are members of the parent club and the North Texas Old English Sheepdog club. Since 1982, Suzy has also had a Treeing Walker dog.

They have four children and all of them appear to be interested in junior handling, and their son Jason is interested in obedience also.

TANGLEWOOL
Tanglewool owners Pamela and Maris Caibe of Anchorage, Kentucky, have been showing Old English Sheepdogs since 1978. It was in 1979 that they finished their first homebred champion, Tanglewools Pepper Mint Shag. She earned her R.O.M. by producing Champions Emmett Kelly, Calico Easter and Hallmark. Out of Hallmark they now have Ch. Tanglewools Precious Juno, and they have just begun showing Tanglewools Heavens To Betsy. Betsy recently won Winners Bitch at the National Specialty in Virginia over 88 bitches.

Betsy's mother, Ch. Grenwal Seraph O'Tanglewool, finished at the 1981 National Specialty in Detroit over an entry of 110 bitches. It seems to run in the family!

Their daughter Jennifer, seen in so many beautiful photos taken by her photographer mother, is training Pepper for 4-H dog training and working toward a C.D. obedience title.

Pam's photographic artistry was seen on a 1985 cover of the *American Kennel Gazette*.

THE HAGOODS
Colonel Lacy E. and Elizabeth Ann Hagood of Clifton, Virginia, have been associated with dogs since 1950, but Bobtails in

particular since 1979. They began showing their Ch. Pooh Bear's Sir Winston then and are members of both the parent club and the Bull Run Old English Sheepdog Club. They also have Miniature Dachshunds, two Siberian Huskies and a Samoyed.

WINDFALL
Arlene Pietrocola told us that "tentatively" her kennel prefix would be Windfall. Perhaps that is appropriate for it truly was a "windfall" for her to acquire a dog like her American and Canadian Champion Lord Sebastian Travis, C.D.

Active in obedience since 1978, she has finished two dogs to their obedience titles and has been showing in conformation since 1982. Arlene calls Travis, or "Sebbie," a Cinderella Fella dog. When she acquired him at three-and-a-half years of age, she brought him out at a match show. Needless to say, he went all the way to the top award. He finished for his American championship quickly and his Canadian championship was earned within 24 hours, over Specials in three shows.

Sebbie is also a prominent figure at 4-H Club gatherings and has appeared in newspapers and on TV, and in Arlene's classes for 1st grade.

Arlene is a member of the parent club, the Twin Colonies Old English Sheepdog club and the Ramapo all-breed Kennel Club.

She started using Sebbie at stud in 1984 and he has an American champion son and a Canadian champion daughter, with more pointed and to come. He has also earned his C.D. obedience title.

WYNSILOT
Dale Meyer has his Wynsilot Kennels in Dorchester, Wisconsin, where he has been showing Bobtails since 1978. His first litter was bred in 1980, the same year he joined the parent club. He is also a member of the Paper Cities all-breed club in his area.

TEE TYME
Jane Newton of Tempe, Arizona, has been in the breed since 1979. She has finished two champions and one obedience titlist since that time. She is a member of the parent club since 1980 and has a daughter who began junior showmanship training, at age

nine, in 1985. Jane considered the dogs as "guardian angels" for her children.

SHASTA

Mrs. Sharon Arbuckle has been in the breed since July 1979. Over the years she has had four litters but only in 1985 did she start showing her dogs. Her son Shawn has been active with their Scarborough's Shasta Daisy in 4-H Club obedience competition since 1984.

Sharon bought her first Bobtail in 1976, the second in 1977, and another in 1983. She is a member of the parent club since 1983 and the Old English Sheepdog Club of Greater Cincinnati. Sharon intends to use the kennel prefix "Shasta" on future litters where she has started her kennel in Elwood, Indiana.

LONDONAIRE

Fred and Karen Stetler have plans to put obedience titles on all their dogs at their Londonaire Kennels in Sacramento, California. Since 1979 this has been their goal and to date they have finished two champions, another with points in the show ring, two C.D. titles and two more moving up in the obedience category.

They belong to the parent club as well as the Old English Sheepdog League of Northern California and have held office in this club as well as other all-breed and breed clubs. Their "other" breed is the Bearded Collie, which joined the fold in 1980.

BLUE MOUNTAIN

Pam Henry has her Blue Mountain Kennel in Citrus Heights, California, where she has been active in the breed since 1979.

She has been breeding since 1981 and in 1984 started her Blue Mountain Boggart in both the obedience and conformation rings.

She is a member of the parent club, the Old English Sheepdog League of Northern California and is membership chairperson and editor of the club Newsletter.

TIMBERMIST

Dr. Steve and Joyce Vanek-Nielsen have their Timbermist Kennels in Evergreen, Colorado.

One of their most recent claims to fame was being winners in "The Most Wonderful Pet" contest, judged by actress Betty White. This national event serves as a public service organization to stress the joys of responsible pet ownership. Their "Tank," for instance, responds to commands in three languages besides English, and has won many friends for the breed.

The Timbermist Bobtails have also been featured on many of the Gaines Calendars over the years and excel in the obedience rings as well as show rings. They also are proficient at backpacking and sometimes accompany the Nielsens on their mountain-climbing escapades.

BRIGADOON

Kirk and Susan Ogden have selected Brigadoon as their kennel since they hope to start breeding very shortly. They started showing in the fall of 1980 and hope to finish their foundation bitch, Tokien Chica Chubb. Their male, Tackleton's Lord Devonshire, or "Devon" prefers the house to the show ring, so his show career is uncertain.

The Ogdens belong to the parent club and also the Twin Colonies Old English Sheepdog Club of Northern New Jersey. Susan also serves as an Old English Sheepdog "contact" through her veterinarian for those interested in the breed. This, of course, is in addition to looking after her infant daughter, Brittany, who also adores her two furry pals. Brigadoon is located in Rockaway Township, New Jersey.

FIELDS

Since February, 1980, when Melanie Mason Fields of Anderson, Indiana, first got into the breed, she has concentrated on obedience training. Her Melanie's Shaggy Bear has his C.D.X. title and another puppy named Loehrs Spoonful of Sugar might well be on his way!

In July 1982 she started showing her dogs, so perhaps we will have Bobtails at her house with two titles. In her spare time, Melanie takes her obedience trained dog to various nursing homes in her area to help entertain the elderly. This is a function of the Anderson Obedience Training Club, to which she has belonged since 1979.

She is also a member of the parent club since 1981 and the Old English Sheepdog Club of Greater Cincinnati since 1984.

PANCELOT

Relative newcomers to the breed, Raymond and Pat Heynis of Hainesville, Illinois, are members of the parent club and also the Chicagoland Old English Sheepdog club.

They bought their first Old English Sheepdog in 1982 as a pet. In January of 1985 they bought another specifically with showing in mind. Both Ray and Pat have had other breeds but they are now addicted to this one and we can look forward to seeing them in the show ring in the future, with dogs and their Pancelot prefix.

McBETH

Mary Beth Smith of Cincinnati, Ohio, chose McBeth for her kennel name for rather obvious reasons. When she started showing in the spring of 1982 she also joined the parent club and has been president of the Old English Sheepdog Club of Greater Cincinnati for two years. In addition she is a member of the Northern Kentucky Kennel Club, serves as a ring steward and is active in the local match shows.

She has also had Maltese dogs since 1984, and intends to become active in obedience work. She also intends to breed Bobtails in the future, and had her first litter in January 1983.

CRESCENDO

Actually Robert and Phyllis Burton of Oak Park, Michigan, started with Yorkshire Terriers back in 1980. But in 1981 they started showing Bobtails and have been hooked on the breed ever since. They have finished two champions to date and had their first litter in 1983 under their Crescendo kennel prefix. They are members of the parent club and a Yorkie club as well.

McDERMOTT

Joan McDermott of New Berlin, Wisconsin, is relatively new to the breed and has not yet selected a kennel name for her Old English Sheepdogs. Since 1983 she has acquired Ch. Windfield Lord Nelson and started showing him to championship.

She is a member of the parent club and the local Old English Sheepdog Club of South Eastern Wisconsin.

Champion Rivermist Dan Patch, a famous dog in the 1960s.

Canadian and American Champion Rivermist Feather Merchant, C.D., and No. 1 Old English Sheepdog in Canada in 1970–71. Feather was a Canadian Best in Show winner, and a multi-U.S. Group and Specialty Winner. Bred by Barry Goodman and Nancie Miller, he is co-owned by Dr. and Mrs. Gary Carter and James McTernan of Calgary, Canada. The win shown here under the late, great dog man, Alva Rosenberg.

Chapter 5

Old English Sheepdogs in Canada

Interest in the breed was growing north of our border in the 1970s. Mrs. Barbara Vanword's Barvan Kennels came up with an American, Canadian and Bermudian Champion named Sir Lancelot of Barvan. He was featured as a cover dog on the magazine *Old English Dispatch* published and edited by Jim Philps in the fall of 1975. This dog had a remarkable show ring record with 39 Canadian Bests in Show along with 63 Group Firsts, 35 Group Seconds, 14 Thirds and approximately 185 Bests of Breed. He was handled by Malcolm Fellows for the owner.

Mrs. Martin Doherty had her Auriga Kennels in Ontario, and Dr. and Mrs. Gary Carter used the prefix Some Buddy's for their Bobtails. John and Edie Shields were also breeding in Calgary, Alberta, under the name of Bugaboo.

SOME BUDDY

Dr. and Mrs. Gary Carter of Calgary, Alberta, started their Some Buddy Old English Sheepdog kennels in 1966. Since that time they have finished 57 Canadian champions and 24 American champions, plus one Danish champion as well as other champions that do not bear their kennel prefix. They have also finished more than 12 obedience titlists.

They are also members of the U.S. parent club since 1968 and the Old English Sheepdog Fanciers of Alberta, and a local all-breed club. They also run local obedience and conformation training classes and hold grooming seminars. At some time in the future Mrs. Terry Carter would like to become a judge. She is also the author of a booklet entitled, *Care of Your Old English Sheepdog*. It includes showing and grooming and tips on raising for the beginner in the breed.

APHRODITE
Since 1971, when Bette Maxwell of Guelph, Ontario got started in the breed, she has amassed a remarkable record of champions in both Canada and the U.S.A. In that time she has finished 21 Canadian and American Champions, 32 American Champions and 41 Canadian Champions. She has owned or bred many others that are pointed.

Along with husband Ken, she started showing in 1971 and breeding in 1974. They have approximately one litter a year, which makes their record all the more impressive. Bette judged the Sweepstakes at the 1985 National Specialty show and she also judges at match shows. She is a member of the parent club in the U.S. since 1984.

WOOLOVER
Everatt and Laurel Basaraba of Winnipeg, Manitoba, use the prefix Woolover for their Old English Sheepdogs. They started showing in 1975, the year they finished their first champion, and have bred one litter. This first champion, Canadian Ch. Moptop's Blue Madam was their brood bitch and the start of the Woolover line. "Minnie," as she is affectionately known, had one litter, in 1978, before her demise. Their second champion was under their own kennel name.

Laurel is Secretary of the Old English Sheepdog Club of Manitoba. They have belonged to the U.S. parent club since 1974.

BENWYCK
Since 1976 when Victor and Kathleen Chan established their Benwyck Kennels in Victoria, British Columbia, they have finished six champions. They have belonged to the parent club in the

A father-daughter picture of two of Canada's best— Champion Farfelu Facsimile, R.O.M., and Canadian and American Champion Snow Dumpling, top producing sire and dam in Canada for 1979. Owned by Bette Maxwell, Ontario, Canada.

U.S.A. and also the Canadian Kennel Club, Barrie Kennel Club, Darthmouth and Newfoundland all-breed. They have also had Afghan Hounds and Pembroke Corgis.

BLUECALEB

Since 1976, when Betty Fast got into the breed, she has finished six champions and four obedience titlists from her Bluecaleb Kennels in Saskatoon, Saskatchewan. While Betty is a member of the Old English Sheepdog Club of America since '1981, she is vice president of the Working Dog Association of Saskatoon, and is an obedience trainer in all breeds of dogs in her area.

Since 1981, she has also had Standard wire-haired Dachshunds. All her dogs have participated as "Mr. Mugs" dogs, a reading series used in the elementary grades. They are also utilized for other demonstration work as well.

While her Ashbee is now quite old, he still is active and watches Betty putting all her dogs through their training at least to the C.D. title level.

WIGGLEBUM

Joyce and Guy Bilodean of Kamloops, British Columbia, have been in the breed since 1980, when they began showing their Bobtails. They have belonged to the Old English Sheepdog Club of America since 1981 and also local clubs in Canada.

Joyce is also a groomer and conditioner, and states that they only breed once in a while to keep a small kennel which offers individual attention to each dog. Since getting into the breed they have finished six champions to date.

Australian Champion Weeack Old Man's Beard, whelped in 1978 and owned by Liris Gaul of New South Wales. Beard won his championship at just 12 months of age and earned more than 1000 points before age three. He is the sire of champions and comes from a litter of three champions.

Chapter 6

The Breed Down Under

Shows are usually held every weekend in Victoria, but the top shows for dog fanciers are the "Royals" which are conducted by the Royal Agricultural Society in each capital city of Australia. They run from seven to ten days, with different breeds being exhibited each day. The shows are benched, and sometimes run from nine in the morning to nine at night. Group and General Specials are judged on the last main show day.

Old English Sheepdog entries usually run from 75 to 200 dogs at the Sydney, Adelaide, and Melbourne shows where the Challenge Certificates are awarded. Males and females are judged separately, as in our country, with classes for Minor puppy (6–9 months); Junior (9–12 months); Intermediate (18 months to 3 years); and Open (any dog over 6 months!).

After breed judging, males and females individually compete for Group Specials. Best Exhibit in Group is awarded plus Best Opposite. The six best exhibits compete for Best in Show and Best Opposite in Show. Judging can vary from state to state.

Bobtails are judged in Group 5 with other herding breeds and most dogs are owner-handled.

OES CLUB OF VICTORIA

The Old English Sheepdog Club of Victoria was formed in 1968 and became affiliated with the Kennel Control Council of Victoria in 1971. One of the major events of the club has been an Open Parade and a championship show each year. The Parade is for dogs which have not as yet attained championship and gives them the opportunity to "strut their stuff." The club tries to obtain an overseas judge for this event and in the past few years has had Mona Berkowitz from the United States, Isobel Lanesen from Britain and several judges from New Zealand.

This club is unique in that it not only caters to the show dogs, but serves the breed in other ways through dedicated committees that address such pursuits as Welfare, Breed Information, Fund Raising, Publicity, Library and Club History, and of course, obedience work. The club regularly conducts obedience classes, grooming, and show handling classes as well. From this effort a team is selected to give a demonstration in obedience at the Melbourne Royal Show, one of the most prestigious shows in Australia.

Their Welfare and Rescue committee does much work, since the ever-present threat of "over population" in the breed has reached this country also. The constant need for finding proper homes for unwanted dogs is a never-ending struggle for that committee.

The club has published two booklets. "A Puppy Buyer's Guide" is one on grooming and care of the Bobtails. There is also a Gazette, of approximately twenty pages of news and happenings in the breed which is of high quality and much value to all in Australia.

The club also conducts a Dog and Bitch of the Year competition and while each section of Australia has a club for its area, there is much cooperation among them toward the good and welfare of the breed throughout all of Australia.

WESTERN AUSTRALIA

The first Old English Sheepdog was registered in Western Australia in 1968. Mr. and Mrs. Ron Slavin acquired Kersbrook Kealia from South Australia. She was sired by Border Riever of Tarras, a British import ex Chandos Polly Perkins and received her first Challenge Certificate the same year. She was to produce three litters for the Slavin's Bonnybow kennels.

In 1968 Harold and Phyllis Harper brought Fettlara Hansom from Victoria and won the Australian championship title in 1971.

70

This made him the first Old English Sheepdog champion in that state. His get did a lot of winning and gained titles, and his name appears on many pedigrees.

By the following year, 1969, Western Australia produced its first homebred champion in Kersbrook Prudence, owned by Mrs. A. Griffin and her Jessmond prefix.

1970 saw more arrivals from Victoria. The Slavins bought a "pal" for Bow, Clarburg Noman, and the Salismans bought a bitch, Clarburg Breman, sired by Mantin Wee Geordie ex Applegate Lady Emma. They both were prepotent breeders.

Three Bobtails arrived in 1971. The first was Saintives Lady Jane from South Australia, purchased by David Hilary for his Thryton prefix. Second came Tumblegum Abigail, owned by the Thompsons. Their prefix from two litters was Appleby. Next was Nellemert Baggins, owned by Tricia and Jim Allender, and she made her title in 1972. These last two produced five champions between them.

1971 also marked the first homebred litters—three litters representing 14 puppies. By 1972 four litters were registered and in 1973, there were nine. 1974 saw eight litters registered in the state, with two championships. By 1977 there was a definite decline in re-registration from state to state, and three imports arrived from England. Tallyham Jumbo, brought out by Mrs. Eames but later owned by Mrs. Causton, was one of them.

In 1974 the Old English Sheepdog Club of Western Australia was formed; Ian MacLean chaired the first meeting with 35 members joining. The first president was David Hillary.

FIRST IMPORTS

1975 marked the date for the first English imports. Joanne Sewell brought out Rollingsea Suzi Bear, bred by Jean Gould. She won her title in 1977 and produced four litters. By 1976, three more English imports arrived on the scene. This year the entry at the Perth Royal was 24; the Challenge Certificate went to Ch. Kenverne Paddy, C.D. and the Bitch Challenge to Ch. Baggins Tessa Tiptoes with 19 bitches entered.

Three seemed to be the magic number since three more English imports arrived in 1978 with re-registrations from all states except Queensland. Charlie and Helen Merrin added Oldash Sea Amber to their kennels, where she was to produce five litters.

Twenty-one litters were registered in 1978 as once again the interest in showing began to decrease. But in 1979, more English imports once again spurred dog show competition. It was also the year that the club became affiliated with the Canine Association, after much hard work by the members.

In 1980, an Old English Sheepdog went Best in Show at the anniversary Classic, and by 1981, two more Bobtails had gained their titles: Barnshaw Macho Man and Regencyblue Miss Eliza.

In 1982 and 1983, less breeding was done since there was the beginning of a feeling of overpopulation among the breeders. 1983 also showed a drop off in show entries. At the fifth Western Classic only 13 dogs were entered, with the Challenge Certificate going to Ch. Woolliwoof Two Knight, and the bitches to Silverstreak Kizmet out of 11 bitches.

1984 and 1985 saw a continued decline—only seven litters were registered and entries were down at the shows. Mrs. Diane Anderson of Norway judged the show again after a few years' absence and awarded the Challenge to Shadyoak Gamblin Man from the Minor Dog Class. Regencyblue Miss Eliza once again won in bitches.

The Hunson Kennels Champion Movama Manhatton, whelped in 1977. The sire was Australian Champion Bluwaldoe Roly Poly, an import from the United Kingdom X Jolifoot Tivoli Star. Owners, Barrie and Jean MacDonald.

Oklahoma Jassy with her friend Champion Beila Miss Dulcibella and Regencyblue The Whig hiding under the hat. Photographed with two human friends in 1977 in Western Australia.

In 1984, the first Canadian import was shown. Owned by P. Robinson, American and Canadian Champion Tarawoods Classic Impression was exhibited at the Royal show.

Other worthy specimens in and around Australia are Prospect-blue Victor, Falconhurst Fuzz Buzz, Barkwith All Agog of Oldash, Shaggyshire Wonder, and Jindella Bags O'Swank, whose dam was Momarvs Misstruss Lufu, an import from the U.S.A.

REMARKABLE DUAL CHAMPION

Australian Champion Flomont Tassyboy Debel, U.D., is the name of Ron and Sue Quayle's dual champion, a dog that has really made history in the breed.

Tassy began his obedience career with the Northern Obedience Dog Club in 1973 at seven months of age. He was the first Old English Sheepdog in Victoria to gain a C.D. title. In September of 1974, he gained his C.D.X. He began Utility Class work in 1975, but it was just not his year. He used this year to earn his show ring championship and to win Open A at the Adelaide Royal. In 1976, he began U.D. points and earned the U.D. title in November, thus becoming the first Bobtail in Australia to achieve the U.D. title. In 1976 he continued training and appeared on a TV show entitled "Young Ramsey" which brought him additional fame.

Champion Shaggywonder Prince Charming, sire of 20 champions. This Belgian import was selected by judge Mrs. Meens, a top European breeder, to be sent to the Marvin Smiths for their Tamara Kennels. He was on the cover of *Dog World* magazine in 1973.

Chapter 7

Old English Sheepdogs Around the World

THE NETHERLANDS

Generally speaking the breed in the Netherlands is said to be of rather poor quality. There seems to be little tendency to breed for quality, and therefore, many of the better dogs are overlooked in the breeding programs—this in spite of the fact the breed is quite popular and there are many individually known dogs that could well enhance the lines.

Coats are said to be poor, conditioning of the dogs poor with the exception of the few top dogs that attend shows rather regularly and travel outside their own country.

There is an Old English Sheepdog Club but, although this single club is all that is allowed (in any breed), the members seem to be almost always at odds with each other and little is accomplished.

Judges abide by the British breed Standard, use the Grading System of four ratings, i.e., Excellent, Very Good, Good, and Poor.

There are two separate championship titles, one for the Netherlands and the International Champion. To become a Netherlands Champion a dog must win four C.A.C. under two different judges. One must be won after nine months of age and the other after 27 months of age.

Entries at show average about 50 to 70 dogs, and are increasing. The classifications are open, junior, champion class, and, occasionally, a breeders class. Sexes are split and dogs may compete in one class only.

The leading dog in the 1980s is Netherlands International Champion Reeuwijkscare for Beauty.

GERMANY AND AUSTRIA

By the turn of the century the Old English Sheepdog had spread across most of Europe. It was popular in Germany where there were some worthy specimens, and in Austria, where it was very rare. In fact, when the first one appeared at a dog show in Vienna, it caused a sensation, and shortly thereafter, many of them were imported to Austria, after which the breed became only slightly more established.

FRANCE

Madame J. Plaim and a Mrs. Gordon showed up with their bobtails at a 1933 dog show in Paris and had their photographs taken with them for a syndicated news release. However, by the later 1930s there were quite a few of the breed in that country where they were often seen on the boulevards as well as on the country farms.

JAPAN

It was in the 1950s that the first Old English Sheepdog was introduced to the Japanese dog fanciers, yet although several could be seen in the major cities, it was not until 1970 or thereabouts that the breed began to appear in the show rings.

It was during this time that two stud dogs were imported to Japan that had a great influence on the quality of the puppies, making them eligible for the show ring. One of these was the British import, King Edward. Another was Reeuwyk's Prince Charming. As a result of this new blood, the breed increased in numbers and the names of these two dogs could be found in almost every bloodline in the bobtails in Japan.

By the mid-1980s, the yearly registrations of the breed became approximately five hundred each year. The first Japanese Old English Sheepdog Specialty show has been held, since the quality has improved after so many years of inbreeding before the influence of the imports could be seen. However, the Japanese breeders and exhibitors in Japan will be the first to admit that there is still room for much improvement in the breed.

One of the leading kennels in Japan today is that of Miss Chieko Kurashima of Tokyo. Her Clutch House Kennels was established in 1974, when she fell in love with the breed after seeing Walt Disney's movie "The Shaggy Dog" featuring an Old English Sheepdog. Her first bobtail, named Aiko, is still alive and well.

Her next was another female named Momoko. She has now acquired all available titles in Japan, namely International Champion Grand Champion and F.C.I.W. Champion. Momoko has been named Best Breed in Japan for 1980 and 1981 and has produced several fine puppies.

Chieko is also a Japanese judge, and has finished two obedience titlists. In 1983, she acquired a son of American and Canadian Champion Marimoor Stormy Weather. "Takeru" and her Momoko produced a Best in Show son named King who is doing well in the all-breed shows.

Another leading kennel in Japan belongs to Fujiko Hasegawa of Shizuoka. She started breeding Old English Sheepdogs in 1965 and began showing her dogs in 1970. She is a member of the Japanese Kennel Club, as is Chieko Kurashima, who joined in 1978.

Two other leading kennels in Japan that cherish the Old English Sheepdog are those of Mr. Ryusuke Kaneko of Aichi, and Mr. Kazuo Ogasawara of Kanagawa.

Today, entries in the classes for Old English Sheepdogs number around ten or twelve, with much enthusiasm and interest in the breed at ringside.

RUSSIA

Russia acknowledges both local and national champions, and these regional titles can be won many times by the same dog, though there is usually only one regional show each year. Every few years there is a show called an All National, and the national champion from this show is the top winning dog. Dogs are rated excellent, very good, fair, poor, or unacceptable, depending on both performance and conformation.

Russia held its first dog show in 1923, and shows have survived all regimes and political changes, though they are on a smaller scale than in other countries. As elsewhere in the world, the dedicated core of devoted breeders and exhibitors managed to preserve most of the important bloodlines during the various wars.

In Russia, if you wish to buy a dog you must do so through a local dog club, and the cost will depend on the quality and success of its sire and dam. You must then register the dog with the club after receiving the dog's papers, and if you wish to breed it you must consult with the Breeding Section of the same local club. Dogs which are permitted to be bred must have a show mark of X, or V.G. for dogs and at least G. for bitches as well as an obedience and/or utility degree. Dogs are registered with three independent branch organizations under Toy, Hunting or Service Dog categories, and then individually by breed.

The service dog clubs can be found in all major cities of Russia, and they are the central body overseeing all the activity under the name of the Federation of Service Dog Breeding.

There is no advertising of "puppies for sale," since there is always a demand for puppies, and no need to advertise!

The city of Moscow provides free veterinary care; however, there is a dog tax of 15 roubles (or $30 U.S. Funds) regardless of the breed, to cover costs. The way the Deputy Chief of the City Veterinary Department explains it is that it is a fee for dog care taken as partial compensation for the expenditures of laying out dogs' walking and training grounds and for vaccination and registrations.

He added that all kinds of veterinary care can be obtained free of charge in the U.S.S.R., whether one needs an emergency call, a consultation in a clinic, or an operation. In the city of Moscow alone there are 29 clubs for the appreciation of different dog breeds, with memberships totalling about 6000. (These statistics date back to about 1982.)

While no name or information was supplied, we do know that there is at least one "Owcharki," or sheepdog, in Russia, since its photograph was used in a feature story in the July 1985 issue of the *American Kennel Gazette*. This most interesting and informa-

Danish Champion Some Buddy's Canadian Ambassador. Bred by Dr. and Mrs. Gary Carter of Calgary, Canada, the owners are Birgette Schoeth and Herdis Thuesen. This dog was No. 1 Working Dog in Denmark and four of his offspring are in the Top Ten Old English Sheepdog. Sire was Canadian American Champion Buddy Catch The Action X Ch. Some Buddy's Love in Symphony.

tive article told of the dog fancy in Russia and a very respectable looking bobtail was shown in a color photograph and had many medals around his collar, apparently for wins.

Since our breed is so often said to be a possible cross from the Russian sheepdogs, we can only assume that they have been further developed to modern, worldwide Standards.

Doing what comes naturally—even as a puppy the herding of sheep is a natural instinct with this breed. Future Canadian Champion BluPrint's Country Squire is on guard. Owned by Don and Coreen Eaton of Ellisville, Missouri.

Chapter 8

Standard of the Breed

OFFICIAL STANDARD FOR THE OLD ENGLISH SHEEPDOG

SKULL—Capacious and rather squarely formed, giving plenty of room for brain power. The parts over the eyes should be well arched and the whole well covered with hair. *Jaw*—Fairly long, strong, square and truncated. The stop should be well defined to avoid a Deerhound face. (The attention of judges is particularly called to the above properties, as a long, narrow head is a deformity.) *Eyes*—Vary according to the color of the dog. Very dark preferred, but in the glaucous or blue dogs a pearl, walleye or china eye is considered typical. (A light eye is most objectionable.) *Nose*—Always black, large and capacious. *Teeth*—Strong and large, evenly placed and level in opposition. *Ears*—Medium-sized, and carried flat to side of head, coated moderately.

LEGS—The forelegs should be dead straight, with plenty of bone, removing the body a medium height from the ground, without approaching legginess, and well coated all around. *Feet*— Small, round; toes well arched, and pads thick and hard.

TAIL—It is preferable that there should be none. Should never, however, exceed 1½ or 2 inches in grown dogs. When not natural-born Bobtails, however, puppies should be docked at the first joint from the body and the operation performed when they are from three to four days old.

NECK AND SHOULDERS—The neck should be fairly long, arched gracefully and well coated with hair. The shoulders sloping and narrow at the points, the dog standing lower at the shoulder than at the loin.

BODY—Rather short and very compact, ribs well sprung and brisket deep and capacious. *Slabsidedness highly undesirable.* The loin should be very stout and gently arched, while the hindquarters should be round and muscular and with well-let down hocks, and the hams densely coated with a thick, long jacket in excess of any other part.

COAT—Profuse, but not so excessive as to give the impression of the dog being overfat, and of a good hard texture; not straight, but shaggy and free from curl. *Quality and texture of coat to be considered above mere profuseness.* Softness or flatness of coat to be considered a fault. The undercoat should be a waterproof pile, when not removed by grooming or season.

COLOR—Any shade of gray, grizzle, blue or blue-merle with or without white markings or in reverse. *Any shade of brown or fawn to be considered distinctly objectionable and not to be encouraged.*

SIZE—Twenty-two inches and upwards for dogs and slightly less for bitches. Type, character and symmetry are of the greatest importance and are on no account to be sacrificed to size alone.

GENERAL APPEARANCE AND CHARACTERISTIC—A strong, compact-looking dog of great symmetry, practically the same in measurement from shoulder to stern as in height, absolutely free from legginess or weaselness, very elastic in his gallop, but in walking or trotting he has a characteristic ambling or pacing movement, and his bark should be loud with a peculiar "potcasse" ring in it. Taking him all round, he is a profusely, but not *excessively* coated, thick-set, muscular, able-bodied dog with a most intelligent expression, free from all Poodle or Deerhound character. *Soundness should be considered of greatest importance.*

SCALE OF POINTS

Skull	5
Eyes	5
Ears	5
Teeth	5
Nose	5
Jaw	5
Foreface	5
Neck and Shoulders	5
Body and Loins	10
Hindquarters	10
Legs	10
Coat (texture, quality and condition)	15
General Appearance and Movement	15
TOTAL	**100**

Approved October 13, 1953

U.S. STANDARD vs. KENNEL CLUB (GREAT BRITAIN) STANDARD

It is interesting to note that while Old English Sheepdogs are sometimes imported and exported between the United States and Great Britain, there are a few discrepancies in the Standards for the breed.

While size is comparable, mention is made in both the British and the U.S. Standard on the characteristic "ambling gait" and "bear-like roll" so desirable to all Old English Sheepdog breeders. Color is also comparable with the emphasis on the undesirability of any tendency toward brown, with the U.S. including an acceptance of a "blue merle." The quality of coat is important in both countries and stress is put on no tendency toward a "curl," or waviness. There is little doubt that a "light" eye, varying only slightly in the U.S. according to the particular color of the dog, is undesirable.

Both countries are agreed on the squareness of body and the rather squarish head, and acknowledge fully the incredible marvelous disposition we have come to know and love in this breed on both sides of the Atlantic.

Chapter 9

The Old English Sheepdog As A Breed

ARTHUR ROLAND

In 1940, in a magazine article entitled "The Story of Pedigreed Dogs," Arthur Roland, dog man and dog columnist for *The New York Sun* newspaper, wrote an amusing piece about Mrs. Lewis Roesler's Champion Merriedip Master Pantaloons, bred at her Merriedip Kennels in Great Barrington, Massachusetts. With his usual tongue-in-cheek style, he wrote in part: "Like the Holy Roman Empire, which wasn't an empire, wasn't Roman, and wasn't holy, the Old English Sheepdog isn't an old breed, isn't English, and isn't a sheepdog so much as a cattle dog."

While he refers to the earliest known record being a Gainsborough portrait circa 1771, he professes the ancestry to be a toss-up between the Scotch Bearded Collie and the Russian Owtchar, even though it was developed in western England. He goes on to tout their herding abilities, he apparently deplores the excess of coat the modern-day dogs carry, and he states that we have been creating "A Society of the Unseeing Eye" since the turn of the century. He declares, however, that in spite of this handicap, the Bobtail remains an excellent house dog, watch dog, and hunter.

In regard to the Bobtail, he recalls the history of their early cattle-driving days when the dogs were not taxable and their tails cut off labeled them as such.

Other attributes with which he blesses the breed consist of their sense of humor, their thoughtfulness, and their fitting into any household situation in spite of their size. He continues with his praise by saying that they are not given to roaming or fighting nor are they boisterous.

In describing the Old English Sheepdog in motion, Mr. Roland waxes poetic as follows: "The Bobtail rolls and shuffles like a bear, moving his hindquarters much more than his headquarters; yet in rapid motion he is singularly free and moves almost without effort."

His words of wisdom on the vocal emanations read as follows: "His bark is queer and loud—if you happen to have a French dictionary around somewhere, look up *potcasse,* which should describe it."

IS THIS THE BREED FOR YOU?

You've decided that you think the Old English Sheepdog is a beautiful animal and you're entranced with its royal heritage in merry olde England. You're impressed with the stories of their performance in the fields and you're convinced you want to share your life with one. Wonderful! But have you and your family considered all aspects of the responsibilities and physical requirements for owning one?

Needless to say, if you want to proudly walk your grown Bobtail down the street, are you physically able to handle yourself and the dog if you encounter another dog? Can you restrain your dog if he is required to defend himself or you, or if he is the instigator in a dog fight where you might end up in the middle of the fracas?

Would other members of your family be physically able to restrain the dog if the situation were theirs? Can you and members of your family handle the dog walking down the aisles past other dogs at a dog show if you buy a show dog to exhibit? You must also ask yourself if there is a danger within your home, are there elderly people or young children that the dog might knock down or jump on and injure, even playfully? You must presume that if you invest in an Old English Sheepdog, it will be sharing your life for the next 15 years or more, and you should be aware of what problems might arise during that period of time.

We all think the Old English Sheepdog is a magnificent animal, and we all love to have beautiful things to look at and enjoy, but this is a large, living creature that must fit into our lives. A family discussion and a long informative talk with the breeder before your purchase are essential if there are any doubts in your mind about your way of life and the part this dog will play in it. Don't buy a dog and become attached to it, only to find you've made a mistake. Preliminary planning is one of the most important parts of bringing a dog into your life.

These questions, by the way, should be passed along to any prospective customers you might have when selling puppies. The young ones suffer the most if they are shunted from home to home, and owner to owner, if they don't fit into their new environment. This is your responsibility as a breeder—or as a prospective buyer. Take it seriously. Don't be sorry.

TEMPERAMENT

Whatever self-praise we might heap upon ourselves today when commenting on the temperament of our dogs, we must just as readily admit that in the early days there might have been some dissention on this opinion. We know Bobtails can be stubborn at times, but obviously many years ago there were definite personality differences.

In *The Book of the Dog*, A.S.L. Wallis writes: ". . . the breed has often an unenviable reputation for moroseness and savagery. I think it may be true that a Bobtail kept without exercise would become short-tempered; but properly cared for, there is no more delightful and tractable companion, and certainly no more intelligent one . . . no, not even the poodle. I know no animal more sensitive to praise or blame; I know no animal more sagacious in its general day to day relations with a human family! I know no breed that shows such astounding comprehension of the inflexions of human speech. And I have kept a lot of dogs in my time. But there is no need to stress the remarkable sagacity of the Old English Sheepdog."

Enough said.

THE HERDING INSTINCT

On occasion you will notice you get a little nip or push in the back from your Old English Sheepdog. This is not in any way to be construed as a mean streak, nastiness, or bad temper, which has been questioned by some over the years. This leaning, bumping, or little act of assertiveness is actually part of the herding instinct, which makes the dog endeavor to corral or herd even people.

Should he sense danger, particularly, you will find him on his feet and circling, ready to do what comes naturally. We must be grateful that he has not lost the instinct to do what the breed was intended to do.

OLD ENGLISH SHEEPDOG SIZE

Whoever said "bigger is better" did not have the Old English Sheepdog in mind. The trend in the show ring for big dogs to be better if they are bigger would certainly be doing our breed a great disservice. While we do not condone the smaller, too-tucked under, almost crippled-looking dogs we sometimes see, we also do not want the over-sized Saint Bernard-type Bobtails that some breeders are pushing. The Standard calls for 22 inches and over—at the withers, that is—and the "over" does not necessarily mean 30 and over.

The general appearance should be of a typey, hairy, sturdy dog, quick on its feet, with a keen desire to herd a flock of sheep with effortless motion.

While today we do not see many Old English Sheepdogs, or "Drover's dogs" in the fields doing their thing, we can see evidences at times as they try to herd children, pets and sometimes owners to their own desires. We can be thankful they have not lost the instinct.

COLOR AND COLOR PATTERNS

With few and rare exceptions, Sheepdogs are born black and white. The black begins to turn a silvery color at about three months of age or later. It usually is noticeable first around the feet and then travels up and over the body. The change in color is noticeable if you separate the hairs and check the undercoat for the lighter hairs.

The Standard, of course, states clearly: "any shade of gray, grizzle, blue or blue-merled with or without white markings or in reverse." A mismarked puppy, or adult dog for that matter, will be easy to spot if you keep this clearly in mind. Any shade of fawn or darker brown is definitely not good. Think blue or gray.

While color and pattern are a matter of choice, if you intend to breed Old English Sheepdogs, two things are of extreme importance, and breeding stock should be of the proper, acceptable kind.

In selecting color, do not be misled by those who will tell you that all-white heads are preferred. Pattern on the head is acceptable and can be most attractive. When considering the head, it is more important to remember that it is the black eye rims that are usually preferred. That is not to say, however, that pink pigment around the eyes makes a dog unacceptable. Only when all other things are equal should eye rim pigmentation be your deciding factor.

YOUR DOG'S SENSE OF SMELL

We've all heard of the famous hunting dogs and the remarkable tales about the dog's wondrous sense of smell. And we know it to be true. Some amazing facts about this have come to light recently.

As we know, sense of smell is directly related to the nervous system, which forms a direct line to the brain via the nasal cavities. And, as we also know, the dog's sense of smell is much more acute than that of their human counterparts. This is due chiefly to the number of olfactory cells found in the nose. A comparison might be something like this:

A German Shepherd has 200 million olfactory cells, a Fox Terrier 148 million, a Dachshund 125 and man a mere five million. Noting this comparison we can understand why the dog usually has its nose either to the ground or high in the air, where it can pick up so many marvelous odors all along the way. In fact, it is said that every dog is able to pick up the odor of a single drop of blood in five quarts of water and can even identify the difference between beef, pork, horsemeat, etc. In case your dog is fussy about meat, there is the reason why—he knows what he likes and knows what he's getting.

OLD ENGLISH NOSES

Several breeds are cursed with occasional pink or Dudley noses. Many owners who are breeding their first litter will think that a puppy with a pink nose or a black nose with a pink pigmentation in it is a candidate for culling. Not necessarily so. A butterfly nose will usually fill in, although it may seem like it's taking too long a time. Perhaps a year or longer is not too long before sacrificing a quality puppy. Even if it means keeping the puppy yourself, hang in there.

We should also be aware of what is sometimes called a "winter" nose. This can be a black nose that definitely takes on a brown or pinkish color in the winter time or during the change in seasons. Seek veterinary or breeder advice on a questionable nose before deciding on the fate of a puppy whose nose is not exactly perfect.

OLD ENGLISH SHEEPDOG EYES

Correct eye color in most breeds is expected to be dark brown. However, the color of the Bobtail's eyes will vary with the color of the coat. Before making a decision on proper or improper eye color, check your Standard with the coat color before making a decision. If you are buying, ask a veterinarian or the breeder—or another breeder. If you are breeding and have a question, do the same.

While folks are inclined to joke about there being two eyes under all that hair anyway, we still want them to be of proper color!

EAR CARE

Any breed with long hair on the ears needs to have its ears cleaned on a regular basis. Our dogs certainly qualify in that category. In addition to keeping the ears free of mats, use a tweezer to pull hairs out of the ear canal, and use cotton swabs to keep the canal clean; any odor from the ear should be investigated immediately. Never be rough with the cleaning, and keep the swab in a straight line with the jawbone. No going around the "corner"! If your dog shakes his head a lot, rubs the side of his face along the floor or furniture, or scratches with those big back feet, it is time to take a look, a sniff, and perhaps a trip to the vet.

TAIL DOCKING

Probably for as long as the breed has been in existence there have been stories from breeders about natural "Bobtails" in their litters on occasion. Perhaps this is true, but we must say that for the most part breeders will also admit that Old English Sheepdogs are born with long tails. ₀

I like to recall the June 1941 issue of *National Geographic Magazine* in which an expert none other than Mr. Freeman Lloyd was quoted in an article entitled, "Working Dogs of the World." His official opinion was as follows:

"The Old English Sheepdog is commonly known as the Bobtail, since his tail is bobbed or cut off close to the rump. This dog carries an enormous coat, and a long hairy tail would gather so much mud as to impede the free movement of a hardworking farm dog. Many are born tailless or with short bobs. For the last fifty years, to my own knowledge, this breed has been producing long-tailed, short-tailed and tailless puppies, often in the same litter."

The accompanying photograph of an oil painting of the breed in this same issue states in part in the caption: "Some are natural-born Bobtails, but others are made so by docking the tail at the first joint when the puppy is three or four days old."

Mr. Freeman Lloyd was right. At three or four days of age, unless you have a litter of weak or premature puppies, the tails should be docked. Docking is a job for a veterinarian since it is considered surgical procedure and might include a stitch. The breeder, of course, can be the best adviser on *where* to cut, so be prepared on *where*.

The slight discomfort this procedure causes passes quickly and once the pups are back with their mothers, all is quickly forgotten. Dew claws can be removed at the same time if it seems feasible.

If you have this done at home, make sure the mother is out of earshot so she does not become distressed at the crying or the smell of blood. Return the pups to her immediately, so that she can determine for herself that they are not too troubled and can calm them down.

Actually, the Old English Sheepdog does not need a tail. In fact, it is better off without one for many reasons, the main one being a matter of cleanliness. All heavily coated breeds are inclined to soil themselves in the tail area, and our breed is certainly no exception. There is less opportunity for this to happen with the tail out of the way.

There is a legend that says that the farm dogs in old England used to have their tails lopped off at the time the owners paid the "license" fee. Perhaps this was the ancient way of paying for a dog license, but I must admit I like our way better.

Hutchinson's *Dog Encyclopedia* presents another version—their tails were cut off to distinguish them from the non-working dogs, or, in relation to the forest laws, the tail was removed to impede the animal's speed in chasing rabbits; without its tail it could not twist and turn so quickly.

SHEEPDOG COMBINGS

Just as with several of the other long-haired breeds of dogs, the combings of the Old English Sheepdog can be spun and made into marvelous knitting wool. This has been done successfully in the past, and with today's remarkable coat conditioners, the results should be even more spectacular than in the past.

After saving several bags of combings from your dog, or dogs, the Yellow Pages of your phone book should put you in contact with a weaver in your area who, I am sure, will be more than willing to give it a try, if only for the personal experience of working with a new medium—dog hair!

CRATE TRAINING

When you are dealing with a dog the size of the Old English Sheepdog, space for running, playing, and developing naturally is essential. However, if you are to have a show dog, which will be expected to travel to shows or which you expect to accompany you and your family on vacations or weekend jaunts, it is absolutely necessary that your dog learn to ride in a car and travel well.

The introduction of a crate of proper size at an early age will assure that your puppy gets used to his "house" to the point where it becomes a place of his own, rather than a place of confinement. Many owners feed their dogs in their crates so they learn that it is a place for food, security, seclusion and wonderful journey in the van or car. Others prefer that their dogs sleep all night in their crates, as a part of housebreaking and for safety. If your dog is to be a watch dog, this will not do, but if the door of the crate is allowed to remain open, it is surprising how many puppies and grown dogs will automatically sleep, and relax, in their crates.

They seem to enjoy having a place of their "very own."

Early on, take your puppy for rides in the car in the crate, with and without his littermates, and each will soon accept it as a way of life. Whether it is an open or closed crate is a matter of choice, or perhaps climate. In hot climates when the summer sun can be a danger, open crates provide the most air for our long-haired breed, but they must be guarded against direct sunlight. Closed crates are warmer for cold climates and they must also be shielded from direct sunlight or they can become "hot houses." Good circulation of air is essential and no direct sunlight is the rule, no matter what season of the year.

If there is a doubt in your mind about the proper size of the crate for your puppy or dog, consult with the salesman at your pet store or supplier, so that he can provide the best dimensions for your car and for the comfort of your dog when it is full grown.

Needless to say, the crate should be washable, sturdy, and have the proper flooring. A carpet is best for winter, along with a piece of blanket or a favorite cushion. In summer, regular newspaper (if the newspaper print doesn't rub off on the coat!), a turkish towel, or bath mat is adequate.

A toy or an object to chew on can be provided to prevent boredom if the trip is long, or you can provide dry dog biscuits for nibbling once you have seen that your dog does not get carsick.

Hook your lead or leash to the handle of the crate for quick walks along the roadways, and carry water in a thermos bottle for periodic drinks along the way.

If your dog truly loves travel, try to position the crate so that he gets to see a little bit of the countryside along the way. Just make sure that wherever you place the crate, a direct current of air is not streaming into the crate. Even in hot weather, the force of a direct current of air or a draft can be harmful. In fact, a direct current of air can be fatal if it interferes with a dog's breathing. There is really no reason why a dog should not like travelling, sleeping, or eating in his own private crate if introduced to it properly. And it certainly will mean easier, safer driving for you.

FENCING AND HOUSING

More than one Old English Sheepdog owner has told me that perhaps better than anything else, Bobtails love to dig in the mud.

A monstrous hole in the ground seems to be one of the most fun things for them to do, rain or shine.

We can suppose that the ideal run, in addition to being large enough, would have a top on it and a well-secured door. Cyclone fences are undoubtedly the best, safest, and most durable, with underground cement blocks around the edges to prevent the dog's digging out. It may be expensive and time-consuming, but a safe yard for our dogs is important—not only to prevent your dog from getting out, but to prevent fence jumpers from getting *in* at your dogs or puppies. A safe, secure fence is a good investment no matter how you look at it. And every dog deserves a place to exercise at its own pace in the fresh air.

While we will all agree our breed looks best on a satin bedspread or plushy couch, they also do well living outdoors, even in cold climates. But they must have adequate housing. They must be protected from the elements, sheltered against direct sun, have dry beds and a house free of dampness and wet ground. Wood platforms in lean-tos are also acceptable. Dog coats are *not* recommended for Old English Sheepdogs; they have incomparable coats of their own!

One of the most important aspects of housing more than one dog is proper accommodations, especially if you own both a male and female. When the bitch is in season, you must have adequate housing in separate quarters or you will end up with a litter of puppies! They should have separate quarters *inside* and *outside* the house.

THE OLD ENGLISH SHEEPDOG IN ART

It was Gainsborough who was credited with having painted the first of the dogs which are now believed to be the first Old English Sheepdogs in art. A portrait, *The Duke of Beucleugh,* dated 1771, depicts a shaggy dog strongly resembling the breed as we know it today, except for its size. There are dissenters who claim that, for this reason, it is not an Old English but rather one of the smaller shaggy, coarse-coated breeds that were also in fashion at that time.

Whatever your belief, we must admit that everything else but the size bears a remarkable resemblance, and we shall never know for sure.

There is the Mathew Dixon painting, *The Duke of Grafton as A Boy,* which comes a little closer, as well as paintings by other artists such as Cooper, Beswick and Philip Reinagle. Reinagle (1749–1833) has the dog actually watching over sheep on a mountainside.

WORLD WAR I HEROS
During the first World War there were two Old English Sheepdogs that were making history for the breed. These dogs were named Haig and Pershing. When they were six months old, Madame Capehart Viseuer, head of the Marme hospital, adopted them, and they were trained for active war duty. They were taught not to bark, and rode the ambulances back and forth to the front, helping to search for the dead and wounded.

Pershing is said to have called attention to 300 wounded men while Haig is credited with saving over 700 lives.

After the War, Haig and Pershing came to the United States and toured this country with Mrs. Walter Colverd and Mrs. Amy Baruch. Mrs. Colverd became their owner, and they all resided in San Francisco after their nationwide tour. Needless to say, the two dogs gained much publicity for their heroic endeavors, and were also lauded for having two sons that served their country during wartime.

COVER DOGS
Over the years the obvious shaggy charm of our breed has resulted in their appearance on many covers of doggie magazines. None were more beautiful than the May 1968 cover of *Popular Dogs* magazine which featured the Howard Payne's Ch. Rivermist Dan Patch with his handler Jack Funk. Jack had guided this dog throughout his ring career, and the mutual respect and admiration these two felt for each other was evident in the charming "nose-to-nose" photograph that graced the cover. The author was editor of this magazine at the time and I can remember the gasp of delight from everyone in the office as I opened the envelope and passed the photograph around for all to see. Needless to say, it was one of my favorite covers in all those years I served as editor.

SEEING STARS
Perhaps the most famous movie star to be associated with the breed was the famous platinum blonde, Jean Harlow. Before her death, Jean Harlow posed for a beautiful photograph for Hutchin-

son's *Encyclopedia* with her two American champions—most certainly good publicity for the breed at the time since, in addition to her fame, she was a bona fide dog lover.

Rod McKuen, the poet and musician, was another champion of the Old English Sheepdog. We can remember the picture of him romping with his Old English Sheepdogs on the cover of the 1973 Calendar and Datebook published by Cheval Books.

A BREED SURVEY

Along with over 1000 invitations to submit photographs of the leading Old English Sheepdogs to be included in this book, a questionnaire was included to get a sampling of opinions on "what's good and what's bad" in our breed today.

Among the questions were two that everyone took much time and thought to answer, and I appreciate this effort and the information that it elicited. The two questions were: "What do you believe are the outstanding characteristics or qualities of the breed today?" and "What do you feel are the breed's outstanding faults?"

Almost unanimously it was agreed that their clownishness and loyalty were their outstanding traits, and while not exactly a "fault," most people mentioned as a concern all the grooming that was necessary to keep them looking good. While their coats are a major part of their beauty, they do require a lot of work, and that in the show ring almost too much emphasis was being put on amount of coat. Most felt that quality and coat pattern, rather than amount, should be of major concern.

It was interesting to note that in answer to the question as to whether or not it was a good dog for children, there was almost a unanimous "yes" on this one. Countless stories have been told over the years about the adventures, companionship, and protection this breed has provided to children. If the temperament of the dog is stable, it is a wonderful worthy companion for children.

A certain amount of concern was expressed over hip dysplasia and eye problems which are found in most all long-haired breeds. There were a few mentions made on the desirability of being both an indoor and outdoor dog, and the fact that they do not seem to bark unnecessarily. A good long life span was also mentioned by a few people.

While questionnaires, polls, and surveys never prove anything 100% sometimes they do give an indication of what is on the minds of the breeders who are so dedicated to continuing to try to breed better dogs. And it is interesting from a comparison aspect. For those reasons, if for no others, we would do well to get other opinions to add to our own store of knowledge and previous experience, and to stimulate our thinking. There is always something to learn!

Prayer For Animals

Hear our humble prayer, O God, for our friends the animals, especially for animals who are suffering;
For any that are hunted or lost or deserted or frightened or hungry;
For all that must be put to death.
We entreat for them all Thy mercy and pity, and for those who deal with them we ask a heart of compassion and gentle hands and kindly words.
Make us, ourselves, to be true friends to animals and so to share the blessings of the merciful.

Albert Schweitzer

← **Overleaf:**

Champion Tanglewool's Emmett Kelly, bred and owned by Pam and Maris Caibe, Anchorage, Kentucky. Olan Mills took this lovely photo.

Overleaf: →

1. "On Guard" at Tanglewool Kennels in Anchorage, Kentucky.

2. Calli and Dr. Steve Nielsen go backpacking in 1982. Calli does it the easy way.

3. Lovely informal shot of Champion Tanglewool's Hallmark with his daughter, Tanglewool's Heavens to Betsy. Photographed in March 1985 by breeder-owner Pam Caibe.

4. Cute puppy picture from the album of Dr. Steve and Joyce Nielsen of Timbermist Kennels, Evergreen, Colorado.

1

2

3

4

HIGH SCORING DOG
SPECIALTY
FEB 1985 FOX & COOK

← Overleaf:

1. The McDonnells' Ch. Hairloom's April Showers, whelped in 1980 and photographed for them by Steven Newell of Kansas City, Missouri.

2. Joanne Knudsen with her Timbermist puppies, Lady Windsong Merry Bear of Timbermist and Tank's Boy.

3. Champion Timbermist's Merry Callisto, C.D., P.T., goes High in Trial at this 1985 Santa Rosa, California, show with a score of 194.5. Owner-handler, Joyce Vanek-Nielsen.

4. Charilyn Cardwell's Sir Raggles poses with a sweater spun from his very own hair. Many Bobtail owners now utilize the coat of their dogs for making clothing. This is a perfect example.

Overleaf: →

1. Dressed for the "silly class" at a fun match is Loehr's the Big Bopper in his 4th of July costume. Owned, bred, and handled by Janet Loehr of Anaconda, Montana.

2. Joanne McDermott and the dog she refers to as her "catalyst." Her first Old English Sheepdog, Barney, at their home in New Berlin, Wisconsin.

3. Mother and puppies—bred and owned by Pam Henry, Blue Mountain Kennels in California. Photo taken in 1981.

4. Champion Piraska's Jesse James, C.D. Bred and owned by Irma Fertl of Houson, Texas.

1 ←

2 →

3 ←

4 →

← Overleaf:

1. Ready for a cookout! Ch. Aphrodite Snow Silver Baron, owned by Bette Maxwell, Ontario, Canada.

2. Jennifer Caibe and Ch. Tanglewool's Hallmark and daughter Tanglewool's Precious Juno. Bred and owned by Maris and Pam Caibe, Anchorage, Kentucky.

3. Sitting pretty in his very own chair. Champion Timbermist's Lord Tanqueray, P.T., hiding behind the Foster Grants at his owners' home in Ever-green, Colorado—owners being J. Vanek-Nielsen and Dr. Steve Nielsen. "Tank" was on his way to Hollywood for the "Most Wonderful Pet" contest judged by TV and movie star Betty White.

4. A run in the sun—Joyce Vanek-Nielsen and Champion Timbermist's Lord Tanqueray take a run on the beach. The Timbermist Kennels are in Evergreen, Colorado.

Overleaf: →

1. 1984 Christmas card photo for Steve and Joyce Nielsen.

2. Two Err-Tails puppies on a lazy afternoon, Sir Champagne Powder Blue and Suiter. Brentwood's Maid Marion, deceased, was their dam.

3. Puppy love! Seven-week-old Bobtail puppy with Mrs. Weitz's grandchild. Photo courtesy of Bobbie Malott.

4. Beautiful head study of one of Joanne McDermott's Bobtails, Ch. Windfield Lord Nelson.

5. A young dog relaxes at the Dollhouse Kennels, Ft. Lauderdale, Florida.

6. Jan Rolfe's Lonestar Sadie Hawkins and Barbara Weber's Lonestar's Hot Gossip pictured during a visit recently.

1

2

3

4

5

6

← **Overleaf:**

1. Five-week-old Londonaire's Ideal Weather poses among the posies in the garden of Karen and Fred Stetler, Sacramento, California.

2. The scholarly type: One of Pam Henry's 6-week-old puppies bred at her Blue Mountain Kennels in Citrus Heights, California.

3. Christmas at Pam Henry's house means dressing up for the occasion.

4. Ain't love grand? Photo courtesy of Pam Caibe, Anchorage, Kentucky.

5. Two Londonaire puppies—these are Mr. Blue Skies and Storm Warning. Fred and Karen Stetler, Londonaire Kennels, Sacramento, California. Photo by Larry and Marge Grant.

6. Yum! Pat Heynis's dog seems to be expressing an opinion of his dinner.

Overleaf: →

1. A winning combination. A beautiful baby with American and Canadian Champion Whisperwood Winslow. "Troy" was handled to both championships by Bob Forsyth. He has five Bests in Show, a Specialty, 17 Group Firsts, and 26 Group Placements to his credit. He was Top Old English Sheepdog in 1978 and among the 15 All-Time Old English Sheepdog. He was retired at Westminster in 1979 after a Group Third. Owned by Mike and Nancy Fournier, Lewiston, Maine.

2. Gayle Schneeweiss of Pembroke Pines, Florida, with Champion Talisman's Rendezvous. Carol Moss, co-owner.

3. Champion Jen-Kris Jenny Lind with her owner Gerry Martin, Columbus, Ohio.

4. Pat Heynis of Hainesville, Illinois, and her Old English.

5. A perfect example of how much Bobtails love the water: A Tanglewool dog and his mistress enjoy a swim.

6. "Devon" with Dad! Devon is Tackleton's Lord Devonshire; Dad is Kirk Ogden, Brigadoon Kennels, Rockaway Township, New Jersey.

1

2

3

4

5

6

1 ←

2 →

3 ←

4 →

5 ←

6 →

← **Overleaf:**

1. Two Whisperwood puppies, namely, Woman of the Year and Midsomer Snow, pictured at nine weeks of age. Sally Shawfrank, owner of Snow.

2. A bevy of beauties at Pam and Maris Caibe's Tanglewool Kennels in Anchorage, Kentucky.

3. A pushover—six-week-old Familytree's Fezziwig My Bess is owned by Jan and David Glossbrenner of Woodstock, Illinois. My Bess was bred by Familytree Kennels, Danna and John Bankovskis. Photo by Danna Bankovskis.

4. Two-year-old littermates—Familytree Timeless and brother, Familytree Fezziwig Sidekick. "Brita" and "Junior" bred and owned by John and Danna Bankovskis of Beavercreek, Ohio, and photographed for them by Louise Lopina.

5. Loehr's Spoonful of Sugar prepares for a nap at the Fields' home in Anderson, Indiana.

6. Familytree Paramour, bred by Danna Bankovskis and co-owned by her with Amy Blackmore. The sire was Fezziwig Walleyed Snow Bob X Champion Fezziwig Familytree. Photo by Danna Bankovskis.

1. A man and his dog—Dr. Steve Nielsen, Timbermist, Evergreen, Colorado, with Lady J's Merry Pippin of Timbermist, C.D.

2. The very best kind of "doggie bag"—an Old English Sheepdog puppy that grew up to be Ch. Timbermist's Merry Callisto, C.D., P.T., "Calli" goes along for the ride. Owned by Joyce and Dr. Steve Nielsen, Evergreen, Colorado.

3. A picture says a thousand words—Jimmie Nielsen with two of Dr. Steve and Joyce Nielsen's Timbermist Old English Sheepdogs.

4. Two Timbermist Bobtails owned by Joanne Knudsen, Pine Junction, Colorado.

1

2

3

4

1. Twelve-week-old puppy named Halston, bred and owned by the Burtons of Oak Park, Michigan.

2. Six-week-old Bobtail puppies belonging to Pam Henry of Citrus Heights, California.

3. Joanne McDermott's Lord Nelson as a puppy.

4. This color photo of Joyce Vanek-Nielsen's Bobtails was the cover of the Gaines calendar for 1985.

Overleaf: →

1. Sir Wilby Daniels, 10 weeks old, bred at the Londonaire Kennels in 1984 by the Stetlers. Wendy Hickman and Karen Stetler, owners.

2. Auditioning for Our Gang Comedy—Lady J (Lady J's Merry Pippin of Timbermist, C.D.) enjoys retirement! Owned by Dr. Steve and Joyce Nielsen, Evergreen, Colorado.

3. Many breeders whose dogs are engaged in motherhood duties cut their dogs back to a sort of "puppy clip" such as this one worn by Ch. To-Jo's Carolina Moon. Moon is co-owned by Joy Kelley and the Ralph Schneeweisses.

4. Champion Windfield's Magnolia is an excellent example of proper coat length when having a litter. Owner, Joanne McDermott.

5. *Siesta* at Judy and Brian Still's Winnoby Kennels in Milford, Michigan.

6. Champion Love'n Stuffs Big Stuff with daughter, Love'n Stuffs Hot Stuff, sitting in one of her Dad's trophies! Owner-breeders of both are Kristi and Marilyn Marshall, Sepulveda, California.

1

2

3

4

5

6

← Overleaf:

1. A happy, healthy nine-week-old puppy bred and owned by Theresa Evans, Keswyck Old English Sheepdogs in Jeffersonville, Indiana. The sire was Familytree Fezziwig Sidekick and the dam was Keswyck Dixieland Delight. Photo by Danna Bankovskis.

2. One of Ray and Pat Heynis's Bobtails. Their Pancelot Kennels are in Hainesville, Illinois.

3. Seven-week-old "Buster," bred and owned by Familytree Kennels in Beavercreek, Ohio. The sire was Champion Fezziwig Joint Venture out of Champion Fezziwig Familytree. Buster is a grandson of Champion Fezziwig Vice Versa.

4. A darling puppy bred and owned by the Tanglewool Kennels.

5. Familytree Kennels' five-week-old Fezziwig Gray Mariah. She is co-owned by breeder Danna Bankovskis and Susan Orlando of Smithtown, Long Island, New York.

6. Mom and the kids—Champion Fezziwig Familytree and her eight-week-old puppies. Photographed by Louise Lopina for breeder-owners Danna and John Bankovskis of Beavercreek, Ohio.

1. One of Julie LaBore's puppies, named "Teddy," owned by Sue Fox and Don Link.

2. Joyce Vanek-Nielsen and actress Betty White with "Calli" and "Tank" at the finals for the "Most Wonderful Pet Contest" in 1985.

3. Marimoor Chaucer Par Avion engages in a bit of play with a friend. Owned by Charilyn Cardwell of Palmer, Arkansas.

4. A family affair—Joanne McDermott with the parents of her Champion Windfield Lord Nelson.

5. A 1984 Old English Sheepdog picnic near Evergreen, Colorado!

6. Not tennis, but baseball anyone? Calamity Jane IV, a C.D.X. titlist owned by Carrlyn Ward Coates, wants to add baseball to her list of accomplishments.

1 ←
2 →
3 ←
4 →
5 ←
6 →

1 ←

2 →

3 ←

4 →

5 ←

6 →

← **Overleaf:**

1. Party time at Fred and Karen Stetler's Londonaire Kennels in Sacramento, California, and everyone wants to get into the act! Photo by Larry and Marge Grant.

2. Now hear this. . . .Champion Benwyck's Buttons and Bows with Victor Chan, Jr., at their home in Victoria, B.C., Canada.

3. A delightful photo taken in Pam Henry's backyard in Citrus Heights, California, in 1980.

4. Champion Dollhouse Ozzie Again shares a secret with one of his many friends. Ozzie is ten years old in this picture. Bred and owned by Helen Dollinger, Ft. Lauderdale, Florida.

5. Sarah Bradford of Kensington, Maryland, with Raggedy Ann.

6. A darling litter of puppies and the young child of Everatt and Laurel Basaraba, photographed in 1978 at their Woolover Kennels in Winnipeg, Manitoba, Canada.

Overleaf: →

1. Mirror, mirror on the wall, who's the fairest of them all? Bobmar's April Luv, of course! Bred and owned by Marilyn Mayfield, Burbank, California.

2. The photographic artistry of Olan Mills captures this charming shot of four doggy pals.

3. Welcome home from school! Champion Baron Sugar Von Bear, C.D., welcomes home his young mistress. Larry and Marge Grant captured this happy moment on film for owners Fred and Karen Stetler.

4. Beautiful Heather Porter and her 8-week-old puppies at home in Burbank, California.

1

2

3

4

← Overleaf:

Champion Love'n Stuffs Grand Illusion at 15 months of age. "Lance" was sired by Champion Love'n Stuffs Big Stuff X Love'n Stuffs Hot Stuff. Co-owned and bred by Kristi and Marilyn Marshall, Sepulveda, California.

Overleaf: ⟶

1. Stephanie Schultes of Mesa, Arizona, with nine-month-old Champion Windfield's Esquire. "Bruce" is pictured here with his young junior handler and his first win in the show ring.

2. Champion Tempest Two, Group winner for the Tamara Kennels, Ocala, Florida.

3. Pinafore Classic Elegance, winning the breed at the December 1984 San Mateo show under judge Joe Tacker. "Ellie" is owned by Fred and Karen Stetler and co-owned by Nancy Smith, Pinafore Kennels.

4. Loehr's Hurricane Hanna pictured winning Best of Winners from the Puppy Class at 10 months of age. Owned, bred, and handled by Janet Loehr, Anaconda, Montana.

DELAWARE OHIO K.C.
WORKING

← **Overleaf:**

1. Timbermist's Merry Moodshadow, C.D., takes her first points. Bred and owned by Dr. Steve and Joyce Nielsen, Evergreen, Colorado.

2. Lady J's Merry Pippin of Timbermist pictured finishing for her C.D. title with a score of 193. Owned and shown by Joyce Vanek-Nielsen, Timbermist Kennels, Evergreen, Colorado.

3. Champion Warwyck Stanley Steamer, owned by Helen and Lyle McDonell of Kansas City, Missouri. The sire was Ch. Aphrodite Snow Sniflik, R.O.M., X Warwyck Surprise Party, R.O.M.

4. Best Brace in Show at the 1982 Albuquerque, New Mexico, event. Joyce Nielsen handles her Lady J's Merry Pippin of Timbermist, C.D., and her Timbermist's Merry Moonshadow, C.D., to this wonderful win.

Overleaf: →

1. In the show ring and winning with owner Marge LaMorte is Champion Shaggypants Basketball Jones. Jones is just eight months old in this photo.

2. Winning the breed is Ch. Midsomers Midnight Surprise, owner-handled to this win by Sally Shawfrank of Jacksonville, Florida.

3. Champion Scalawag Hellzapoppin, owned by Pat and Mike Bolen of Encinitas, California. The sire was Ch. Moptops Thunder of Ragbear X Ch. Scalawagg Shady Lady.

4. Crescendo's Brigadoon pictured at eight months of age, owner-handled for major points. "Zack" was bred and is owned by Robert and Phyllis Burton of Oak Park, Michigan. Photo by Martin Booth.

5. Champion Loyalblu Scalawagg All In One, shown finishing for her championship at a 1984 Old English Sheepdog Southern California Club show.

6. Talisman's Summers Last Song, C.D. "Suzie" is shown going Best of Winners and Best Opposite Sex at a recent Berks County dog show. Her sire was Canadian Champion Talisman's Junket X Canadian Champion Talisman's Holly of Shaggyacre. Owned by Dawn Largent of Marion, Pennsylvania.

OLD ENGLISH SHEEP DOG
CLUB OF CANADA

← **Overleaf:**

1. Tied for Top Producing Bitch in 1984 with the Old English Sheepdog Club of America was Jen-Kris Dapper Darby. Sired by Champion Barrelroll Blues in the Night X Jen-Kris Blackeyed Susan. Owned by Jen-Kris Kennels in Columbus, Ohio.

2. Top Junior Handler in the Old English Sheepdog Club of America show in 1984. Jennifer Martin with her dog "Annie," better known as Jen-Kris Some Where In Time. Jennifer is 15 years old in this August 1984 photo taken at the National Specialty Show.

3. Jen-Kris St. Marc Whitechapel, co-owned by Ron and Carol Ranus and Laura Martin. This remarkable dog obtained both his American and Canadian championships and American and Canadian C.D. titles before he was two years old.

4. Ch. To-Jo's Carolina Moon, co-owned by Mr. and Mrs. Ralph Schneeweiss and Joy Kelley. Moon is handled here by Adrienne Schneeweiss to a Group win from the classes at a 1983 show.

5. Ch. Talisman's Rendezvous, co-owned with Carol Moss and Mr. and Mrs. Ralph Schneeweiss of Pembroke Pines, Florida. "Roni" is handled for them by Joseph Napolitano. She was the No. 1 bitch in the country in 1982.

6. Canadian Champion Jen-Kris Fluffy Delight, handled by Laura Martin and co-owned by her and Don Jarrett.

Overleaf: →

1. On the way to championship is Grey Bear, a daughter of Mexican and American Champion Bobmar Midnight Cowboy. Owned by Vicki Saito, and pictured winning a major under breeder-judge Marilyn Mayfield in November 1984.

2. Four-point major for Marilyn Mayfield's Ch. Bobmar Maggie Lee under judge Thelma Von Thaydon.

3. "Tank," better known as Ch. Timbermist's Lord Tanqueray, photographed winning points toward his championship at the 1982 Salt Lake City show. Owned and handled by Joyce Vanek-Nielsen, Evergreen, Colorado.

4. One of Pam Henry's show dogs on the way to championship, winning at the 1985 Sir Francis Drake Kennel Club show under judge Peggy Adamson.

1

2

3

BEST OF
WINNERS

4

1

2

3

4

← Overleaf:

1. Champion Crescendo's Red Hot and Blue, pictured winning Best in Sweepstakes allowed by a five-point major at the 1984 National Specialty. At just barely one year of age, "Brooke" won these first points at a major show. Owned by Robert and Phyllis Burton, Crescendo Kennels, Oak Park, Michigan.

2. American and Canadian Champion Lord Sabastian Travis, C.D., is pictured here winning his 85th Best of Breed under judge Mrs. Thomas Powers. This "Cinderella Fella" started his career with a Best in Match, first time out, and became a Canadian champion in three shows over Specials within 24 hours. He also appears on TV and at 4-H Club meetings. Owned by Arlene Pietrocola of New Milford, New Jersey.

3. Champion It's Magic Shaggy Illusion, pictured winning on the way to championship at a 1983 Old English Sheepdog Club of Southern California show. Bred and owned by Ann Marie Levin, It's Magic Kennels, Reseda, California.

4. Summer of 1982 meant a Group 3rd win for Marilyn Mayfield's Bobmar Alice Blue Gown. Photo by Missy Yuhl.

Overleaf: →

1. Ch. Midsomer Champagne Delight, handled by Dick Shawfrank and owned by Sally Shawfrank of Jacksonville, Florida. Judge, Ed Dixon.

2. A couple of prizewinners—Susan Smith, Top Junior Handler in 1973, Cleveland, Ohio, with her Old English Sheepdog Pal.

3. Champion Tamara's Memory of Suzanne, whelped in 1966, pictured finishing her championship in 1968 at a Heart of America Kennel Club show in Kansas City. She is 17 months old here and was Best of Winners for a five-point major under famous dog man, Alva Rosenberg.

4. Nob-Lee's Great Expectations pictured going Best of Winners on the way to his championship at a 1985 Muncie Kennel Club show. Handled by Earl Goheen for owner Rosemary Goheen.

5. Marilyn Mayfield's Champion Bobmar Moon, a big winner in 1974. Photo by Rich Bergman.

6. Will Scarlett of Sherwood, C.D., with his team mates at a training exhibition class. "Ruff" was sired by Ch. Sweet William of Sherwood X Minnesota's Dipiddy Doo, and his owner-trainer is Julie LaBore of St. Paul, Minnesota.

1

2

3

4

5

6

BEST OF BREED
8A VARIETY
WEST VIRGINIA

BEST OF
WINNERS

BEST OF
WINNERS
MUNCIE
KENNEL CLUB
RITTER PHOTO
BY KATHY

9 TO 12 PUPPY BITCH
PUPPY SWEEPSTAKES
OESCSC SPECIALTY
SEPT 20 1974
JUDGE MRS TERRY CARTER

1

2

3

4

BEST OF BREED
COULEE K.C.
AUGUST 6, 1978
OLSON PHOTO

BEST OF BREED
FARGO - MOORHEAD K.C.
JUNE 6, 1982
OLSON PHOTO

BEST OF WINNERS
LAUREL HIGHLANDS
KENNEL CLUB SHOW
MAY 1985
PHOTO BY ALVERSON

5

6

Old English Sheepdog League
Northern California
SPECIALTY
SWEEPSTAKES
DATE

VARIETY GROUP
FIRST
WEST VOLUSIA
KENNEL CLUB
JUNE 1984
PHOTO BY Graham

HERDING

← Overleaf:

1. American and Canadian Champion Sherwood's Sure is Shapely was the first champion for Julie LaBore of St. Paul, Minnesota. She won numerous Breeds and finished her U.S. championship by taking the breed over Best in Show specials. For her Canadian championship she won a Group two days in a row and had multiple Group placings. At that time she was also No. 1 bitch in the Breed in Canada. In her one and only litter she is the dam of champions.

2. Best Brace in Show at the 1980 Oshkosh show was Julie LaBore's American and Canadian Champion Sherwood's Ruff All Over, American and Canadian Champion Sherwood's Classy Chassis. This was their first time out as a brace and it was quite a thrill for their owner. These two dogs were also shown as specials together and won the Breed and Best Opposite Sex nine different times.

3. American and Canadian Champion Sherwood's Classy Chassis owned by Julie LaBore of St. Paul, Minnesota.

4. Nob-Lee Perfection of Lamluv at 11 months of age. Shown in Bred-by Exhibitor Class from nine months of age, he has taken three point majors on the way to championship. Owned by George Lytle, Barry Deist, and Jere Marder.

5. Best in Sweepstakes, 1982 goes to Bobmar Molly O'Mally, bred by Marilyn Mayfield and Carolyn Harich.

6. Champion Whisperwoods Midsomer Snow, owner-handled by Sally Shawfrank of Jacksonville, Florida. Snow is co-owned by Joyce Wetzler.

Overleaf: ⟶

1. Ch. Tanglewool's Pepper Mint Shag, R.O.M., and Ch. Glenwal Seraph O'Tanglewools. Magnificent photograph of two Old English Sheepdogs in a sylvan setting by Pamela Caibe, Anchorage, Kentucky.

2. Champion Pickwick's Mandy, R.O.M., shown finishing with a five-point major under judge Eileen Pimlot. Mandy was ranked No. 3 Brood Bitch in 1983. Sire was Champion Alamanda's My Boy Jonathon X Champion Fancy Pants Proud Lady. Owner-handled by Barry Deist of Carnegie, Pennsylvania.

3. Ch. Royalty Blu Ragedy Andy, ranked in the Top Twenty-five Old English Sheepdogs in the December 1984 AKC Report. Andy always placed in the Group and was never less than a Group Third. Sire was Champion J. R. Tunk of Moptop X Ch. Pickwick's Mandy, R.O.M. Owned by Mike and Mary Godfrey, Barry Deist, and Dave Erickson.

4. Pettibone's Talisman Dream On pictured at 15 months winning on the way to her championship. Handled by Ann Bowley for Dawn Largent of Marion, Pennsylvania. Judge was Marie Moore.

1

2

3

GROUP 3RD
BUTLER
KENNEL CLUB
SEPT 1984

4

← Overleaf:

1. 1985 Westminster show found Champion "Sootie" as Best of Opposite Sex. Sire was Shaggypants Top Hat No Tails X Shaggypants Dyna Might. Owned by Dan and Joyce Trunk, now residing in England.

2. Canadian Champion Bluprint's Country Squire by sitting up says thanks to the judge for the win. Owned and shown here by Coreen Eaton of Ellisville, Missouri.

3. American and Canadian Champion Sherwood's Little Lambchop, "Snarfy" finished her Canadian championship with three Bests of Breed wins in a row. Her Group Third was over 117 dogs in competition. She was also a *Dog World* magazine award winner for championship titles in two countries. Bred and owned by Julie LaBore of St. Paul, Minnesota.

4. Larame's Checkerboard Square, owned and trained by Barbara Weber of Mukwonago, Wisconsin. The sire was Champion Maidstone's Lonestar Rebel X Barkshire's Little Angel. Checkerboard was second ranking obedience dog in the Delaney System in 1980.

Overleaf: →

1. The winning line-up at the 1979 Old English Sheepdog Club of America Match show was Oriole Lane's Lady Amanda, U.D., (clipped down) who went high score in Match with owner Barbara Weber of Mukwonago, Wisconsin, and Champion Jamark's British Sterling, C.D., who was first in Novice under judge Chuck Gear and is pictured with owner-trainer Kathy D'Onofrio.

2. Loehr's The Ring Master winning his second four-point major at 15 months of age under famous dog judge Anne Rogers Clark. The sire was Champion Shaggylamb's Bagel X Champion Loehr's Lady Mindi. Owned by Janet Loehr, his breeder and handler, of Anaconda, Montana.

3. American and Canadian Champion Mari Moor Regal Sir Raggles pictured winning at a 1979 show. The sire was Champion Sir Lancelot of Barwan X Champion Maid Missy of Mari Moor. Owned by Charilyn Cardwell of Palmer, Arkansas.

4. Ch. Pembridge Cheerio Li'l Rascal wins Best Puppy in Match at the 1979 Old English Sheepdog Club of New York show under breeder-judge Joyce Wetzler. Bred by Cheryl Whitacre and Paula Leach; owned by Walter Sommerfelt, the Ken Leachs, and Cheryl Whitacre.

5. A Prince Charming son taking the Working Group, handled by Susan Smith, daughter of the Marvin Smiths, Tamara Kennels, Ocala, Florida. Photo by Martin Booth.

6. Best of Winners and Best of Breed over Specials is Love'n Stuff's Big Stuff and Winners Dog to littermate Love'n Stuff's Ragdoll. Breeder-owners, Kristi and Marilyn Marshall, Love'n Stuff Kennels, Sepulveda, California. Photo by Missy Yuhl.

1

2

3

4

BEST
PUPPY

5

ANN ARBOR
KENNEL CLUB

JUNE 2 1974

WORKING
GROUP

JUDGE
MR JAMES TRULLINGER

PHOTO BY BOOTH

6

BEST OF WINNERS
BEST OF BREED
LIVINGSTON
KENNEL CLUB
KLEIN   JAN 1983

OPP. SEX
GAN K.C.
28, 1985
ON PHOTO

GROUP
FIRST

← **Overleaf:**

1. Britain Blue Magic Wizard pictured winning at a recent California show. Owned by Ann Marie Levin of Reseda, California.

2. Champion Pinafore Dubble Bubble winning at the Old English Sheepdog League of Northern California show in 1984. Judge Lou Harris awarded this Best of Winners to her breeder–handler–co-owner Nancy Smith. Also pictured is owner Karen Stetler, Londonaire Kennels, Sacramento, California.

3. Champion Loehr's Sissy Britches pictured winning a four-point major at a 1983 show. She finished in 10 shows, always breeder-owner-handled by Janet Loehr, Anaconda, Montana. Also pictured is True Grit.

4. Love'n Stuff's Wooly Bully, pictured winning toward his championship at a 1985 show. Bully is owned by Kristi and Marilyn Marshall of Sepulveda, California. Photo by Missy Yuhl.

5. Lonestar's Hot Gossip, co-owned by Barbara Weber of Mukwonago, Wisconsin, and Shirley Sturm. "Scooby" had six points toward championship at this point.

6. American and Canadian Champion Whisperwood Winslow, bred by Joyce Wetzler and co-owned by her and Mike and Nancy Fournier of Lewiston, Maine. Winslow is pictured here winning a Group First during his show ring career.

Overleaf: →

1. Dale Meyer's Wynsilot's Mission of Motion pictured going Best in Sweep-stakes at the 1985 Mattaponi Kennel Club Show.

2. Champion Bobmar Blockbuster, C.D., R.O.M. pictured winning RWD at a Specialty in Beverly Hills, California, under judge Fred Young. Bred and owned by Marilyn Mayfield, Burbank. This dog was featured on the Kal Kan TV Commercials run in 1985. Sired by Mexican and American Champion Bobmar Midnight Cowboy, R.O.M., X Champion Bobmar Daisy Muffit. Photo by Missy Yuhl.

3. Canadian Champion Bluecaleb's Signature, bred and owned by Betty Fast of Saskatoon, Saskatchewan, Canada. The sire was Canadian and American Champion Somebuddy Leading the Parade X Canadian Champion Shuffleshag's Chivas Regal.

4. Canadian and American Champion Snow Dude at Aphrodite, R.O.M. owned by Betty Maxwell of Guelph, Ontario, Canada, Dude was No. 2 Old English Sheepdog in Canada in 1981. He was also Best in Show at Oxford County Kennel Club in July 1982, the Old English Sheepdog Club of Can-ada National Specialty in November 1980, and Chicagoland Old English Sheepdog Club in the USA in June 1980.

1 ←

2 →

3 ←

4 →

← **Overleaf:**

1. Tolkien Chica Chubb, pictured winning toward her championship at a 1983 show under judge Joe Gregory. "Solo" is co-owned by the Larry Steins and the Kirk Ogdens.

2. Olan Mills photographed two Tanglewool dogs for owners Pam and Maris Caibe, Anchorage, Kentucky.

3. Champion Windfield Lord Nelson, owned by Joanne McDermott of New Berlin, Wisconsin, pictured winning on the way to his championship.

4. Champion Wynsilot's Ski Bum shown taking 1st in Bred-by-Exhibitor Class at the Los Angeles Old English Sheepdog Club of America Specialty Show in 1983. Dale Meyer, owner, whose Wynsilot Kennels are in Dorchester, Wisconsin.

Overleaf: →

1. A magnificent photograph of American and Canadian Champion Qubic's Crossfire, owned by Paula Coffman of Liberty, Indiana. "Gunner" was photographed for her by Pam Caibe. He is a Specialty and Best in Show winner.

2. Beautiful informal pose of Champion Baron Sugar von Bear, C.D., in his backyard in Sacramento, California. The Stetlers are the owners.

1 ↑   2 ↓

← **Overleaf:**

Pictured are Tanglewool's This Is Sirius and Champion Tanglewool's Th'Life of Riley, bred and owned by Pam and Maris Caibe of Anchorage, Kentucky.

Overleaf: →

1. Pooh Bear's Gandalf the Grey at 12 weeks, winning Best Junior Puppy and Best of Opposite Sex at the 1984 National Specialty Match Show. Owners and breeders, Robert and Kathie Dhuey of Mantua, Ohio.

2. A prestigious win under world-renowned breeder-judge Serena Van Rensselear for handler Alan Levine and American and Canadian Champion Lord Sabastian Travis, C.D. This remarkable dog is owned by Arlene Pietrocola of New Milford, New Jersey.

3. Talisman SnoShu's Finest Hour, C.D.X., pictured at one of his "finest hours," High in Trial at the 1984 Greater Portland Old English Sheepdog Specialty show. Larry Foster co-owns with Barbara Foster.

4. Ch. Amiable's Star Warrior, C.D., and Ch. Amiable's No Tails To Tell, C.D., both bred by Carol Cooke of Chesapeake, Virginia. "Rascal" and "Marie" are pictured here finishing for their obedience titles. Marie was highest scoring Champion of Record at the Merrimac Dog Training Club and other shows.

5. Whirlwind's Prince Charles was killed shortly after this picture was taken. The dam of this promising dog was sired by Champion Sir Lancelot of Barvan, Best in Show winner at Westminster in 1975. Owned by Susan Bethards of Cleburne, Texas.

6. Champion Tojo Light My Fire of Piroska, pictured winning the Group the day he finished for his championship. Owned by Irma Fertl of Houston, Texas.

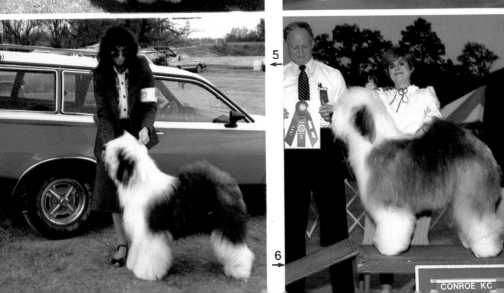

← Overleaf:

1. Multiple Group-placing Champion Dollhouse Beau Baily, co-owned and co-bred by Helen and Carla Dollinger of Ft. Lauderdale, Florida.

2. Show Downe Forget Me Not, C.D., earning High in Trial at the Old English Sheepdog Club of America Specialty in Denver in 1982. Co-owned by Barbara (handling) and Larry Foster and pictured here with judge Charles Mulock.

3. Ch. Loehr's Custom Blend, C.D., pictured winning this time in the conformation ring with owner-handler-breeder Janet Loehr.

4. Multiple Best-in-Show–winning bitch, Champion Dollhouse Maggie, bred by Helen and Howard Dollinger; owned and handled by Richard Chaboudy, who co-owns with Kathy Chaboudy.

5. American and Venezuelan Champion Dollhouse David Copperfield, shown with co-breeder and owner Helen Dollinger, Dollhouse Kennels, Ft. Lauderdale, Florida.

6. American and International Three-time Best-in-Show–winning bitch, Dollhouse Pearl Bailey, bred by Helen and Carla Dollinger, Dollhouse Kennels, Ft. Lauderdale, Florida, and owned by Dr. Miguel Correa.

Overleaf: →

1. A winning duo,—No. 1 Old English Sheepdog for 1984 and his daughter, No. 1 Old English Sheepdog in obedience for 1984! American and Canadian Champion Winnoby's Dictator of Talisman, R.O.M., and American Champion Winnoby's A Star Is Born. Father handled by Brian Still and daughter handled by owner-breeder Judy Still of Milford, Michigan.

2. Best in Show Ch. Dollhouse Bill Bailey, R.O.M., multiple group-winning Old English Sheepdog bred and owned by Helen Dollinger of Dollhouse Kennels, Ft. Lauderdale, Florida. This dog was awarded the "Ch. Ceiling Zero Award" for having produced group-placing offspring.

1↑   2↓

1 ↑   2 ↓

←— **Overleaf:**

1. Champion Pooh Bear's Special Edition, the No. 1 Old English Sheepdog and No. 4, all-breeds, in 1981. A Westminster, 1982, Breed winner as well. Bred and owned by Robert and Kathie Dhuey of Mantua, Ohio.

2. Champion Rollingview's Rising Star, owned by Joyce and Guy Bilodeau of B.C., Canada. She is pictured here taking a Group Fourth at a 1982 Canadian show. Star is the foundation bitch for the Bilodeau's Wigglebum Kennels.

1. Canadian and American Champion Some Buddy Bring on the Clowns, co-owned by Dr. and Mrs. Gary Carter and Mr. and Mrs. Jim Murdoch of Calgary, Alberta, Canada. This dog has won both all-breed and National Specialty Bests in Show.

2. Canadian and American Champion Aphrodite Snow Fresh, Top Old English Sheepdog in Canada for 1984 and an all-breed Best in Show winner in the U.S.A. Owners are Tris and Tony Lett and Bette Maxwell, Ontario, Canada.

3. Canadian Ch. Bluecaleb Putting on the Ritz, bred by Betty Fast and co-owned by her and Doug and Linda Smith. The sire was Canadian Ch. Somebuddy Ready to Ruffit, R.O.M., X Can. Ch. Shuffleshag's Chivas Regal.

4. Canadian Champion Moptop's Blue Madam, foundation bitch at Everatt and Laurel Basaraba's Woolover Kennels in Winnipeg, Manitoba, Canada. This photo of "Winnie" was taken on the way to her championship in December 1976.

5. Canadian and American Champion Some Buddy's Cotton Candy, R.O.M. Bred and owned by Dr. and Mrs. Gary Carter of Calgary, Alberta, Canada, she is the dam of three all-breed Best in Show winners and five Group winners. The sire was American and Canadian Champion Rivermist Feather Merchant, C.D. X Ch. Peace Hill's Princess Michelle, C.D.

6. Sherwood's Papa's Pride goes over the high jump in Open obedience class. Owned and trained by Julie LaBore of St. Paul, Minnesota. In 1975 "Tumbl" was second highest scoring Old English Sheepdog in Canada for Open and Utility work. At 11 years of age he competed in the Veterans Class and was second oldest qualifying dog. At the age of 13 years, he did a modeling job for Anheuser Busch.

1

2

ERMONT COUNTY
ENNEL CLUB INC
SEPT. 8. 1984
ERDING GROUP 2
JUDGE

WINNERS
DEL MONTE
KENNEL CLUB

3

4

NKC
BEST
IN
SHOW

NENT KNL CLUB
A OKLAHOMA
RIL 13 1980
ACE IN SHOW
H E GREGORY
LIS

5

6

← Overleaf:

1. Champion Tanglewools Hallmark, bred and owned by the Caibes and shown for them by Robert Helton.

2. Champion Blue Mountain Boggart, owned by Pam Henry and pictured winning on the way to championship with Karen Stetler at the 1985 Del Monte Kennel Club Show where he was Winners Dog under judge Chet Collier.

3. Champion Benwyck's Lord Albert being shown to championship by Victor Chan, Victoria, British Columbia.

4. In 1980 at the Mid-continent Kennel Club Show of Tulsa, Best Brace in Show went to Champion Bellewood Farms Blue Tango, C.D., and her daughter, Trick O'Treat, C.D., under judge Joe Gregory. Owners, Larry and Melinda Dugan, Roanoke, Texas.

5. Tanglewool's Just For Fun, bred and owned by Pamela and Maris Caibe, Anchorage, Kentucky.

6. Barrelroll B.G. Molly McGuirk, owned by Eugene and Barbara McGuirk of Cold Spring, New York.

1. To the victor goes the spoils. . . a reward for a job well done! Calamity Jane IV, C.D.X. is owned and trained by Carrlyn Ward Coates, Lakewood, Colorado.

2. Carrlyn Ward Coates's Calamity Jane IV, C.D.X., goes over the jump during an obedience trial.

3. Up, up and away! Calamity Jane IV, C.D.X., is owned by Carrlyn Ward Coates of Lakewood, Colorado.

4. Talisman's SnoShu's Finest Hour, C.D.X., earning High in Trial in August 1983 at the Greater Seattle Old English Sheepdog Club Specialty show. Larry Foster, handling, co-owns with Barbara Foster. Judge, Janice Thomas.

1

2

3

4

1

2

3

4

← Overleaf:

1. Champion Barrelroll B.G. Dress Blues pictured winning at a show in 1984. Owned by Barbara and Eugene McGuirk, Cold Spring, New York.

2. Best in Show, fifth time out as a Special is Ch. Cobbystock Lord Chumly, C.D., handled by 16-year-old Patricia Gipson. His record to date is two Group Firsts, three Group Seconds, one Group Third, aand 15 Bests of Breed, plus the Best in Show. He was No. 13 Old English Sheepdog in the nation for 1984 and also qualified for "Showdog of the Year" that same show season. Pat and her mother, Lorraine, own Cobbystock Kennels in Firth, Idaho.

3. Champion Pembridge Doing My Thing, C.D. with owner-handler Patricia Gipson of Firth, Idaho. This remarkable duo won three majors in three days and won the C.D. title in three shows.

4. Champion Dandia Sheer Delight, C.D., pictured finishing for her championship with JoEllen Spaeth of West Bend, Wisconsin.

Overleaf: →

1. Relaxing at the Perth, Western Australia Royal show—Regencyblue Lord Byron and Edgebaston Ebonnie with George Goldfinch.

2. Four generations in one family at the Shagmore Kennels in Victoria, Australia. Left to right, Australian Champion Tansprey Faithful Joy, Australian Champion Shagmor Blue Joy, Australian Champion Shagmor Royal Joy and Cooken Gentle Joy.

3. Australian Champion Elkeef Hanky Panky, whelped in 1976 and one of the breed's most consistent winners. He had over 1,000 challenge points, though only 100 are necessary to make an Australian championship. His titles, too numerous to mention, include Best Dog, Best Exhibits, and Best of Breeds at all the major shows. Owned by Sue and Tony Webster, Victoria, Australia.

4. Australian Champion Baluchistan Ben Jason, sired by Australian Champion Applegate Ribald X Lameda Sea Mist. Owned by C. Barton, Victoria, Australia.

5. Australian Champion Foggyday Ascot pictured at 18 months of age with his friend, Matthew Merrin, in Wanneroo, Western Australia.

6. Regencyblue Miss Eliza at 3½ weeks of age with darling Stacey Sewell in Western Australia. Photo taken in 1980.

← Overleaf:

1. One of Miss Chieko Kurashima's International Champions in Tokyo, Japan.

2. Miss Chieko Kurashima and her Best in Show Bobtail Puppy at a 1985 dog show in Tokyo, Japan.

3. Three of Miss Chieko Kurashima's Old English Sheepdogs at her Clutch House Bobtail Kennels in Tokyo, Japan.

4. Another Best in Show win for Chieko Kurashima's Bobtail. Her Clutch House Kennels in Tokyo, Japan, is the home of several International and Japanese champions.

5. One of Chieko Kurashima's International and Japanese Champions getting a last look before going into the show ring in Tokyo, Japan.

6. Three Bobtails belonging to Fujiko Hasegawa in Shizuoka, Japan.

Overleaf: →

1. Six-week-old Familytree Paramour and his sister, Brita, also known as Familytree Timeless, were captured on film by Louise Lopina as they chewed on a squash vine. Puppies owned by John and Danna Bankovskis of Beavercreek, Ohio.

2. American and Canadian Champion Lord Sabastian Travis, C.D., with his adoring owner, Arlene Pietrocola of New Milford, New Jersey.

1↑ 2↓

1↑ 2↓

← **Overleaf:**

1. Three puppies bred and owned by Pamela and Maris Caibe, Anchorage, Kentucky. The sire was Moptop's Hullabaloo X Champion Glenwal Seraph O'Tanglewool.

2. On the road again! Champion Timbermist's Merry Callisto, C.D., P.T., and Ch. Timbermist's Lord Tangueray, P.T. This dynamic duo was the winner of The Most Wonderful Pet Contest, judged by actress Betty White. Owned by Joyce and Dr. Steve Nielsen, Evergreen, Colorado.

Overleaf: →

1. Champion Tanglewool's Precious Juno photographed at nine months of age. Bred and owned by Pam and Maris Caibe, Anchorage, Kentucky.

2. Benwyck's Lord Arden, photographed with owner Kathleen Chan one autumn in Nova Scotia.

1↑ 2↓

← **Overleaf:**

1. Champion Aphrodite Snow Doll, owned by Bette Maxwell of Guelph, Ontario, Canada.

2. Tackleton's Lord Devonshire, owned by Kirk and Susan Ogden of Rockaway Township, New Jersey.

Overleaf: →

1. A charming trio—Julie, seven, Jill, five, and Mindy the Old English Sheep-dog, belonging to Pam Henry of Citrus Heights, California.

2. Heidi Spaeth and "Rory," or Jo-Jo's Keepsake. JoEllen Spaeth, owner.

3. This photograph was used in a Hero Dog Food advertisment and featured Margaret LaMorte's Champion Shaggypant's Basketball Jones.

4. Idaho's first team to compete at Westminster—Pat Gipson and her C.D.X., Gipson's Big Moses. Pat and Moses competed two years in a row at this leading dog show when Pat was just 11 years old in 1979.

1

2

3

4

Chapter 10

The Dog Show World

Let us assume that after a few months of tender loving care you realize your dog is developing beyond your wildest expectations and that the dog you selected is very definitely a show dog. Of course every owner is prejudiced, but if you are sincerely interested in going to dog shows with your dog and making a champion of him, now is the time to start casting a critical eye on him from a judge's point of view.

There is no such thing as a perfect dog. Every dog has some faults, perhaps even a few serious ones. The best way to appraise your dog's degree of perfection is to compare him with the Standard for the breed or when he is before a judge in the show ring.

Keep in mind that dog show terminology varies from one place to another and even from one time to another. If you plan to show your dog, it always makes sense to check with your local or national breed club or with the national dog registry for the most complete, most up-to-date information regarding dog show regulations. In Great Britain, for example, match shows are known as limit shows. Age limit also differs, as dogs less than six months old may not be shown in Britain. Additionally, Britain has no point system for dogs, rather the dogs compete for championship certificates (C.C.s). Thus, point shows are known as championship shows in Great Britain.

MATCH SHOWS

For the beginner there are "mock" shows, called match shows, where you and your dog go through many of the procedures of a regular dog show but do not gain points toward championship. These informal events are usually held by kennel clubs, annually or semiannually, and much ring poise and experience can be gained there. The minimum age limit at most matches is usually two months, in order to give puppies four months of training before they compete at the regular shows when they reach six months of age. (It should be noted, however, that at some match shows the minimum age requirement varies, so be sure to inquire about this before you fill out the entry form.) Classes range from two to four months, four to six months, six to nine months, and nine to twelve months. Puppies compete with others of their own age for comparative purposes. Many breeders evaluate their litters in this manner, choosing which is the most outgoing, the most poised, the best showman, and so on.

For those seriously interested in showing their dogs to full championship, match shows provide important experience for both the dog and the owner. Class categories may vary slightly, according to number of entries, but basically include all the classes that are included at a regular point show. There is a nominal entry fee and, of course, ribbons and trophies usually are given for your efforts as well. Unlike the point shows, entries can be made on the day of the show right on the show grounds. Matches are unbenched and provide an informal, congenial atmosphere for the amateur, and this helps to make the ordeal of one's first adventure in the show ring a little less nerve-wracking.

THE POINT SHOWS

It is not possible to show a puppy at an American Kennel Club sanctioned point show before the age of six months. When your dog reaches this eligible age, your local kennel club can provide you with the names and addresses of the show-giving superintendents in your area who will be staging the club's dog show for them, and they can tell you where to write for an entry form.

The forms are mailed in a pamphlet called a premium list. This also includes the names of the judges for each breed, a list of the prizes and trophies, the name and address of the show-giving club and where the show will be held, as well as rules and regulations set up by the American Kennel Club.

A booklet containing the complete set of show rules and regulations, *Rules Applying to Registration and Dog Shows*, may be obtained by writing to the American Kennel Club, Inc., 51 Madison Avenue, New York, NY, 10010.

When you write to the dog-show superintendent, request not only your premium list for this particular show, but ask that your name be added to their mailing list so that you will automatically receive all premium lists in the future. List your breed or breeds and they will see to it that you receive premium lists not only for all-breed shows, but for specialty shows as well.

Unlike the match shows where your dog will be judged on ring behavior, at the point shows he will be judged on conformation to the breed Standard. In addition to being at least six months of age (on the day of the show) he must be purebred for a point show. This means both of his parents and he are registered with the American Kennel Club. There must be no alterations or falsifications regarding his appearance, for example, no dyes or powders may be used to enhance or alter the natural color, the shade of natural color, or the natural markings of the dog's coat. Females cannot have been spayed and males must have both testicles in evidence. Any lameness, deformity, or major deviation from the Standard for the breed constitutes a disqualification.

With all these things in mind, groom your dog to the best of your ability in the specified area for this purpose in the show hall and *exercise your dog before taking him into the ring!* Too many dog show people are guilty of making their dogs remain in their crates so they do not get dirty, and the first thing the animals do when they are called into the ring is to stop and empty themselves. There is no excuse for this. All it takes is a walk *before* grooming. If your dog is clean, well groomed, *empty*, and leash-trained, you should be able to enter the show ring with confidence and pride of ownership, ready for an appraisal by the judge.

The presiding judge on that day will allow each and every dog a certain amount of time and consideration before making his decisions. It is never permissible to consult the judge, regarding either your dog or his decision, while you are in the ring. An exhibitor never speaks unless spoken to, and then only to answer such

Champion Sniflik Warwyck Darwen winning the Breed at the 1983 Old English National Specialty Show under breed specialist Caj Haakansson. This dog is also a Best in Show winner, all breeds, and finished among the Top Ten Old English Sheepdog for 1984. His daughter Champion Moptops Willywonder Melody Was Winners and his son, Champion Moptops Just is also a top dog, taking the breed at the 1985 Old English Sheepdog League of Northern California. Owned by Susan Davis of Ellicott City, Maryland.

196

questions as the judge may ask—the age of the dog, the dog's bite, or to ask you to move your dog around the ring once again.

However, before you reach the point where you are actually in the ring awaiting the final decisions of the judge, you will have had to decide in which of the five classes (five for each sex) your dog should compete.

POINT SHOW CLASSES

The regular classes of the AKC are: Puppy, Novice, Bred-By-Exhibitor, American-bred, and Open; if your dog is undefeated in any of the regular classes (divided by sex) in which it is entered, he or she is *required* to enter the Winners Class. If your dog is placed second in the class to the dog which won Winners Dog or Winners Bitch, hold the dog or bitch in readiness, as the judge must consider it for Reserve Winners.

● THE PUPPY CLASS shall be for dogs which are six months of age and over but under twelve months, and which are not champions. Classes are often divided, thus: six and (under) nine, and nine and (under) 12 months. The age of a dog shall be calculated up to and inclusive of the first day of a show. For example, a dog whelped on January 1 is eligible to compete in a Puppy Class on July 1, and may continue to compete up to and including December 31 of the same year. He is not eligible to compete January 1 of the following year.

● THE NOVICE CLASS is for dogs six months of age or over, whelped in the USA or Canada, which have not, prior to the closing entries, won three first prizes in the Novice Class, a first prize in Bred-by-Exhibitor, American-bred or Open Class, nor one or more points toward a championship title.

● THE BRED-BY-EXHIBITOR CLASS is for dogs whelped in the USA (or, if individually registered in the AKC Stud Book, for dogs whelped in Canada) that are six months of age and over, that are not champions, and that are owned wholly or in part by the person or by the spouse of the person who was the breeder or one of the breeders of record. Dogs entered in the BBE Class must be handled by an owner or by a member of the immediate family of an owner, i.e., the husband, wife, father, mother, son, daughter, brother, or sister.

197

- THE AMERICAN-BRED CLASS is for all dogs (except champions) six months of age or over, whelped in the USA by reason of a mating that took place in the USA.
- THE OPEN CLASS is for any dog six months of age or over, except in a member specialty club show held for only American-bred dogs, in which case the class is for American-bred dogs only.
- WINNERS DOG and WINNERS BITCH After the above male classes have been judged, the first-place winners are then *required* to compete in the ring. The dog judged "Winners Dog" is awarded the points toward his championship title.
- RESERVE WINNERS are selected immediately after the Winners Dog. In case of a disqualification of a win by the AKC, the Reserve Dog moves up to "Winners" and receives the points. After all male classes are judged, the bitch classes are called.
- BEST OF BREED or BEST OF VARIETY COMPETITION is limited to Champions of Record or dogs (with newly acquired points, for a 90-day period prior to AKC confirmation) which have completed championship requirements, and Winners Dog and Winners Bitch (or the dog awarded Winners if only one Winners prize has been awarded), together with any undefeated dogs which have been shown only in non-regular classes; all compete for Best of Breed or Best of Variety (if the breed is divided by size, color, texture, or length of coat hair, etc.).
- BEST OF WINNERS: If the WD or WB earns BOB or BOV, it automatically becomes BOW; otherwise they will be judged together for BOW (following BOB or BOV judging).

Best of Opposite Sex is selected from the remaining dogs of the opposite sex to Best of Breed or Best of Variety.

Other Classes may be approved by the AKC, such as Stud Dogs, Brood Bitches, Brace Class, Team Class; classes consisting of local dogs and bitches may also be included in a show if approved by the AKC (special rules are included in the AKC Rule Book).

- THE MISCELLANEOUS CLASS is for purebred dogs of such breeds as designated by the AKC. No dog shall be eligible for entry in this class unless the owner has been granted an Indefinite Listing Privilege (ILP) and unless the ILP number is given on the entry form. Application for an ILP shall be made on a form pro-

Champion Cheerio Olde English Jester, winning Best Opposite at the 1978 Greater Seattle Specialty show, under breeder-judge J. Richard Schneider. Bred by the Cheerio Kennels and owned by Walter J. Sommerfelt and Ken and Paula Leach.

vided by the A.K.C. and when submitted must be accompanied by a fee set by the Board of Directors.

All Miscellaneous breeds shall be shown together in a single class except that the class may be divided by sex if so specified in the premium list. There shall be *no* further competition for dogs entered in this class. Ribbons for 1st, 2nd, 3rd, and 4th places shall be rose, brown, light green and gray, respectively.

OBEDIENCE TRIALS

Some shows also offer Obedience Trials, which are considered as separate events. These give the dogs a chance to compete and score by performing a prescribed set of exercises intended to display their training in doing useful work.

There are three obedience titles for which they may compete: First, the Companion Dog or CD title; second, the Companion Dog Excellent or CDX; and third, the Utility Dog or UD. Detailed information on these degrees is contained in a booklet entitled *Obedience Regulations* and may be obtained by writing to the American Kennel Club.

JUNIOR SHOWMANSHIP

Junior Showmanship competition is for boys and girls in different age groups who handle their own dogs or ones owned by their immediate family. There are four divisions: Novice A (10-to-12-year-olds) and Novice B (13-to- 17-year-olds) for competitors with no previous Junior Showmanship wins, Open A (10 to 12-year-olds) and Open B (13-to 17-year-olds) for competitors with one or more JS awards.

As Junior Showmanship at the dog shows increased in popularity, certain changes and improvements had to be made. The American Kennel Club issues a pamphlet, *Regulations for Junior Showmanship*, which may be obtained by writing to the AKC at 51 Madison Avenue, New York, NY 10010.

DOG SHOW PHOTOGRAPHERS

Every show has at least one official photographer who will be more than happy to take a photograph of your dog with the judge, ribbons, and trophies, along with you or your handler. These make marvelous remembrances of your top show wins and are frequently framed along with the ribbons for display purposes. Photographers may be paged at the show over the public address system if you wish to obtain this service. Prices vary, but you will probably find it costs little to capture these happy moments, and the photos can always be used in various dog magazines to advertise your dog's wins.

ALL-BREED VS. SPECIALTY

There are two types of dog shows licensed by the American Kennel Club. One is the all-breed show which includes classes for all of the AKC recognized breeds and groups of breeds, i.e., all Terriers, all Toys, etc. Then there are the specialty shows, for one particular breed, which also offer championship points.

BENCHED VS. UNBENCHED SHOWS

The show-giving clubs determine, usually on the basis of what facilities are offered by their chosen show site, whether their show will be benched or unbenched. A benched show is one where the dog show superintendent supplies benches or cages dogs. Each bench is numbered and its corresponding number appears on your entry identification slip which is sent to you prior to the show date. The number also appears in the show catalog. Upon entering the show, you should take your dog directly to the bench where he should remain until it is time to groom him prior to judging. After he has been judged, he must be returned to the bench until the official time of dismissal from the show. At an unbenched show, the club makes no provision whatsoever for your dog other than an enormous tent (if an outdoor show) or an area in a show hall where all crates and grooming equipment must be kept.

Benched or unbenched, the moment you enter the show grounds, you are expected to look after your dog and have it under complete control at all times. This means short leads in crowded aisles or when getting out of cars. In the case of a benched show, a "bench chain" is needed. It should allow the dog to move around but not get down off the bench. Please refrain from having small tots lead dogs around the show grounds where they might be dragged into the middle of a dog fight. Show dogs should be supervised at all times by a responsible adult or adolescent, never by a young child.

American and Canadian Champion Silvermist Peek-a-Boo, owned by Anne Weisse of LaCrosse, Wisconsin, shown handling her to her championship in 1965. The sire was Champion Greyfriar's Lord Fauntleroy X Ch. Silvershag Sally Snow-Boots.

IF YOUR DOG WINS A CLASS

Study the classes to make certain your dog is entered in a proper class for his or her qualifications. If your dog wins his class, *you are required*—for no additional fee—to enter classes for Winners, Best of Breed and Best of Winners. No eligible dogs may be withheld from competition. It is not mandatory that you stay for group judging, *if your dog wins a group,* however, *you must stay for Best in Show competition.*

THE PRIZE RIBBONS

No matter how many entries there are in each class at a dog show, if you place in the first through fourth positions you will receive a ribbon. These ribbons commemorate your win, and, when collected and displayed they can be impressive to prospective buyers when and if you have puppies for sale or if you intend to use your dog at public stud.

All ribbons from the American Kennel Club licensed dog shows will bear the AKC seal, the name of the prize, the name of the show-giving club, the date of the show, and the name of the city or twon where the show is being held. In the classes the colors are blue for first, red for second, yellow for third, and white for fourth. Winners Dog or Winners Bitch ribbons are purple, while Reserve Winners Dog and Reserve Winners Bitch ribbons are purple-and-white. Best of Winners ribbons are blue-and-white, Best of Breed and Best of Variety of Breed are purple-and-gold, and Best of Opposite Sex ribbons are red-and-white.

In the six groups, first prize is a blue rosette or ribbon, second placement is red, third is yellow, and fourth is white. The Best in Show rosette is either red, white, and blue or incorporates the colors used in the show-giving club's emblem.

QUALIFYING FOR CHAMPIONSHIP

Championship points are given for Winners Dog and Winners Bitch in accordance with a scale of points established by the American Kennel Club, based on the popularity of the breed in entries and the number of dogs competing in the classes. This scale of points varies with the breed, its sex, and the geographical location of the show, but the scale is published in the front of each dog show catalog. You may win additional points by winning Best of Winners, if there are fewer dogs than bitches entered, or vice versa. Points never exceed five at any one show and a total of 15 points must be won to constitute a championship. These 15 points must be won under at least three different judges, and you must acquire at least two major wins. Anything from a three-to-five point win is a major, while one and two point wins are minor wins. Two major wins must be won under two different judges to meet championship requirements.

PROFESSIONAL HANDLERS

If you are new in the fancy and do not know how to handle your dog to his best advantage, or if you are too nervous or physically unable to show your dog, you can hire a reliable professional handler who will do it for you for a specified fee. The more successful or well-known handlers charge slightly higher rates, but generally speaking there is a uniform charge for this service. As the dog progresses with his wins in the show ring, the fee increases proportionately. Included in this service is professional advice on when and where to show your dog, grooming, a statement of your wins at each show, and all trophies and ribbons that the dog accumulates. Usually any cash award is kept by the handler as a sort of "bonus."

When engaging a handler, it is advisable to select one who does not take more dogs to a show than he can properly and comfortably handle. You want your dog to receive his individual attention and not be rushed into the ring at the last moment because the handler has been busy with too many other dogs in other rings. Some handlers require you to deliver the dog to their establishment a few days ahead of the show so they have ample time to groom and train him. Other handlers will accept well-behaved and trained dogs that have been groomed by their owners at ringside— if they are familiar with the dog and the owner. This should be determined well in advance of the show date. *Never* expect a handler to accept a dog at ringside that is not groomed to perfection!

There are several sources for locating a professional handler. Dog magazines carry their classified advertising. A note or telephone call to the American Kennel Club will also put you in touch with several in your area.

Another great Bobtail from the Tamara Kennels—Champion Tamara's Alex the Great, pictured taking the Breed. This Prince Charming son was bred and owned by the Marvin Smiths, Ocala, Florida.

DO YOU REALLY NEED A HANDLER?

The answer to that question is sometimes yes, sometimes no. However, the answer that must be determined first of all is, "Can I *afford* a professional handler?" or "I want to show my dog myself. Does that mean my dog will never do any big winning?"

Do you *really* need a handler to win? If you are mishandling a good dog that should be winning and isn't because it is made to look bad in the ring by its owner, the answer is yes. If you don't know how to handle a dog properly, why make your dog look bad when a handler could show it to its best advantage?

Some owners simply cannot handle a dog well and wonder why their dogs aren't winning in the ring no matter how hard they try. Others are nervous, and this nervousness travels down the leash to the dog and the dog behaves accordingly. Some people are extroverts by nature, and these are the people who usually make excellent handlers. Of course, dogs that do all of the winning at the shows usually have a lot of "show off" in their nature, too, and this helps a great deal.

THE COST OF CAMPAIGNING A DOG

At present, many champions are shown an average of 25 times before completing a championship. In entry fees at today's prices, that adds up to a few hundred dollars. This does not include motel bills, traveling expenses, or food. There have been dog champions finished in fewer, say five to ten, shows, but this is the exception rather than the rule. When and where to show should be thought out carefully so that you can perhaps save money on entries. This is one of the services a professional handler provides that can mean considerable savings. Hiring a handler can save money in the long run if you just wish to make a champion. If your dog has been winning reserves and not taking points and a handler can finish him in five to ten shows, you would be ahead financially. If your dog is not really top quality, the length of time it takes even a handler to finish it (depending upon competition in the area) could add up to a large amount of money.

Campaigning a show specimen that not only captures the wins in his breed but wins Group and Best in Show awards gets up into the big money. To cover the nation's major shows and rack up a record as one of the top dogs in the nation usually costs an owner thousands of dollars a year. This includes not only the professional handler's fee for taking the dog into the ring, but the costs of conditioning and grooming, boarding, and advertising him in magazines and so forth.

There is great satisfaction in winning with your own dog, especially if you have trained and cared for it yourself. With today's enormous entries at the dog shows and so many worthy dogs competing for top wins, many owners who have said "I'd rather do it myself!" and meant it have become discouraged and have eventually hired a handler anyway.

However, if you really are in it just for the sport, you can and should handle your dog if you want. You can learn the tricks by attending training classes, and you can learn a lot by carefully observing the more successful professional handlers as they perform in the ring. Model yourself after the ones who command respect as being the leaders in their profession. But, if you find you'd really rather be at ringside looking on, do get a handler so that your worthy dog gets his deserved recognition in the ring. To own a good dog and win with it is a thrill, so good luck, no matter how you do it.

DOG CLUBS

In addition to getting involved with the parent club for your breed, it is advisable for owners to join other clubs if they wish to keep informed and abreast of all the latest information pertaining to the fancy.

It is wise to belong to an all-breed club in your area, as well as to dog training clubs, if you are interested in obedience work. These clubs can usually be located through your telephone book listing in the Yellow Pages.

There is also the Owner-Handler Association of America, Inc. Founded in 1967, this group has members throughout the United States (including Puerto Rico) and Canada. Their objectives are to encourage and promote the sport of owner-handling and the training of purebred dogs and to communicate with and educate purebred dog fanciers. Membership is open to all who advocate these principles.

Any interested group of 15 or more members may form a chapter in their area with the approval of the Board. Chapters hold training classes in obedience and show training, offer educational programs, and hold symposiums of benefit to the fancier.

Champion Glenwal Seraph O'Tanglewool's and Ch. Tanglewool's Pepper Mint Shag, R.O.M. Owned by Maris and Pam Caibe, Anchorage, Kentucky. Photo by Pam Caibe.

Chapter 11

Statistics and the Phillips System

As Old English Sheepdogs continued to grow in popularity, it was only natural that the entries at dog shows continued to increase, and competition got keener. The larger the entries, the more coveted the wins. In 1956, when Irene Phillips created her Phillips System of evaluating show dogs, Old English Sheepdog fanciers fell in love with her point system and began keeping records of their dogs' wins to compare them not only with other bobtails, but with the other Working Dogs, and even other dogs of all breeds.

To this day, dog fanciers are still keeping score on the top winners in the breeds, and while many a system of making it to the top of a winner's list has been recorded and publicized, there is no denying that they are all based on the fairest, most popular, and most recognized and remembered ever devised for naming the top-winning dogs in the country.

True, records are made to be broken, and we can all look forward to the day when another magnificent Old English Sheepdog will come on the show scene and cut a path through the crowds of show dogs to triumph as the newest top-winning dog in our breed. There is always room for another great dog to bring additional glory to the Old English and, just as naturally as night follows day, we all hope that extra special specimen will be our very own.

Today we have a remarkable list of excellent dogs that can already claim fame as having reached the top of the list of all-time winners in the history of the breed to date. This book would be less than complete if it did not pay tribute in both word and picture to those dogs that have earned their titles by accumulation of Phillips System points in the past, as well as those that are skyrocketing to the tops of other lists today. But first, let's talk about the Phillips System, on which all other systems are based.

WHAT IS THE PHILLIPS SYSTEM?

In the mid-1950s, Mrs. John Phillips, a woman famous for her Haggiswood Irish Setter kennels and a judge of many breeds, devised a point system, based on show records published in the American Kennel Club *Gazette*, to measure the wins of the nation's show dogs.

As in all sports, competition and enthusiasm in the dog fancy run high, and Irene Phillips (now Mrs. Harold Schlintz) came up with a simple, yet certainly true, method of measuring wins for this competition, which over the years has provided many thrills for dog lovers interested in the good sportsmanship so essential to a competitive sport.

The Phillips System, which Mrs. Phillips not only devised but also compiled during the early years, was sold as an annual feature to *Popular Dogs* magazine, whose editor at that time, Mrs. Alice Wagner, did much to make it the most important rule of success for a show dog. When I took over as editor of *Popular Dogs* in 1967, the tradition was carried on. For the five years I was tallying the finals for the Phillips System, it was a constant source of enjoyment to watch the leading dogs in this country, in all breeds, climb to the top, with one dog, at the end of the year, reaching the pinnacle of success as the No. 1 dog in America. Because so many feel the same way, and since the competition increases with each passing year, I feel that a healthy sampling of the Old English Sheepdogs which have achieved their honors should be represented in this book so that their success would become a matter of permanent record.

HOW THE SYSTEM WORKS

The Phillips System was designed to measure, with fairness, the difference between a dog-show win scored over many dogs and one scored over just a few dogs. For example, a Best In Show win over 1000 dogs should obviously have more significance than a Best In Show scored over 200 dogs. The Phillips System acknowledged this difference by awarding points in accordance with the number of dogs over which the win was scored. Points were awarded for Best In Show and Group placings only. Best of Breed wins did not count, as they do today in many of the other systems.

The Best in Show dog earned a point for each dog in actual competition; absentees or obedience dogs were not counted. The first place winner in each of the six Groups earned a point for each dog defeated in his Group. The dog that placed second earned a point for each dog in the Group less the total of the breeds that were first. Third in the Group earned a point for each dog in the Group less the total of the breeds that were first and second. Fourth in the Group earned a point for each dog in the Group less the total of the brees that were first, second, and third.

Sources for the count were the official records for each dog show as published each month in the American Kennel Club *Gazette*, the magazine which is the official publication for the American Kennel Club. An individual card was kept on every dog that placed in the Group or won a Best in Show during the entire year. Figures were tallied for publication at the end of each 12-month period, and a special Phillips System issue of *Popular Dogs* magazine was devoted each year to presenting the Top Ten winners in each breed, along with the total number of points accrued to each.

In the beginning, only a few of the top dogs were published, but by 1966 the phrase "Top Ten" was firmly established in dog-show jargon, and the system had captured the imagination of dog fanciers all over the nation—many striving to head the list of the top-winning dog in the country for that year.

The published figures included not only the total number of points (or number of dogs defeated), but the number of Bests in Show, and the number of Group Placements. It is extremely interesting to note that, as each year passed, there was a tremendous increase in the amount of points each dog had won. There is proof positive of the amazing success and increase in the number of entries at the dog shows from the mid-50s, when the System was first created, to the mid-70s, when it became a matter of record that the No. 1 dog in the nation had amassed over 50,000 points to claim the title of Top Show Dog in the Nation for that year. Today the number of dogs defeated is even higher!

Melanie's Shaggy Bear, C.D.X., owned and trained by Melanie Mason Fields of Anderson, Indiana. Bear is a dog that Mrs. Fields takes into nursing homes in her area to visit the elderly.

Chapter 12

Old English Sheepdogs in Obedience

The history of dog show obedience goes back to 1933. Dog shows and their conformation classes had a big head start on obedience work, and it wasn't until 1933 that the first obedience tests were held in Mount Kisco, New York. It was Mrs. Helene White-house Walker who inaugurated these initial all-breed obedience tests that she had brought from England. She and her kennelmaid at that time, the famous Blanche Saunders, were responsible for the staging of the first four obedience tests held in the United States.

Obedience training and tests for dogs were an immediate success from the moment those first 150 spectators saw the dogs go through their paces.

Mrs. Walker was instrumental in getting the American Kennel Club to recognize and even sponsor the obedience trials at their dog shows, and her discussions with Charles T. Inglee (then the vice president of the A.K.C.), ultimately led to their recognition. In 1935, she wrote the first booklet published on the subject called simply *Obedience Tests*. These tests were eventually incorporated into the rules of the A.K.C. obedience requirements in March 1936. It developed into a 22-page booklet that served as a manual for judges, handlers and the show-giving clubs. The larger version was called "Regulations and Standards for Obedience Test Field Trials."

Mrs. Walker, Josef Weber (another well-known dog trainer), and Miss Saunders added certain refinements, basic procedures, and exercises, and these were published in the April 1936 issue of the *American Kennel Gazette.* Obedience training for dogs was officially off and running, and it hasn't stopped since!

On June 13 of that same year, the North Westchester Kennel Club held the first American Kennel Club licensed obedience test in conjunction with their all-breed dog show. At that very first show there were 12 entries for judge Mrs. Wheeler H. Page. The exercises for Novice and Open classes remain virtually unchanged today—over half a century later—a remarkable tribute to the time and thought put behind the original exercises. Only Tracking Dog and Tracking Dog Excellent have been added in the intervening years.

By June 1939, the A.K.C. realized obedience was here to stay and saw the need for an advisory committee. One was established and chaired by Donald Fordyce, with enthusiastic members from all parts of the country willing to serve on it. George Foley of Pennsylvania was on the board. He was one of the most important men in the fancy, being superintendent of most of the dog shows on the Eastern seaboard. Mrs. Radcliff Farley, also of Pennsylvania, was on the committee with Miss Aurelia Tremaine of Massachusetts, Mrs. Bryant Godsell of California, Mrs. W. L. McCannon of Massachusetts, Samuel Blick of Maryland, Frank Grant of Ohio, as well as Josef Weber and Mrs. Walker from the original starters of obedience. Their contribution was to further standardize judging procedures and utility exercises.

A little of the emphasis on dog obedience was diverted with the outbreak of World War II, when talk switched to the topic of dogs serving in defense of their country. As soon as peace was declared, however, interest in obedience reached new heights. In 1946, the American Kennel Club called for another Obedience Advisory Committee, this time headed by John C. Neff. This committee included Blanche Saunders, Clarence Pfäffenberger, Theodore Kapnek, L. Wilson Davis, Howard P. Claussen, Elliott Blackiston, Oscar Franzen and Clyde Henderson.

11-year-old Chris Cebelak and Champion Loehr's Custom Blend, C.D. Chris had borrowed the dog for a 4-H project and they worked so well together that breeder Janet Loehr let Chris put his C.D. title on him. "Wisky" and Chris are inseparable pals after their 5-show obedience title wins!

Hi, Mom! Lady J's Pippin of Timbermist, C.D., R.O.M., and her newest baby. Bred and owned by Dr. Steve and Joyce Nielsen, Timbermist, Evergreen, Colorado.

Under their leadership, the obedience booklet grew to 43 pages. Rules and regulations were even more standardized than before, and there was the addition of the requirements for the Tracking Dog title.

In 1971, an obedience department was established at the American Kennel Club offices to keep pace with the growth of the sport and for constant review and guidance for show-giving clubs. Judge Richard D'Ambrisi was the director until his untimely death in 1973, at which time his duties were assumed by James E. Dearinger, along with his two special consultants: L. Wilson Davis for Tracking and Reverend Thomas O'Connor for Handicapped Handlers.

The members of this 1973 committee were Thomas Knott of Maryland, Edward Anderson of Pennsylvania, Jack Ward of Virginia, Lucy Neeb of Louisiana, William Phillips of California, James Falkner of Texas, Mary Lee Whiting of Minnesota, and Robert Self of Illinois, co-publisher of the important *Front and Finish* obedience newspaper.

While the committee functions continuously, meetings of the board are tentatively held every other year, unless a specific function of obedience question comes up, in which case a special meeting is called.

During the 1975 session, the committee held discussions on several old and new aspects of the obedience world. In addition to their own ever-increasing responsibilities to the fancy, they discussed seminars and educational symposiums, the licensing of tracking clubs, a booklet with suggested guidelines for obedience judges, Schutzhund training, and the aspects of a Utility Excellent Class degree.

Through the efforts of succeeding Advisory Committee members, the future of the sport has been insured, as well as the continuing emphasis on the working abilities for which dogs were originally bred. Obedience work also provides novices an opportunity to train and handle their dogs in an atmosphere that provides maximum pleasure, knowledge and accomplishment at minimum expense—which is precisely what Mrs. Walker intended.

When the Advisory Committee met in December 1980, many of the familiar names were among those listed as attending and continuing to serve the obedience cause. James E. Dearinger, James

C. Falkner, Rev. Thomas V. O'Connor, Robert Self, John Ward, Howard Cross, Helen Phillips, Samuel Kodis, George S. Pugh, Thomas Knott, and Mrs. Esme Treen were present and accounted for.

As we look back now at over more than a half century of obedience trials, we can only surmise that the pioneers—Mrs. Helene Whitehouse Walker and Blanche Saunders—would be proud of the progress made in the obedience rings.

MRS. WALKER HONORED

Everyone in obedience circles was delighted when Mrs. Walker received the 1983 Gaines Obedience Fido Award. She was honored for her contribution to the dog fancy and for 50 years of interest in the obedience field. The award was presented to her by Mr. Steve Willett, Director of Professional Services for Gaines at their Dog Care Center in White Plains, New York. The citation read, in part, ". . . for outstanding service and contributions to the advancement of obedience training and competition."

Mrs. Walker also received a framed engraved scroll presented to her by William Stifel, president of the American Kennel Club.

It was noted that Mrs. Walker and Blanche Saunders drove more than 10,000 miles in 1937 in a car and trailer, giving exhibitions in obedience all across the country which certainly helped fanciers to understand and become enthusiastic about obedience work. It is interesting, too, that in that same year, 95 dogs received their Companion Dog titles, and by 1982, more than 8000 dogs had earned this title. Catherine Riley, a protege of the late Blanche Saunders, arranged the affair which culminated in a standing ovation for Mrs. Walker, which was both fitting and proper!

THE OBEDIENCE RATING SYSTEMS

Just as the Phillips System mushroomed out of the world of show dogs, it was almost inevitable that a system to measure the successes of obedience dogs would become a reality.

By 1974, Nancy Shuman and Lynn Frosch had established the "Shuman System" of recording the Top Ten All Breed Obedience Dogs in the country. They also listed the Top Four in every breed, if each dog had accumulated a total of 50 or more points according to their requirements. Points were accrued on a scale based upon qualifying scores from 170 and up.

THE DELANEY SYSTEM

In 1975, *Front and Finish, The Dog Trainer's News* published an obedience rating system compiled by Kent Delaney to evaluate and score the various obedience dogs which had competed during the previous year. The system was devised primarily to measure the significance of a win made over a few dogs against one made over many dogs.

Points were given for both High in Trial or Class Placements, as recorded and published in the *American Kennel Gazette* magazine. The dog that scores the highest in the trial receives a point for each dog in competition, and first place winner in each class receives a point for each dog in the class. The dog placing second receives a point for each dog in the class less one, the third place winner a point less two, the fourth place winner a point less three.

During 1975, when the first obedience ratings were being compiled, there were no Old English Sheepdogs that made the Top Ten in either the all-breed category or the Top Ten Working Breeds. Ten Bobtails were mentioned, with several C.D.X. titlists among them.

They were Scottbar Kipling, C.D.X., owned by S. and D. Werford III; second was Mother Nature of Beau Cheval, owned by J. and L. Landis. Ranking third was Queen Victoria IV, owned by A. Heiner, and fourth was Miss Nana Pan, C.D.X., owned by J. Winkel. Fifth and sixth place went to Sir Pilbert of Surrey, owned by K. Lambert, and Ensigns Lady Penelope, C.D.X., owned by G. and P. Ensign. D. and D. Blanchard's Shaggy Lady Gwenivere was seventh, and R. and T. Brandau's Scottbar Black Eyed Susan was eighth. Ninth place went to S. and D. Lloyd's Old Weird Wendy II, C.D.X. There was a three-way tie for tenth place with Bluehavens Easy Going, Silverviews Gentle Streak and Sir Sherlock Shepton, owned by the Finnegans, the Norvos, and the Ritters respectively.

1976

During the second year of the Delaney System, no Old English Sheepdog had made it to the Top Ten all-breed or Working Group lists, but there was the full list of ten within the breed. The No. 1 position went to the previous year's eighth place winner, Scottbar Black Eyed Susan, owned by the Brandaus. K. Knox's Smokey was No. 2, P. Ziegler's CoryJoe Beck was No. 3 and No. 4 was Wee Bonnie Lassie, C.D.X., owned by R. Crossley. No. 5 was last year's second place winner, Mother Nature of Beau Cheval. S. Fischer's Breezy Bruan was No. 6, I. Martin's Ingers Lady Alhambra was No. 7, and J. Winkel's Miss Nana Pan, U.D., was No. 8. The No. 9 spot went to B. Fosters Cheerio Poetry Man, and the No. 10 to J. Brusseau's Sugar Trees Frosty Morn. It is interesting to note that Miss Nana Pan had moved up from her C.D.X. title to U.D., but dropped from her previous No. 4 spot to No. 8.

1976 was also the year that *Front and Finish* printed the Shuman System, a slight variation on the Delaney System, and no Old English Sheepdog qualified for top ten all-breed listings or top ten working group. The system found only three or four dogs in each breed qualifying, and we had four in our breed. No. 1 was the Crossley's Wee Bonnie Lassie, No. 2 was J. T. Winkel's Miss Nana Pan, U.D., No. 3 was the Brandaus' Scottbar Black Eyed Susan, U.D., and tieing for No. 4 were the D. L. Smiths' Smiths Misty Lady, U.D., and C. and J. Bells' Wright's Isles Susie Bell, U.D.

1977

In 1977 the Shuman System found Miss Nana Pan, U.D., to be No. 1. The No. 2 place went to A. R. Tucker's Arlo Gaitefeathers, No. 3 to C. M. Sheriff's Harry Woolybear Sheriff and No. 4 to Sherwoods Papa Pride, owned by J. LaBore.

1978

The 1978 Shuman System found no Bobtails in the top spots in the all-breed listings or in the working group, but four qualified for the breed. Again Miss Nana Pan, U.D., was No. 1, Ingers Lady Alhambra was No. 2, and two newcomers to the lists were No. 3 and No. 4 respectively. They were Shaggydrovers Miss Muffett, owned by the K. Schotters, and Double JJs Spellbinder, owned by H. McKee.

1979

The leading four in 1979 were: No. 1, Scottbar Funny Girl, owned by L. V. Ansell; No. 2, Ingers Lady Alhambra, owned by I. Martin; and the only repeater, No. 3, Gipson's Big Moses, owned by P. L. Gipson; and No. 4, J. Speath's Sir Benjamin Jasha Log.

The Delaney System in 1979 produced similar results—no Old English Sheepdogs in the Top Ten all-breeds or in the Working Group. There were ten dogs in the breed, and heading the list was M. and K. Keller's Sir Osker of Carnaby. No. 2 was D. and V. Gray's Sir Patch of Mill, and No. 3 was Gramelhills Mauldin Gold, owned by J. Bramel. No. 4 was P. Gipson's Big Moses, C.D., No. 5 was Blue Pandas Pooh A Party of One, owned by L. Long and D. McKee. The No. 6 spot went to D. Moore's Shaggymor Andys Molleo; the No. 7 to C. Miller's Sugarbear XIX; the No. 8 to Beefeater Sunshine Jenny, C.D., owned by R. and G. Manucy, who tied for points with Heinemans Lady Macbeth, owned by C. Heineman; and the No. 10 went to Christopher Robin VIII, owned by F. Townsend.

THE DECADE OF THE EIGHTIES

Records, listings and individual point counts clearly illustrate that the decade of the '70s saw a tremendous surge in obedience titles and training. The beginning of the 1980s saw those keeping score seeking help for their tabulations due to the ever-increasing number of participants, and these include the Old English Sheepdog. Their numbers in all titles continue to increase and certainly will in the future.

WEBER

Barbara Weber of Mukwonago, Wisconsin, has been active in the obedience rings since 1973. She is the proud owner of Wisconsin's first, and still the only, Utility Dog titlist in the breed. Her Oriole Lanes Lady Amanda, U.D., was also the first to obtain Conformation class points.

Barbara also owns Larame's Checkerboard Square, a C.D. titlist who was second in the Delaney System in 1980. She is also training a young male, Lonestar's Hot Gossip, who at this time has six points toward championship. He's been scoring as high as 197 at match shows so far.

221

Barbara is also a member of the parent club since 1980 and the Old English Sheepdog Club of South Eastern Wisconsin since 1978. She has had Golden Retrievers since 1979 and is also training them in obedience. She has also won *Dog World* awards with the Goldens.

COBBLESTONE

Barb and Larry Foster of Beaverton, Oregon, started their Cobblestone Old English Sheepdog kennel in 1975. Their first dog that year finished to a C.D. title within one weekend. In 1976, when he was 16 months old, he earned the title, and the Fosters became hooked on obedience training.

Since that time they have finished a U.D. on one dog, a C.D. on another one, and a C.D.X. on still another.

Cheerio Poetry Man was their C.D. who qualified for three out of four shows in September 1976. Chardee Prinde's Messenger earned his C.D.X. in 1980, and the U.D. in 1982. He was the 24th Bobtail to earn a U.D. in the history of the breed to that time.

Their bitch, ShowDoune Forget MNot, is their C.D. dog which earned the title in July 1982. She was High In Trial at the parent club specialty in Denver that year, with a score of 193 in Novice B Class.

Talisman Sno Shu's Finest Hour is their C.D.X. winner who made the grade in June 1983. As of this writing, their Winnoby's Promises to Keep promises to win a title also, and was in training.

Barb Foster is also the author of a book entitled *Companions, Competitors and Clowns—The Old English Sheepdog in Obedience.*

PAULA BUSH

Paula Bush has been interested in the breed and active in obedience since 1976. Her Jendowers Union Jack, C.D., is her pride and joy, and it was Paula that put his C.D. title on him. She also belongs to the parent club and lives with her dog and family in Herndon, Virginia.

WINDOM

Dawn E. Largent of Marion, Pennsylvania, started in the breed in 1976, at which time she also joined the parent club. Since then

Blueprints Holly Go Lightly, owned by Don and Coreen Eaton of Ellisville, Missouri. Holly was High Scoring Dog at the 1978 National Specialty.

Lady Guinnevere of Sommer, C.D. shown completing her C.D. title at the parent club national specialty in August 1976. Owned and shown to her degree by Walter J. Sommerfelt, Colliersville, Tennessee.

she has finished two obedience titlists and is training one of those for C.D.X. In 1985 she began thinking about breeding Bobtails, and in the short time she has been in the breed has accomplished excellent results in the obedience ring. Her Charity's Lady Tamara Windom is a C.D. and finished in just four trials. Her Talisman's Summers Last Song completed her obedience title in 1983 and has points toward championship. Pettibone's Talisman Dream On will also be put through her paces in the obedience rings to earn her title like her kennel mates.

TEC TYME

Jill Schultes of Mesa, Arizona, started in the obedience ring in 1979, and she now has two bitches with their C.D. titles. She has two daughters showing in the junior showmanship classes, one with a Sheepdog and a Shih Tzu, and other with a Shih Tzu. Shih Tzu were added to their Tec Tyme Kennel in 1981.

Stephanie, who works with the Old English Sheepdog, started training their future Ch. Windfields' Esquire when he was just three months old. "Bruce," as he is called, was nine months old when Stephanie won two of her three wins, in the novice classes,

224

the first and second times he was shown. They really work well together.

Stephanie, was the Top Junior Handler in the Novice Class in 1981, and in 1982 was Top Junior Handler in the Open Junior Class in the Old English Sheepdog Club of America.

When Bruce finished his championship, Stephanie began showing her Shih Tzu and is also showing several dogs for other people. She is obviously a young lady who is great at what she does!

COATES

In 1982, Carrlyn L. Ward Coates of Lakewood, Colorado, began training her Calamity Jane in obedience. Her first time out she won the Novice A class at the Old English Sheepdog Club of Denver Specialty show. Jane is also the only Bobtail in Colorado that also herds. Carrlyn Coates is a member of the Stockdog Club in her area as well as the parent club, the Old English Sheepdog Fanciers of Central Arizona, and the Mountain States Dog Obedience Club.

Carrlyn got her foundation bitch in 1985, but has not yet decided on a kennel name.

Oriole Lanes Lady Amanda, U.D., going through her paces at a 1978 Wisconsin Kennel Club obedience trial. Owned by Barbara Weber.

American and Mexican Champion Bobmar Midnight Cowboy and his friend Tina.

226

Chapter 13

Buying Your First Old English Sheepdog

In searching for that special puppy, there are several paths that will lead you to a litter from which you can find the puppy of your choice. If you are uncertain as to where to find a reputable breeder, write to the parent club and ask for the names and addresses of members who have puppies for sale. The addresses of various breed clubs can be obtained by writing directly to the American Kennel Club, Inc., 51 Madison Avenue, New York, NY 10010. They keep an up-to-date, accurate list of breeders from whom you can seek information on obtaining a good, healthy puppy. The classified ad listings in dog publications and the major newspapers may also lead you to that certain pup. The various dog magazines generally carry a monthly breed column which features information and news on the breed that may aid in your selection.

It is advisable that you become thoroughly acquainted with the breed prior to purchasing your puppy. Plan to attend a dog show or two in your area, at which you can view purebred dogs of just about every breed at their best in the show ring. Even if you are not interested in purchasing a show-quality dog, you should be familiar with what the better specimens look like so that you will at least purchase a decent representative of the breed for the money. You can learn a lot from observing show dogs in action in the ring, or in some other public place, where their personalities can be clearly shown. The dog show catalog is also a useful tool to put you in contact with the local kennels and breeders. Each dog that is entered in the show is listed along with the owner's name and address. If you spot a dog that you think is a particularly fine and pleasing specimen, contact the owners and arrange to visit their kennel to see the types of dogs they are breeding and winning with at the shows. Exhibitors at the dog shows are usually more than delighted to talk to people interested in their dogs and the specific characteristics of their breed.

Once you've decided that this is the breed for you, read some background material so that you become thoroughly familiar with it. When you feel certain that this puppy will fit in with your family's way of life, it is time to start writing letters and making phone calls and appointments to see those dogs that may interest you.

Some words of caution: don't choose a kennel simply because it is near your home, and don't buy the first cute puppy that romps around your legs or licks the end of your nose. All puppies are cute, and naturally some will appeal to you more than others. But don't let preferences sway your thinking. If you are buying your puppy to be strictly a family pet, preferences can be permissible. If you are looking for a top-quality puppy for the show ring, however, you must evaluate clearly, choose wisely, and make the best possible choice. Whichever one you choose, you will quickly learn to love your puppy. A careful selection, rather than a "love at first sight" choice will save you from disappointment later on.

To get the broadest idea of what puppies are for sale and what the going market prices are, visit as many kennels as possible in your area and write to others farther away. With today's safe and rapid air flights on the major airlines, it is possible to purchase dogs from far-off places at nominal costs. While it is safest and wisest to first see the dog you are buying, there are enough reputable breeders and kennels to be found for you to take this step with a minimum of risk. In the long run, it can be well worth your while to obtain the exact dog or bloodline you desire.

It is customary for the purchaser to pay the shipping charges, and the airlines are most willing to supply flight information and prices upon request. Rental on the shipping crate, if the owner does not provide one for the dog, is nominal. While unfortunate incidents have occurred on the airlines in the transporting of animals by air, the major airlines are making improvements in safety measures and have reached the point of reasonable safety and cost. Barring unforeseen circumstances, the safe arrival of a dog you might buy can pretty much be assured if both seller and purchaser adhere to and follow up on even the most minute details from both ends.

WHAT TO LOOK FOR IN YOUR DOG

Anyone who has owned a puppy will agree that the most fascinating aspect of raising him is to witness the complete and extraordinary metamorphosis that occurs during his first year of maturing. Your puppy will undergo a marked change in appearance, and during this period you must also be aware of the puppy's personality, for there are certain qualities visible at this time that will generally make for a good adult dog. Of course no one can guarantee nature, and the best puppy does not always grow up to be a great dog; however, even the novice breeder can learn to look for certain specifics that will help him choose a promising puppy.

Should you decide to purchase a six-to-eight-week-old puppy, you are in store for all the cute antics that little pup can dream up for you! At this age, the puppy should be well on its way to being weaned, wormed, and ready to go out into the world with its responsible new owner. It is better not to buy a puppy that is less than six weeks old; it simply is not ready to leave its mother or the security of the other puppies. By eight to twelve weeks of age, you will be able to notice much about the behavior and appearance of the dog. Puppies, as they are recalled in our fondest childhood memories, are amazingly active and bouncy—and well they should be! The normal puppy should be alert, curious, and interested, especially when a stranger is present. However, if the puppy acts a little reserved or distant, don't necessarily construe these acts to be signs of fear or shyness. It might merely indicate that he hasn't quite made up his mind whether he likes you as yet. By the same token, though, he should not be openly fearful or terrified by a stranger—and especially should not show any fear of his owner!

In direct contrast, the puppy should not be ridiculously over-active, either. The puppy that frantically bounds around the room and is never still is not especially desirable. And beware of the "spinners." Spinners are the puppies or dogs that have become neurotic from being kept in cramped quarters or in crates and behave in an emotionally unstable manner when let loose in adequate space. When let out they run in circles and seemingly "go wild." Puppies with this kind of traumatic background seldom ever regain full composure or adjust to the big outside world. The puppy which has had proper exercise and appropriate living quarters will have a normal, though spirited, outlook on life and will do its utmost to win you over without having to go into a tailspin.

If the general behavior and appearance of the dog thus far appeal to you, it is time for you to observe him more closely for additional physical requirements. First of all, you cannot expect to find in the puppy the coat he will bear upon maturity. That will come with time and good food and will be additionally enhanced by the many wonderful grooming aids which can be found in pet shops today. Needless to say, the healthy puppy's coat should have a nice shine to it, and the more dense at this age, the better the coat will be when the dog reaches adulthood. Look for clear, sparkling eyes that are free of discharge.

It is important to check the bite. Even though the puppy will cut another complete set of teeth somewhere between four and seven months of age, there will already be some indication of how the final teeth will be positioned.

Puppies take anything and almost everything into their mouths to chew on, and a lot of diseases and infections start or are introduced in the mouth. Brown-stained teeth, for instance, may indicate the puppy has had a past case of distemper, and the teeth will remain that way. This fact must be reckoned with if you have a show puppy in mind. The puppy's breath should be neither sour nor unpleasant. Bad breath can be a result of a poor food mixture in the diet, or of eating low quality meat, especially if it is fed raw. Some people say that the healthy puppy's breath should have a faint odor that is vaguely reminiscent of garlic. At any rate, a puppy should never be fed just table scraps, but should be raised on a well-balanced diet containing a good dry puppy chow and a good grade of fresh meat. Poor meat and too much cereal or fillers tend to make the puppy grow too fat. Puppies should be in good flesh but not fat from the wrong kind of food.

Needless to say, the puppy should be clean. The breeder that shows a dirty puppy is one to steer away from. Look closely at the skin. Make sure it is not covered with insect bites or red, blotchy sores and dry scales. The vent area around the tail should not show evidences of diarrhea or inflammation. By the same token, the puppy's fur should not be matted with feces or smell strongly of urine.

True enough, you can wipe dirty eyes, clean dirty ears, and give the puppy a bath when you get it home, but these things are all indications of how the puppy has been cared for during the important formative first months of its life, and they can vitally influence the pup's its future health and development. There are many reputable breeders raising healthy puppies that have been reared in proper places and under the proper conditions in clean housing, so why take a chance on a series of veterinary bills and a questionable constitution?

MALE OR FEMALE?

The choice of sex in your puppy is also something that must be given serious thought before you buy. For the pet owner, the sex that would best suit the family life you enjoy would be the paramount choice to consider. For the breeder or exhibitor, there are other vital considerations. If you are looking for a stud to establish a kennel, it is essential that you select a dog with both testicles evident, even at a tender age. If there is any doubt, have a vet verify this before the sale is finalized.

The visibility of only one testicle, known as monorchidism, automatically disqualifies the dog from the show ring or from a breeding program, though monorchids are capable of siring. Additionally, it must be noted that monorchids frequently sire dogs with the same deficiency, and to knowingly introduce this into a bloodline is an unwritten sin in the fancy. Also, a monorchid can sire dogs that are completely sterile. Such dogs are referred to as cryptorchids and have no testicles.

An additional consideration in the male versus female decision for private owners is that with males there might be the problem of leg-lifting and with females there is the inconvenience while they are in heat. However, this need not be the problem it used to be—pet shops sell "pants" for both sexes, which help to control the situation.

THE PLANNED PARENTHOOD
BEHIND YOUR PUPPY

Never be afraid to ask pertinent questions about the puppy, nor questions about the sire and dam. Feel free to ask the breeder if you might see the dam; the purpose of your visit is to determine her general health and her appearance as a representative of the breed. Also, ask to see the sire, if the breeder is the owner. Ask what the puppy has been fed and should be fed after weaning. Ask to see the pedigree, and inquire if the litter or the individual puppies have been registered with the American Kennel Club, how many of the temporary and/or permanent inoculations the puppy has had, when and if the puppy has been wormed, and whether it has had any illness, disease, or infection.

You need not ask if the puppy is housebroken; it won't mean much. He may have gotten the idea as to where "the place" is where he lives now, but he will need new training to learn where "the place" is in his new home! You can't really expect too much from puppies at this age anyway. Housebreaking is entirely up to the new owner. We know puppies always eliminate when they first awaken and sometimes dribble when they get excited. If friends and relatives are coming over to see the new puppy, make sure he is walked just before he greets them at the front door. This will help.

The normal elimination time for puppies is about every two or three hours. As the time draws near, either take the puppy out or indicate the newspaper for the same purpose. Housebreaking is never easy, but anticipation is about 90 percent of solving the problem. The schools that offer to housebreak your dog are virtually useless. Here again the puppy will learn   "the place" at the schoolhouse, but coming home he will need special training for the new location.

A reputable breeder will welcome any and all questions you might ask and will voluntarily offer additional information, if only to brag about the tedious and loving care he has given the litter. He will also sell a puppy on a 24-hour veterinary approval basis. This means you have a full day to get the puppy to a veterinarian of your choice to get his opinion on the general health of the

On the way to her championship, Barrelroll Dame Judith takes a 5-point major under the late renowned dog man Percy Roberts. She is pictured here with handler Laura Martin. She was the foundation bitch for the Jen-Kris Kennels in Columbus, Ohio.

The Centenary
presentation to
Miss F. Tilley,
President of the
O.E.S. Club
1966-1981, at the
Club's
Championship
Show on July 25,
1981 at the Royal
Bath and West
Showground.
Presentation
made by the
Chairman, Mr.
Ivor Thick.

Best in Show at a Saratoga Springs dog show several decades ago was Mrs. Helen Margery Lewis's Ch. Merriedip Master Pantaloons, J. McKercher handled and famous dog man David Wagstaff was the judge. With Mrs. Lewis is E. B. Taylor, president of the Wildwood Kennel Club. William Brown photograph.

puppy before you make a final decision. There should also be veterinary certificates and full particulars on the dates and types of inoculations the puppy has been given up to that time.

PUPPIES AND WORMS

Let us give further attention to the unhappy and very unpleasant subject of worms. Generally speaking, most puppies—even those raised in clean quarters—come into contact with worms early in life. The worms can be passed down from the mother before birth or picked up during the puppies' first encounters with the earth or their kennel facilities. To say that you must not buy a puppy because of an infestation of worms is nonsensical. You might be passing up a fine animal that can be freed of worms in one short treatment, although a heavy infestation of worms of any kind in a young dog is dangerous and debilitating.

The extent of the infection can be readily determined by a veterinarian, and you might take his word as to whether the future health and conformation of the dog has been damaged. He can prescribe the dosage and supply the medication at this time, and you will already have one of your problems solved.

VETERINARY INSPECTION

While your veterinarian is going over the puppy you have selected, you might just as well ask him for his opinion of it as a breed, as well as the facts about its general health. While few veterinarians can claim to be breed-conformation experts, they usually have a good eye for a worthy specimen and can advise you where to go for further information. Perhaps your veterinarian could also recommend other breeders if you should want another opinion. The veterinarian can point out structural faults or organic problems that affect all breeds and can usually judge whether an animal has been abused or mishandled and whether it is oversized or undersized.

I would like to emphasize here that it is only through this type of close cooperation between owners and veterinarians that we can expect to reap the harvest of modern research.

Most reliable veterinarians are more than eager to learn about various breeds of purebred dogs, and we in turn must acknowledge and apply what they have proved through experience and research in their field. We can buy and breed the best dog in the world, but when disease strikes we are only as safe as our veterinarian is capable—so let's keep him informed, breed by breed and dog by dog. The veterinarian can mean the difference between life and death!

THE CONDITIONS OF SALE

While it is customary to pay for the puppy before you take it away with you, you should be able to give the breeder a deposit if there is any doubt about the puppy's health. Depending on local laws, you might also postdate a check to cover the 24-four hour veterinary approval. If you decide to take the puppy, the breeder is required to supply you with a pedigree, along with the puppy's registration papers. He is also obliged to supply you with complete information about the inoculations and American Kennel Club instructions on how to transfer ownership of the puppy to your name.

For convenience, some breeders will offer buyers time payment plans if the price on a show dog is very high or if deferred payments are the only way you can purchase the dog. However, any such terms must be worked out between buyer and breeder and should be put in writing to avoid later complications.

You will find most breeders cooperative if they believe you are sincere in your love for the puppy and that you will give it the proper home and the show ring career it deserves (if it is sold as a show-quality specimen of the breed). Remember, when buying a show dog, it is impossible to guarantee what mother nature has created. A breeder can only tell you what he *believes* will develop into a show dog, so be sure your breeder is an honest one.

Also, if you purchase a show prospect and promise to show the dog, you definitely should show it! It is a waste to have a beautiful dog that deserves recognition in the show ring sitting at home as a family pet, and it is unfair to the breeder. This is especially true if the breeder offered you a reduced price because of the advertising his kennel and bloodlines would receive by your showing the dog in the ring. If you want a pet, buy a pet. Be honest about it, and let the breeder decide on this basis which is the best dog for you. Your conscience will be clear and you'll both be doing a real service to the breed.

Five 4-week-old puppies at the Londonaire Kennels in Sacramento, California.

BUYING A SHOW PUPPY

If you are positive about breeding and showing, make this point clear so that the breeder will sell you the best possible puppy. If you are dealing with an established kennel, you will have to rely partially, if not entirely, on their choice, since they know their bloodlines and what they can expect from the breeding. They know how their stock develops, and it would be foolish of them to sell you a puppy that could not stand up as a show specimen representing their stock in the ring.

However, you must also realize that the breeder may be keeping the best puppy in the litter to show and breed himself. If this is the case, you might be wise to select the best puppy of the opposite sex so that the dogs will not be competing against one another in the show rings.

THE PURCHASE PRICE

Prices vary on all puppies, of course, but a good show prospect at six weeks to six months of age will usually sell for several hundred dollars. If the puppy is really outstanding, and the pedigree and parentage are also outstanding, the price will be even higher. Honest breeders, however, will all quote around the same figure, so price should not be a strong deciding factor in your choice. If you have any questions as to the current price range, a few telephone calls to different kennels will give you a good average. Reputable breeders will usually stand behind the health of their puppies should something drastically wrong develop. Their obligation to make an adjustment or replacement is usually honored. However, this must be agreed to in writing at the time of the purchase.

237

American and Canadian Champion Tamara's Shaggy Shoes Mac Duff takes a Best in Show in 1970 under Judge Reid. Owned and handled by Don and Jean McColl of Birmingham, Michigan.

238

Chapter 14

Grooming Your Old English Sheepdog

It is the complete responsibility of the seller of an Old English Sheepdog to point out to a prospective buyer the amount of grooming involved to keep a bobtail in good condition. Regardless of how conscientious and dedicated a new owner may be, a high percentage of dogs will become dirty and matted, with no alternative left except to be cut down to the skin to remove mats before the adult coat ever reaches full bloom.

While pets, or city dogs, may look adorable in their puppy clip coats, or with one or two inches all over, anyone entertaining an idea of having a show dog should be aware of the care that must be expended to keep their coats in proper condition.

We all admire the beautiful coats on the Old English Sheepdogs we see in the ring today, but it represents time and money. Anyone can learn to do it—it is up to the owner to decide.

GROOMING A PUPPY

Teach puppies right away to learn to stay put on a grooming table. When they get big enough, teach them to jump up and down on the table by themselves and save your back. Puppies, however, should be lifted, like lambs, up on to it and taught to stay. Don't allow the puppy to become restless due to a slippery surface, or by attaching him to a grooming pole so that even a show lead around his neck will send him into fits of fear or resistance. Talk to the puppy, perhaps have a radio or TV turned on nearby, for your benefit even more than his, and make sure all distractions (other dogs, food, toys, etc.) are out of sight. Let it be a sort of "private time" between the two of you, when you let the dog know you mean business in getting this grooming over and done with, and that later is play time. Patience is a prerequisite; don't take out your hostilities on your dog by hard, heavy brushing. Give the coat lots of tender loving care and you will see the fruits of your labor as time goes by.

Which end you start with is up to you, but if you start in the rear, you will teach your dog to get used to being "handled" here and it won't be immediately distressed by seeing that brush flashing past its eyes. You must be sure to brush in layers and to get all the way down to the skin so the undercoat won't mat. A surface grooming is not good enough!

Bear in mind that correct color in the Old English Sheepdog can be affected by your grooming procedure. Caution must be taken not to remove that undercoat. This thick undercoat is of a different color than the outercoat and can change the "shade" of your dog's appearance.

It will be necessary to teach your dog to stand on the table as well as lying down, first on one side and then the other. In the beginning, pick up the dog and lay him down, pat him, tell him to "stay," and gently brush him. After he gets used to the idea, you will find that he will doze off while you're brushing, and that's when you've got it made!

HOW OFTEN TO GROOM

For as many owners of dogs there are in the world, there are that many "theories" on how often to groom, how often to bathe, and so it goes. The best possible answer, for any breed, is when they need it. But if you have a show dog or want your dog to always look its best, you will find yourself developing a routine that will accomplish the effect you want.

Puppies should be groomed lightly each day to get them used to the process; older dogs may come to expect it, and even to like it. Here again, *when* they need it always counts. If you share close quarters with your dog, and he's a part of your household, you will want him clean and looking good all the time.

Good health will also play a part in your grooming. A healthy dog will have a lustre and a coat that will reflect his general condition. The proper amount of oil will be present in the coat and it will automatically look better. Matting will be your biggest concern, especially if you live in the suburbs, if your dog has a yard, or if you walk it in fields or along garden paths.

GETTING RID OF MATS

Both comb and brush are needed for mats. Take the mat between your fingers and try to gently pull it apart from all sides; a little brushing between pulls will help. The process may have to be repeated several times before you make any headway, but do it until you feel the hairs can be combed to the edge of the coat without leaving a "hole." Then brush the remaining hairs (you'll always lose some hair in a mat) back into the rest of the coat. Only in *extreme cases* should you ever use a pair of scissors on a mat. Next, gently split the center of the mat in a direction *away from the body*. Then begin your hair splitting, gently brushing, and eventually, at the end, use a comb to get out the remaining hairs before brushing the spot back into the rest of the coat.

This should be done *before* a bath. Do not depend on soap and water to remove the mats. You will wind up at the end of the bath with a dog full of foamy balls of suds. The process of bathing means grooming, bathing and then grooming again. There is no shortcut.

THE BATH

After a thorough brushing out, place the dog in the tub and thoroughly water it down, making sure it is wet to the skin all over. Our breed needs special attention around the eyes, so be careful with the soap when doing the head. Hold the head up and back until the soap is all rinsed off.

Here again we recommend starting at the rear end and the legs of the dog before spraying water and suds around the head. One or two shampoos and thorough rinsings are a matter of personal choice; squeeze, rather than rub, shampoo through the coat so you don't tangle the coat unnecessarily. We cannot recommend strongly enough that you not only shampoo every part of the dog, but that you make sure that *every part of the dog is thoroughly rinsed clean of shampoo*. Shampoo or soapy residue left in the coat will dry it, make it brittle and affect the beauty and shine.

While the dog is still in the tub, gently squeeze excess water out of the coat, then throw a turkish towel over it and pat it dry, especially the feet, before lifting it out of the tub onto the grooming table.

A hand dryer will usually do the trick as you gently brush dry. Don't keep it on one spot; brush dry all over the body. With your rounded scissors cut out the hair between the toes and shape the feet until they brush dry and resemble big powder puffs. If you wish to learn this as well as the other trimming some people do, get expert instruction from another breeder so that you do it correctly. In fact, don't use scissors on your dog at all until another breeder-exhibitor has shown you how.

Make sure all parts of the dog are dry before you finish, or the dog's damp coat will pick up dirt again and you will risk the dog's catching cold if the weather and circumstances aren't exactly right.

If you choose to have your dog with a topknot to keep the hair out of its eyes—some people now put bows on them!—make sure that none of the hair is pulling the eye rims or skin out of place. If it is, the dog will not give up until he has scratched it off and he will lose a lot of hair in so doing.

CLIPPING

Some people choose to keep their bobtails clipped down, especially in warmer weather and climates, and this is perfectly all right. Bobtails look good no matter how they wear their hair! Some prefer an all-over clip about one to three inches from the skin. This protects from sun and insects and looks plushy.

Shaving a dog down to the skin can be a dangerous thing. Using a clipper leaves a dog exposed to the elements and can result in skin burns. This drastic a measure is usually only necessary in severe cases of matted coat. I have never seen a dog of any longhaired breed that did not look self-conscious when shaved to the skin—they just seem to look guilty about being "naked." A short length coat may take a little bit more time and trouble but will still leave your dog looking like a bobtail.

In other words, get instruction for any use of clippers!

GROOMING SALONS

While grooming the Old English Sheepdog may become a relatively simple matter after practice, there may be those who do not feel they can, or want to, do it to their satisfaction. For those who do not enjoy grooming their dogs, there is an alternative.

Grooming shops can be located through the Yellow Pages of the telephone book, and a schedule can be set up with one of them to have your dog groomed on a regular basis. Visit the shops in your area until you find the one that appeals most to you, after asking if they are experienced at handling and grooming bobtails. Tell them what you want, how often you want it, and *ask the price!* Some shops will pick up and deliver, and some nowadays even bring a van to your driveway and do the grooming at home! I like this the best. You can watch the procedure, and the dog likes the familiar surroundings.

While at the shop, observe if it is clean, the brand of products used, if the personnel is kind and gentle with the dogs they are working on during your visit, and if possible, get the opinions of others about satisfaction with their work. Indeed, your veterinarian may be able to tell you something about their reputation. Some grooming parlors will want to tranquilize a dog that "acts up" or is excessively fearful or aggressive. *Make sure you explain that you do not want this for your dog,* and take it elsewhere! The dangers of overdose, the dog falling off the table, etc., are not to be tolerated. If your dog is fearful or aggressive, stay with it! Tranquilizing is an unnecessary procedure designed with the groomers' own convenience in mind. Do not jeopardize your dog's health for their ease in doing their job.

Word of mouth is the best advertising—satisfied customers and your own inspection should be your guide. And best of all, let them do it *while you wait.* A good book will help you pass the time.

Photographed in 1942, these adorable shaggy Merriedip puppies were bred and owned by Mrs. Helen Margery Lewis of Massachusetts and New York.

Chapter 15

Breeding Your
Old English Sheepdog

Let us assume the time has come for your dog to be bred, and you have decided you are in a position to enjoy producing a litter of puppies that you hope will make a contribution to the breed. The bitch you purchased is sound, her temperament is excellent and she is a most worthy representative of the breed.

You have a calendar and have counted off the ten days since the first day of red staining and have determined the tenth to 14th day, which will more than likely be the best period for the actual mating. You have additionally counted off 60 to 65 days before the puppies are likely to be born to make sure everything necessary for their arrival will be in good order by that time.

From the moment the idea of having a litter occurred to you, your thoughts should have been given to the correct selection of a proper stud. Here again, the novice would do well to seek advice on analyzing pedigrees and tracing bloodlines for the best breedings. As soon as the bitch is in season and you see color (or staining) and a swelling of the vulva, it is time to notify the owner of the stud you selected and make appointments for the breedings. There are several pertinent questions you will want to ask the stud owners after having decided upon the pedigree. The owners, naturally, will also have a few questions they wish to ask you. These questions will concern your bitch's bloodlines, health, age, how many previous litters she's had, if any, and so forth.

GENETICS

No one can guarantee nature! But, with facts and theories at your command you can at least, on paper, plan a litter of puppies that should fulfill your fondest expectations. Since the ultimate purpose of breeding is to try to improve the breed, this planning, no matter how uncertain, should be earnestly attempted.

There are a few terms you should be familiar with to help you understand the breeding procedure and the structure of genetics. The first thing that comes to mind is the Mendelian Law—or the Laws of Mendelian Inheritance. Who was Mendel?

Gregor Mendel was an Austrian clergyman and botanist born in Brunn, Moravia. He developed his basic theories on heredity while working with peas. Not realizing the full import of his work, he published a paper on his experiments in a scientific journal in the year 1866. That paper went unnoticed for many years, but the laws and theories put forth in it have been tried and proven. Today they are accepted by scientists, as well as dog breeders.

To help understand the Mendelian law as it applies to breeding dogs, we must acquaint ourselves with certain scientific terms and procedures. First of all, dogs possess glands of reproduction which are called gonads. The gonads of the male are in the testicles which produce sperm or spermatozoa. The gonads of the female are the ovaries and produce eggs. The bitch is born with these eggs and, when she is old enough to reproduce, she comes into heat. The eggs descend from the ovaries, via the fallopian tubes in to the two horns of the uterus. There they either pass out during the heat cycle or are fertilized by the male sperm in the semen deposited during a mating.

In dog mating, there is what we refer to as a tie, which is a time period during which the male pump s about 600 million spermatozoa into the female to fertilize the ripened eggs. When the sperm and the ripe eggs meet zygotes are created, and the little one-celled future puppies descend from the fallopian tubes into the uterus, where they attach themselves to the walls of the uterus and begin to develop. With all inherited characteristics deter-

246

mined when the zygote was formed, the dam must now assume her role as incubator for her babies, which are organisms in their own right. The bitch has been bred and is now in whelp!

Let us take a closer look at what is happening during the breeding phenomenon. We know that while the male deposits as many as 600 million sperm into the female, the number of ripe eggs she releases will determine the number of puppies in the litter. Therefore, those breeders who advertise their stud as "producer of large litters" do not know the facts. The bitch determines the size of the litter; the male, the sex of the puppies. It takes only one sperm of the 600 million to produce a puppy.

Each dog and bitch possesses 39 pairs of chromosomes in each reproductive germ cell. The chromosomes carry the genes, like peas in a pod, and there are approximately 150,000 genes in each chromosome. These chromosomes split apart and unite with half the chromosomes from the other parent, and the puppy's looks and temperament are created.

To understand the procedure more thoroughly, we must understand that there are two kinds of genes—dominant and recessive. A dominant gene is one of a pair whose influece is expressed to the exclusion of the effects of the other. A recessive gene is one of a pair whose influece is subdued by the effects of the other. Most of the important qualities we wish to perpetuate in our breeding programs are carried on by the dominant genes. It is the successful breeder who becomes expert at eliminating recessive or undesirable genes and building up the dominant or desirable ones. This principle holds true in every phase of breeding—inside and outside the dog!

There are many excellent books available which will take you deeper into the fascinating subject of canine genetics. You can learn about your chances of getting so many black, so many white, and so many black and white puppies. etc. Avail yourself of this information before your next, or hopefully, first breeding. I have merely touched upon genetics here to point out the importance of planned parenthood. Any librarian can help you find further information, or books may be purchase offering the very latest findings in canine genetics. It is a fascinating and rewarding field toward creating better dogs.

THE POWER IN PEDIGREES

Someone in the dog fancy once remarked that the definition of a show prospect puppy is one third the pedigree, one third what you see and one third what you *hope* it will be! Well, no matter how you break down your qualifying fractions, we all quite agree that good breeding is essential if you have any plans at all for a show career for your dog. Many breeders will buy on pedigree alone, counting largely on what they themselves can do with the puppy by way of feeding, conditioning, and training. Needless to say, that very important piece of paper is reassuring to a breeder or buyer new at the game or to one who has a breeding program in mind and is trying to establish his own bloodline.

One of the most fascinating aspects of tracing pedigrees is the way the names of the really great dogs of the past keep appearing in the pedigrees of the great dogs of today—proof positive of the strong influence of heredity and witness to a great deal of truth in the statement that great dogs frequently reproduce themselves, though not necessarily in appearance only. A pedigree represents something of value when one is dedicated to breeding better dogs.

To the novice buyer or one who is perhaps merely switching to another breed and sees only a frolicking, leggy, squirming bundle of energy in a fur coat, a pedigree can mean everything! To those of us who believe in heredity, a pedigree is more like an insurance policy—so always read it carefully and take heed.

For the more serious breeder who wishes to make a further study of bloodlines in relation to his breeding program, the American Kennel Club library stud books can and should be consulted.

THE BREEDING STOCK

Some of your first questions should concern whether the stud has already proven himself by siring a normal healthy litter. Also inquire as to whether the owners have had a sperm count made to determine just exactly how fertile or potent the stud is. Determine for yourself whether the dog has two normal testicles.

When considering your bitch for this mating, you must take into consideration a few important points that lead to a successful breeding. You and the owner of the stud will want to recall whether she has had normal heat cycles, whether there were too many runts in the litter and whether a Caesarean section was ever necessary. Has she ever had a vaginal infection? Could she take care of her puppies by herself, or was there a milk shortage? How many surviving puppies were there from the litter, and what did they grow up to be in comparison to the requirements of the breed Standard?

Don't buy a bitch that has problems in heat and has never had a live litter. Don't be afraid, however, to buy a healthy maiden bitch, since chances are, if she is healthy and from good stock, she will be a healthy producer. Don't buy a monorchid male, and certainly not a cryptorchid. If there is any doubt in your mind about his potency, get a sperm count from the veterinarian. Older dogs that have been good producers and that are for sale are usually not too hard to find at good, established kennels. If they are not too old and have sired quality show puppies, they can give you some excellent show stock from which to establish your own breeding lines.

The best advice used to be not to breed a bitch until her second heat. Today, with our new scientific knowledge, we have become acutely aware of such things as hip dysplasia, juvenile cataracts, and other congenital diseases. The best advice now seems to be aimed at not breeding your dogs before two years of age, when both the bitch and the sire have been examined by qualified veterinarians and declared, in writing, to be free and clear of these conditions.

The stud fee will vary considerably—the better the bloodlines and the more winning the dog does at shows, the higher the fee. Stud service from a top winning dog could run up to $500. Here again, there may be exceptions. Some breeders will take part cash and then, say, third pick of the litter. The fee can be arranged by a private contract rather than the traditional procedure we have described. Here again, it is wise to get the details of the payment of the stud fee in writing to avoid trouble.

THE DAY OF THE MATING

Now that you have decided upon the proper male and female combination to produce what you hope will be, according to the pedigrees, a fine litter of puppies, it is time to set the date. You have selected the two days (with a one day lapse in between) that you feel are best for the breeding, and you call the owner of the stud. The bitch always goes to the stud, unless, of course, there are extenuating circumstances. You set the date and the time and arrive with the bitch *and* the money.

Standard procedure is payment of a stud fee at the time of the first breeding if there is a tie. For the stud fee, you are entitled to two breedings with ties. Contracts may be written up with specific conditions on breeding terms, of course, but this is general procedure. Often a breeder will take the pick of a litter to protect and maintain his bloodlines. This can be especially desirable if he needs an outcross for his breeding program or if he wishes to continue his own bloodlines, if he sold you the bitch to start with and this mating will continue his line-breeding program. This should all be worked out ahead of time and written and signed before the two dogs are bred. Remember that the payment of the stud fee is for the services of the stud—not for a guarantee of a litter of puppies. This is why is it so important to make sure you are using a proven stud. Also bear in mind also that the American Kennel Club will not register a litter of puppies sired by a male that is under eight months of age. In the case of an older dog, they will not register a litter sired by a dog over 12 years of age, unless there is a witness to the breeding in the form of a veterinarian or other responsible person.

Many studs over 12 years of age are still fertile and capable of producing puppies, but if you do not witness the breeding there is always the danger of a "substitute" stud being used to produce a litter. This brings up the subject of sending your bitch away to be bred if you cannot accompany her.

The disadvantages of sending a bitch away to be bred are numerous. First of all, she will not be herself in a strange place, so she'll be difficult to handle. Transportation, if she goes by air (while reasonably safe), is still a traumatic experience. There is always the danger of her being put off at the wrong airport, not being fed or watered properly, and so on.

Some bitches get so upset that they go out of season and the trip—which may prove expensive, especially on top of a substantial stud fee—will have been for nothing.

If at all possible, accompany your bitch so that the experience is as comfortable for her as it can be. In other words, make sure, before setting this kind of schedule for a breeding, that there is no stud in the area that might be as good for her as the one that is far away. Don't sacrifice the proper breeding for convenience, since bloodlines are so important, but put the safety of the bitch above all else. There is always a risk in traveling, since dogs are considered cargo on a plane.

THE ACTUAL MATING

It is always advisable to muzzle the bitch. A terrified bitch may fear-bite the stud or one of the people involved, and the wild or maiden bitch may snap or attack the stud to the point where he may become discouraged and lose interest in the breeding. Muzzling can be done with a lady's stocking tied around the muzzle with a half knot, crossed under the chin and knotted at the back of the neck. There is enough "give" in the stocking for her to breathe or salivate freely and yet not open her jaws far enough to bite. Place her in front of her owner, who holds on to her collar and talks to her and calms her as much as possible.

If the male will not mount on his own initiative, it may be necessary for the owner to assist in lifting him onto the bitch, perhaps even in guiding him to the proper place. The tie is usually accomplished once the male gets the idea. The owner should remain close at hand, however, to make sure the tie is not broken before an adequate breeding has been completed. After a while the stud may get bored and try to break away. This could prove injurious. It may be necessary to hold him in place until the tie is broken.

We must stress at this point that, while some bitches carry on physically and vocally during the tie, there is no way the bitch can be hurt. However, a stud can be seriously or even permanently damaged by a bad breeding. Therefore, the owner of the bitch must be reminded that she must not be alarmed by any commotion. All concentration should be devoted to the stud and to a successful and properly executed service.

Many people believe that breeding dogs is simply a matter of placing two dogs, a male and a female, in close proximity, and letting nature take its course. While this is often true, you cannot count on it. Sometimes it is hard work, and in the case of valuable stock it is essential to supervise to be sure of the safety factor, especially if one or both of the dogs are inexperienced. If the owners are also inexperienced, it may not take place at all.

ARTIFICIAL INSEMINATION

Breeding by means of artificial insemination is usually unsuccessful, unless under a veterinarian's supervision, and can lead to an infection for the bitch and discomfort for the dog. The American Kennel Club requires a veterinarian's certificate to register puppies from such a breeding. Although the practice has been used for over two decades, it now offers new promise, since research has been conducted to make it a more feasible procedure for the future.

Great dogs may eventually look forward to reproducing themselves years after they have left this earth. There now exists a frozen semen concept that has been tested and found successful. The study, headed by Dr. Stephen W.J. Seager, MVB, an instructor at the University of Oregon Medical School, has the financial support of the American Kennel Club, indicating that organization's interest in the work. The study is being monitored by the Morris Animal Foundation of Denver, Colorado.

Dr. Seager announced in 1970 that he had been able to preserve dog semen and to produce litters with the stored semen. The possibilities of selective world-wide breedings by this method are exciting. Imagine simply mailing a vial of semen to the bitch! The perfection of line-breeding by storing semen without the threat of death interrupting the breeding program is exciting also.

As it stands today, the technique for artificial insemination requires the depositing of semen (taken directly from the dog) into the bitch's vagina, past the cervix and into the uterus by syringe. The correct temperature of the semen is vital, and there is no guarantee of success. The storage method, if successfully adopted, will present a new era in the field of purebred dogs.

THE GESTATION PERIOD

Once the breeding has taken place successfully, the seemingly endless waiting period of about 63 days begins. For the first ten days after the breeding, you do absolutely nothing for the bitch—just spin dreams about the delights you will share with the family when the puppies arrive.

Around the tenth day it is time to begin supplementing the diet of the bitch with vitamins and calcium. We strongly recommend that you take her to your veterinarian for a list of the proper or necessary supplements and the correct amounts of each for your particular bitch. Guesses, which may lead to excesses or insufficiencies, can ruin a litter. For the price of a visit to your veterinarian, you will be confident that you are feeding properly.

The bitch should be free of worms, of course, and if there is any doubt in your mind, she should be wormed before the third week of pregnancy. Your veterinarian will advise you on the necessity of this and proper dosage as well.

PROBING FOR PUPPIES

Far too many breeders are overanxious about whether the breeding "took" and are inclined to feel for puppies or to persuade a veterinarian to radiograph or X-ray their bitches to confirm it. Unless there is reason to doubt the normalcy of a pregnancy, this is risky. Certainly 63 days is not too long to wait, and why risk endangering the litter by probing with your inexperienced hands? Few bitches give no evidence of being in whelp, and there is no need to prove it for yourself by trying to count puppies.

ALERTING YOUR VETERINARIAN

At least a week before the puppies are due, you should telephone your veterinarian and notify him that you expect the litter and give him the date. This way he can make sure that there will be someone available to help, should there be any problems during the whelping. Most veterinarians today have answering services and alternative vets on call when they are not available themselves. Some veterinarians suggest that you call them when the bitch starts labor so that they may further plan their time, should they be needed. Discuss this matter with your veterinarian when you first take the bitch to him for her diet instructions, etc., and establish the method that will best fit in with his schedule.

Even if this is your first litter, I would advise that you go through the experience of whelping without panicking and calling desperately for the veterinarian. Most animal births are accomplished without complications; you should call for assistance only if you run into trouble.

When having her puppies, your bitch will appreciate as little interference and as few strangers around as possible. A quiet place, with her nest, a single familiar face, and her own instincts are all that is necessary for nature to take its course. An audience of squealing and questioning children, other pets nosing around, or strange adults should be avoided. Many a bitch that has been distracted in this way has been known to devour her young. This can be the horrible result of intrusion into the bitch's privacy. There are other ways of teaching children the miracle of birth, and there will be plenty of time later for the whole family to enjoy the puppies. Let them be born under proper and considerate circumstances.

LABOR

Some litters, and many first litters, do not run the full term of 63 days. Therefore, at least a week before the puppies are actually due and at the time you alert your veterinarian as to their expected arrival, start observing the bitch for signs of the commencement of labor. This will manifest itself in the form of ripples running down the sides of her body that will come as a revelation to her as well. It is most noticeable when she is lying on her side. She will be sleeping a great deal as the arrival date comes closer. If she is sitting or walking about, she will perhaps sit down quickly or squat peculiarly. As the ripples become more frequent, birth time is drawing near, and you would be wise not to leave her. Usually within 24 hours before whelping she will stop eating, and as much as a week before she will begin digging a nest. The bitch should be given something resembling a whelping box with layers of newspaper (black and white only) to make her nest. She will dig more and more as birth approaches, and this is the time to begin making your promise to stop interfering unless your help is specifically required. Some bitches whimper and others are silent, but whimpering does not necessarily indicate trouble.

The sudden gush of green fluid from the bitch indicates that the water or fluid surrounding the puppies has "broken" and that they are about to start down the canal and come into the world. When the water breaks, the birth of the first puppy is imminent. The first puppies are usually born within minutes to half an hour of each other, but a couple of hours between the later ones is not uncommon. If you notice the bitch straining constantly without producing a puppy, or if a puppy remains partially in and partially out for too long, it is cause for concern. Breech births (puppies born feet first instead of head first) can often cause delay or hold things up, and this is often a problem that requires veterinary assistance.

BREECH BIRTHS

Puppies are normally delivered head first; however, some are presented feet first or in other abnormal positions, and they are referred to as a "breech births." Assistance is often necessary to get the puppy out of the canal, and great care must be taken not to injure the puppy or the dam.

Aid can be given by grasping the puppy with a piece of turkish toweling and pulling gently during the dam's contractions. Be careful not to squeeze the puppy too hard; merely try to ease it out by moving it gently back and forth. Because even this much delay in delivery may mean the puppy is drowning, do not wait for the bitch to remove the sac. Do it yourself by tearing the sac open to expose the face and head. Then cut the cord anywhere from one-half to three-quarters of an inch away from the navel. If the cord bleeds excessively, pinch the end of it with your fingers and count five. Repeat if necessary. Then pry open the mouth with your finger and hold the puppy upside down for a moment to drain any fluid from the lungs. Next, rub the puppy briskly with turkish or paper toweling. You should get it wriggling and whimpering by this time.

If the litter is large, this assistance will help conserve the strength of the bitch and will probably be welcomed by her. However, it is best to allow her to take care of at least the first few herself to preserve the natural instinct and to provide the nutritive values obtained by her consumption of one or more of the afterbirths as nature intended.

Occasionally the sac will break before the delivery of a puppy and will be expelled while the puppy remains inside, thereby depriving the dam of the necessary lubrication to expel the puppy normally. Inserting vaseline or mineral oil via your finger will help the puppy pass down the birth canal. This is why it is essential that you be present during the whelping so that you can count puppies and afterbirths and determine when and if assistance is needed.

CAESAREAN SECTION

Should the whelping reach the point where there is complication, such as the bitch's not being capable of whelping the puppies herself, the "moment of truth" is upon you and a Caesarean section may be necessary. The bitch may be too small or too immature to expel the puppies herself, her cervix may fail to dilate enough to allow the young to come down the birth canal, there may be torsion of the uterus, a dead or monster puppy, a sideways puppy blocking the canal, or perhaps toxemia. A Caesarean section will be the only solution. No matter what the cause, get the bitch to the veterinarian immediately to insure your chances of saving the mother and/or the puppies.

The Caesarean section operation (the name derived from the idea that Julius Caesar was delivered by this method) involves the removal of the unborn young from the uterus of the dam by surgical incision into the walls through the abdomen. The operation is performed when it has been determined that for some reason the puppies cannot be delivered normally. While modern surgical methods have made the operation itself reasonably safe, with the dam being perfectly capable of nursing the puppies shortly after the completion of the surgery, the chief task lies in the ability to spark life into the puppies immediately upon their removal from the womb. If the mother dies, the time element is even more important in saving the young, since the oxygen supply ceases upon the death of the dam, and the difference between life and death is measured in seconds.

After surgery, when the bitch is home in her whelping box with the babies, she will probably nurse the young without distress. You must be sure that the sutures are kept clean and that no redness or swelling or ooze appears in the wound. Healing will take place naturally, and no salves or ointments should be applied, unless prescribed by the veterinarian, for fear the puppies will get it into their systems. If there is any doubt, check the bitch for fever, restlessness (other than the natural concern for her young), or a lack of appetite, but do not anticipate trouble.

Even though most dogs are generally easy whelpers, any number of reasons might occur to cause the bitch to have a difficult birth. Before automatically resorting to Caesarean section, many veterinarians are now trying the technique known as episiotomy.

Used rather frequently in human deliveries, episiotomy (pro-nouced e-pease-e-ott-o-me) is the cutting of the membrane be-tween the rear opening of the vagina back almost to the opening of the anus. After delivery it is stitched together, and barring complications, heals easily, presenting no problem in future births.

FALSE PREGNANCY

The disappointment of a false pregnancy is almost as bad for the owner as it is for the bitch. She goes through the gestation period with all the symptoms—swollen stomach, increased appetite, swollen nipples—and even makes a nest when the time comes. You may even take an oath that you noticed the ripples on her body from the labor pains. Then, just as suddenly as you made up your mind that she was definitely going to deliver puppies, you will know that she definitely is not! She may walk around carrying a toy as if it were a puppy for a few days, but she will soon be back to normal and will act as if nothing happened—and nothing did!

FEEDING THE BITCH
BETWEEN BIRTHS

Usually the bitch will not be interested in food for about 24 hours before the arrival of the puppies, and perhaps as long as two or three days after their arrival. The placenta that she cleans up after each puppy is high in food value and will be more than am-ple to sustain her. This is nature's way of allowing the mother to feed herself and her babies without having to leave the nest and hunt for food during the first crucial days. In the wild, the mother always cleans up all traces of birth so as not to attract other ani-mals to her newborn babies.

However, there are those of us who believe in making food available should the mother feel the need to restore her strength during or after delivery—especially if she whelps a large litter. Raw chopped meat, beef bouillon, and milk are all acceptable and may be placed near the whelping box during the first two or three days. After that, the mother will begin to put the babies on a sort of schedule. She will leave the whelping box at frequent intervals, take longer exercise periods and begin to take interest in other things. This is where the fun begins for you. Now the babies are no longer soggy little pinkish blobs. They begin to crawl around and squeal and hum and grow before your very eyes! It is at this time, if all has gone normally, that the family can be introduced gradually and great praise and affection given to the mother.

THE TWENTY-FOUR HOUR CHECKUP

It is smart to have a veterinarian check the mother and her puppies within 24 hours after the last puppy is born. The veterinarian can check the puppies for cleft palates or umbilical herniae and may wish to give the dam—particularly if she is a show dog—an injection of Pituitin to make sure of the expulsion of all afterbirths and to tighten up the uterus. This can prevent a sagging belly after the puppies are weaned when the bitch is being readied for the show ring.

REARING THE FAMILY

Needless to say, even with a small litter there will be certain considerations that must be adhered to in order to insure successful rearing of the puppies. For instance, the diet for the mother should be appropriately increased as the puppies grow and take more and more nourishment from her. During the first few days of rest, while the bitch looks over her puppies and regains her strength, she should be left pretty much alone. It is during these first days that she begins to put the puppies on a feeding schedule and feels safe enough about them to leave the whelping box long enough to take a little extended exercise.

It is cruel, however, to try to keep the mother away from the puppies any longer than she wants to be because you feel she is being too attentive or to give the neighbors a chance to peek in at the puppies. The mother should not have to worry about harm coming to her puppies for the first few weeks. The veterinary checkup will be enough of an experience for her to have to endure until she is more like herself again.

A show puppy prospect should be outgoing (probably the first one to fall out of the whelping box!), and all efforts should be made to socialize the puppy that appears to be the most shy. Once the puppies are about three weeks old, they can and should be handled a great deal by friends and members of the family.

During the third week the puppies begin to try to walk instead of crawl, but they are unsteady on their feet. Tails are used for balancing, and they begin to make sounds.

The crucial period in a puppy's life occurs when the puppy is from 21 to 28 days old, so all the time you can devote to them at this time will reap rewards later on in life. This is the age when several other important steps must be taken in a puppy's life. Weaning should start if it hasn't already, and this is the time to check for worms. Do not worm unnecessarily. A veterinarian should advise on worming and appropriate dosage and he can also discuss with you at this time the schedule for serum or vaccination, which will depend on the size of the puppies as well as their age.

Exercise and grooming should be started at this time, with special care and consideration being given to the diet. You will find that the dam will help you wean the puppies, leaving them alone more and more as she notices that they are eating well on their own. Begin by leaving them with her during the night for comfort and warmth; eventually, when she shows less interest, keep them separated entirely.

By the time the fifth week arrives, you will already be in love with every member of the litter and desperately searching for reasons to keep them all. They recognize you—which really gets to you and they box and chew on each other, try to eat your finger, and have a million other captivating antics that are special with puppies. Their stomachs seem to be bottomless pits, and their weight will rise. At eight to ten weeks, the puppies will be weaned and ready to go.

SOCIALIZING YOUR PUPPY

The need for puppies to get out among other animals and people cannot be stressed enough. Kennel-reared dogs are subject to all sorts of idiosyncrasies and seldom make good house dogs or normal members of the world around them when they grow up.

The crucial age that determines the personality and general behavior patterns that will predominate during the rest of the dog's life are formed between the ages of three and ten weeks. This is particularly true between the 21st and 28th day. It is essential that the puppy be socialized during this time by bringing him into family life as much as possible. Walking on floor surfaces, indoor and outdoor, should be experienced; handling by all members of the family and visitors is important; preliminary grooming gets him used to a lifelong necessity; light training (such as setting him up on tables and cleaning teeth and ears and cutting nails, etc.) has to be started early if he is to become a show dog. The puppy should be exposed to car riding, shopping tours, a leash around its neck, children (your own and others), and in all possible ways, relationships with humans.

It is up to the breeder, of course, to protect the puppy from harm or injury during this initiation into the outside world. The benefits reaped from proper attention will pay off in the long run with a well-behaved, well-adjusted adult dog capable of becoming an integral part of a happy family.

SPAYING AND CASTRATING

A wise old philosopher once said, "Timing in life is everything!" No statement could apply more readily to the age-old question that every dog owner is faced with sooner or later—to spay or not to spay.

For the one-bitch pet owner, spaying is the most logical answer, for it solves many problems. The pet is usually not of top breeding quality, and therefore there is no great loss to the bloodline; it takes the pressure off the family if the dog runs free with children, and it certainly eliminates the problem of repeated litters of unwanted puppies or a backyard full of eager males twice a year.

But for the owner or breeder, the extra time and protection that must be afforded a purebred quality bitch can be most worthwhile—even if it is only until a single litter is produced after the first heat. It is then not too late to spay; the progeny can perpetuate the bloodline, the bitch will have been fulfilled—though it is merely an old wives' tale that bitches should have at least one litter to be "normal"—and she may then be retired to her deserved role as family pet once again.

With spaying, the problem of staining and unusual behavior around the house is eliminated, as is the necessity of having to keep her in "pants" or administering pills, sprays, or shots, of which most veterinarians do not approve anyway.

A quiet moment in Calgary with Kyle Carter and his pals Hero, Justy, Poppy, and Song. All owned by Dr. Gary and Terry Carter.

In the case of males, castration is seldom contemplated, which to me is highly regrettable. The owners of male dogs overlook the dog's ability to populate an entire neighborhood, since they do not have the responsibility of rearing and disposing of the puppies. When you take into consideration the many females the male dog can impregnate, it is almost more essential that the males rather than the females be taken out of circulation. The male dog will still be inclined to roam but will be less frantic about leaving the grounds, and you will find that a lot of *wanderlust* has left him.

When considering the problem of spaying or castrating, the first consideration after the population explosion should actually be the health of the dog or bitch. Males are frequently subject to urinary diseases, and sometimes castration is a help. Your veterinarian can best advise you on this problem. Another aspect to consider is the kennel dog that is no longer being used at stud. It is unfair to keep him in a kennel with females in heat when there is no chance for him to be used. There are other, more personal, considerations for both kennel and one-dog owners, but when making the decision, remember that it is final. You can always spay or castrate, but once the deed is done there is no return.

TOP-PRODUCING OLD ENGLISH SHEEPDOGS

There are many, many quality specimens that have produced beautiful puppies, even though as parents they may never have been placed on a "top producer" list. However, if you are intent upon "buying by the book" from a sire or dam that is on such a list, here is the current one based on males having produced three or more champions and dams having produced two or more champions in a one-year period.

Champion Aphrodite Snow Sniflik was Top Producing Stud Dog in the nation for two consecutive years, (1981 and 1982) and has been placed in the Top Ten for 1983. His record of 29 champion get to date finds him the only living stud dog on the list. He has produced two National Specialty winners also. He is owned by Bob and Linda Burns of Grain Valley, Missouri, and was bred by Bette Maxwell.

Sires

Ch. Cobby Stone Marshl the Marshl	5
Ch. Loyalblu Hendihap Sund A Best	5
Ch. Pockethall Silver Sovereign	5
Ch. Whisperwood's Wildwon	5
Ch. Vidmar's Visibility Zero	4
Ch. Aphrodite's Snow Sniflik	3
Ch. Blueacre Legend of Marimoor	3
Ch. Brightcut Limited Edition	3
Brightcut Rhythm 'N Blues	3
Ch. Greyfriar's Holier Than Thou	3
Ch. Shagglamb's Bagel	3
Ch. Some Buddy Catch the Action	3

Dams

Ch. Agincourt Circe of Marimoor	3
Ch. Barrellroll Am I Blue	3
Candy Kane Loyalblu Babe Ruth	3
Ch. Cobbystone Just Call Me Maxi	3
Jen Kris Dapper Darby	3
Ch. Maidstone Debutant of To Jo	3
Ch. Snow Dumpling Aphrodite	3
Whisperwood's Wildwood	3
Alamandas Tiffany Star	2
Bear Dance Miranda Panda	2
Ch. Brightcut Hallelujah	2
Ch. Bugaboo's Just For Me	2
Graybear's Miss Muppet	2
Greyfriar's Trafford Lass, C.D.	2
Ch. Loyalblu This One is Mine	2
Ch. Moptop's Upper Crust	2
Pamela's Lady of Loehr	2
Rholenwood's Ode to Whitby	2
Ch. Shershag Lady Peppermnt Tanker	2
Ch. Sleepy Hollow's Potpourri	2
Ch. Sniflik's Breeze of Warwyck	2
Ch. Some Buddy Just My Style	2
Talisman's Maggie My Love	2
Ch. Warwyck's Exclusive Edition	2
Whisperwood's White Bear	2
Ch. Windfield Scarborough Jill	2

Champion Marimoor Regal Sir Raggles, photographed in 1979 with his Chihuahua pal "Ribbon." Owned by Charilyn Cardwell of Palmer, Alaska.

Chapter 16

Feeding and Nutrition

FEEDING PUPPIES

There are many diets today for young puppies, including all sorts of products on the market for feeding the newborn, for supplemental   feeding of the young, and for adding "this or that" to diets, depending on what is lacking in the way of a complete diet.

When weaning puppies it is necessary to put them on four meals a day, even while you are tapering off with the mother's milk. Feeding at six in the morning, noontime, six in the evening, and midnight is about the best schedule since it fits in with most human eating plans. Meals for the puppies can be prepared immediately before or after your own meals without too much of a change in your own schedule.

Two meat and two milk meals serve best and should be served alternately, of course. Assuming the six a.m. feeding is a milk meal, the contents should be as follows: dilute two parts evaporated milk and one part water along with raw egg yolk, honey, or Karo syrup, sprinkled with high-protein baby cereal and wheat germ. Goat's milk is the very best milk to feed puppies, but is expensive and usually available only at drug stores, unless you live in farm country where it may be readily available fresh and less expensive. If goat's milk is not available, use evaporated milk (which can be changed to powdered milk later on). As the puppies mature, cottage cheese may be added or, at one of the two milk meals, it can be substituted for the cereal.

At noon, a puppy chow that has been soaked in warm water or beef broth (according to the time specified on the wrapper) should be mixed with raw or simmered chopped meat in equal proportions with vitamin powder added.

At six p.m. repeat the milk meal—perhaps varying the type of cereal from wheat to oats, corn, or rice.

At midnight, repeat the meat meal. If raw meat was fed at noon, the evening meal might be simmered.

Please note that specific proportions on this suggested diet are not given; however, it's safe to say that the most important ingredients are the milk and cereal, and the meat and puppy chow that form the basis of the diet. Your veterinarian can advise on the portion sizes if there is any doubt in your mind as to how much to use.

If you notice that the puppies are cleaning their plates, you are perhaps not feeding enough to keep up with their rate of growth. Increase the amount at the next feeding. Observe them closely; puppies should each "have their fill," because growth is very rapid at this age. If they have not satisfied themselves, increase the amount so that they do not have to fight for the last morsel. They will not overeat if they know there is enough food available. Instinct will usually let them eat to suit their normal capacity.

If there is any doubt in your mind as to any ingredient you are feeding, ask yourself, "Would I give it to my own baby?" If the answer is no, then don't give it to your puppies. At this age, the comparison between puppies and human babies can be a good guide. If there is any doubt in your mind, ask your veterinarian in order to be sure.

Many puppies will regurgitate their food, perhaps a couple of times, before they manage to retain it. If they do bring up their food, allow them to eat it again, rather than clean it away. Sometimes additional saliva is necessary for them to digest it, and you do not want them to skip a meal just because it is an unpleasant sight for you to observe.

This same regurgitation process sometimes holds true with the bitch, who will bring up her own food for her puppies every now and then. This is a natural instinct on her part that stems from the days when dogs were giving birth in the wild. The only food the mother could provide at weaning time was too rough and indigestible for her puppies; therefore, she took it upon herself to predigest the food until it could be taken and retained by her young. Bitches today will sometimes resort to this, especially bitches that love having litters and have a strong maternal instinct. Some dams will help you wean their litters and even give up feeding entirely once they see you are taking over.

WEANING PUPPIES

When weaning the puppies, the mother is kept away from the little ones for longer and longer periods of time. This is done over a period of several days. At first she is separated from the puppies for several hours, then all day, staying   with them only at night for comfort and warmth. This separation aids in helping the mother's milk to dry up gradually, and she suffers less distress after feeding a litter.

If the mother continues to carry a great deal of milk with no signs of its tapering off, consult your veterinarian before she gets too uncomfortable. She may cut the puppies off from her supply of milk too abruptly if she is uncomfortable; this may occur before they should be completely on their own.

There are many opinions on the proper age to start weaning puppies. If you plan to start selling them between six and eight weeks, weaning should begin between two and three weeks of age. (Here again, each bitch will pose a different situation.) The size and weight of the litter should help determine the time, and your veterinarian will have an opinion as he determines the burden the bitch is carrying by the size of the litter and her general condition. If she is being pulled down by feeding a large litter, he may suggest that you start at two weeks. If she is glorying in her motherhood without any apparent taxing of strength, he may suggest three to four weeks. You and he will be the best judges. But remember, there is no substitute that is as perfect as mother's milk—and the longer the puppies benefit from it, the better. Other food helps, but mother's milk first and foremost makes the healthiest puppies.

ORPHANED PUPPIES

The ideal solution to feeding orphaned puppies is to put them with another nursing dam who will take them on as her own. If this is not possible within your own kennel, or a kennel that you know of, it is up to you to care for and feed the puppies. Survival is possible but requires a great deal of time and effort on your part.

Your substitute formula must be precisely prepared, always served heated to body temperature, and refrigerated when not being fed. Esbilac, a vacuum-packed powder with complete feeding instructions on the can, is excellent and about as close to mother's milk as you can get. If you can't get Esbilac, or until you do get Esbilac, there are two alternative formulas that you might use.

Mix one part boiled water with five parts evaporated milk and add one teaspoonful of dicalcium phosphate per quart of formula. Dicalcium phosphate can be secured at any drug store. If they have it in tablet form only, you can powder the tablets with the back part of a tablespoon. The other formula for newborn puppies is a combination of eight ounces of homogenized milk mixed well with two egg yolks.

You will need baby bottles with three-hole nipples. Sometimes doll bottles can be used for the newborn puppies, which should be fed at six-hour intervals. If they are consuming sufficient amounts, their stomachs should look full, or slightly enlarged, though never distended. The amount of formula to be fed is proportionate to the size, age, growth, and weight of the puppy, and is indicated on the can of Esbilac; or consult the advice of your veterinarian if necessary. Many breeders like to keep a baby scale nearby to check the weight of the puppies to be sure they are thriving on the formula.

At two to three weeks you can start adding pablum or some other high protein baby cereal to the formula. Also, baby beef can be licked from your finger at this age, or added to the formula. At four weeks the surviving puppies should be taken off the diet of Esbilac and put on a more substantial diet, such as wet puppy meal or chopped beef; however, Esbilac powder can still be mixed in with the food for additional nutrition. Baby foods of pureed meats in jars also make for a smooth changeover, and can be blended into the diet.

HOW TO FEED THE NEWBORN PUPPIES

When the puppy is a newborn, remember that it is vitally important to keep the feeding procedure as close to the natural mother's routine as possible. The newborn puppy should be held in your lap in your hand in an almost upright position with the bottle at an angle to allow the entire nipple area to be full of the formula. Do not hold the bottle upright so the puppy's head has to reach straight up toward the ceiling. Do not let the puppy nurse too quickly or take in too much air; this may cause colic. Once in awhile take the bottle away and let him rest a moment and swallow several times. Before feeding, test the nipple to see that the fluid does not come out too quickly, or by the same token, too slowly so that the puppy gets tired of feeding before he has had enough to eat.

When the puppy is a little older, you can place him on his stomach on a towel to eat, and even allow him to hold on to the bottle or to "come and get it" on his own. Most puppies enjoy eating and this will be a good indication of how strong an appetite he has and his ability to consume the contents of the bottle.

It will be necessary to "burp" the puppy. Place a towel on your shoulder and hold the puppy on your shoulder as if he were a human baby, patting and rubbing him gently. This will also encourage the puppy to defecate. At this time, you should look for diarrhea or other intestinal disorders. The puppy should eliminate after each feeding, with occasional eliminations between times as well. If the puppies do not eliminate on their own after each meal, massage their stomachs and under their tails gently until they do.

You must keep the puppies clean. Under no circumstances should fecal matter be allowed to collect on their skin or fur.

All this, plus your determination and perseverance, might save an entire litter of puppies that would otherwise have died without their real mother.

FEEDING THE ADULT DOG

The puppies' schedule of four meals a day should drop to three by six months and then to two by nine months; by the time the dog reaches one year of age, it is eating one meal a day.

The time when you feed the dog each day can be a matter of the dog's preference or your convenience, so long as once in every 24 hours the dog receives a meal that provides it with a complete, balanced diet. In addition, of course, fresh clean water should be available at all times.

There are many brands of dry food, kibbles, and biscuits on the market that are all of good quality. There are also many varieties of canned dog food that provide a balanced diet for your dog. But for those breeders and exhibitors who show their dogs, additional care is given to providing a few "extras" that enhance the good health and appearance of show dogs.

A good meal or kibble mixed with water or beef broth and raw meat is perhaps the best ration to provide. In cold weather, many breeders add suet or corn oil (or even olive or cooking oil) to the mixture, and others make use of the bacon fat after breakfast by pouring it over the dog's food.

Salting a dog's food in the summer helps replace the salt "panted away" in the heat. Many breeders sprinkle the food with garlic powder to sweeten the dog's breath and prevent gas, especially in breeds that gulp or wolf their food and swallow a lot of air. I prefer garlic powder; the salt is too weak and the clove is too strong.

There are those, of course, who cook very elaborately for their dogs, which is not necessary if a good meal and meat mixture is provided. Many prefer to add vegetables, rice, tomatoes, etc., to everything else they feed. As long as the extras do not throw the nutritional balance off, there is little harm, but no one thing should be fed to excess. Occasionally, liver is given as a treat at home. Fish, which most veterinarians no longer recommend even for cats, is fed to puppies, but should not be given in excess of once a week. Always remember that no one food should be given as a total diet. Balance is most important; a 100% meat diet can kill a dog.

THE ALL-MEAT DIET CONTROVERSY

In March 1971 the National Research Council investigated a great stir in the dog fancy about the all-meat dog-feeding controversy. It was established that meat and meat by-products constitute a complete balanced diet for dogs only when it is further fortified.

Therefore, a good dog chow or meal mixed with meat provides the perfect combination for a dog's diet. While the dry food is a complete diet in itself, the fresh meat additionally satisfies the dog's anatomically and physiologically meat-oriented appetite. While dogs are actually carnivores, it must be remembered that when they were feeding themselves in the wild they ate almost the entire animal they captured, including its stomach contents. This provided some of the vitamins and minerals we must now add to the diet.

In the United States, the standard for diets that claim to be "complete and balanced" is set by the Subcommittee on Canine Nutrition of the National Research Council (NRC) of the National Academy of Sciences. This is the official agency for establishing the nutritional requirements of dog foods. Most foods sold for dogs and cats meet these requirements and manufacturers are proud to say so on their labels, so look for this when you buy. Pet food labels must be approved by the Association of American Feed Control Officials (AAFCO) Pet Foods Committee. Both the Food and Drug Administration and the Federal Trade Commission of the AAFCO define the word "balanced" when referring to dog food as follows:

"Balanced is a term which may be applied to pet food having all known required nutrients in a proper amount and proportion based upon the recommendations of a recognized authority (the National Research Council is one) in the field of animal nutrition, for a given set of physiological animal requirements."

With this much care given to your dog's diet, there can be little reason for not having happy, well-fed dogs in proper weight and proportions for the show ring.

OBESITY

As we mentioned before, there are many "perfect" diets for your dogs on the market today. When fed in proper proportions, they should keep your dogs in "full bloom." However, there are those owners who, more often than not, indulge their own appetites and are inclined to overfeed their dogs as well. A study in Great Britain in the early 1970s found that a major percentage of obese people also had obese dogs. The entire family was overfed and all suffered from the same condition.

Obesity in dogs is a direct result of the animal's being fed more food that he can properly "burn up" over a period of time, so it is stored as fat or fatty tissue in the body. Pet dogs are more in-

Canadian and American Ch. Some Buddy Leading the Parade, R.O.M., was Top Old English Sheepdog in Canada for 1980–81 and No. 4 Working Dog. He was also winner of the Stud Dog Class at the Parent Club Specialty in Denver in 1982. Bred and owned by Dr. and Mrs. Gary Carter, Calgary, Canada. He is also a multi-Best in Show winner.

clined to become obese than show dogs or working dogs, but obesity also is a factor to be considered with the older dog since his exercise is curtailed.

A lack of "tuck up" on a dog or not being able to feel the ribs, or great folds of fat that hang from the underside of the dog can all be considered as signs of obesity. Genetic factors may enter into the picture, but usually the owner is at fault.

The life span of the obese dog is decreased on several counts. Excess weight puts undue stress on the heart as well as on the joints. The dog becomes a poor anesthetic risk and has less resistance to viral or bacterial infections. Treatment is seldom easy or completely effective, so emphasis should be placed on not letting your dog get fat in the first place!

GASTRIC TORSION

Gastric torsion or bloat, sometimes referred to as "twisted stomach," has become more and more prevalent. Many dogs that in the past had been thought to die of blockage of the stomach or intestines, because they had swallowed toys or other foreign objects, are now suspected of having been the victims of gastric torsion and the bloat that followed.

Though life can be saved by immediate surgery to untwist the organ, the rate of fatality is high. Symptoms of gastric torsion are unusual restlessness, excessive salivation, attempts to vomit, rapid respiration, pain, and the eventual bloating of the abdominal region.

The cause of gastric torsion can be attributed to overeating, excess gas formation in the stomach, poor function of the stomach or intestine, or general lack of exercise. As the food ferments in the stomach, gases form which may twist the stomach in a clockwise direction so that the gas is unable to escape. Surgery, where the stomach is untwisted counter-clockwise, is the safest and most successful way to correct the situation.

To avoid the threat of gastric torsion, it is wise to keep your dog well exercised to be sure the body is functioning normally. Make sure that food and water are available for the dog at all times, thereby reducing the tendency to overeat. With self-service dry feeding, where the dog is able to eat intermittently during the day, there is not the urge to "stuff" at one time.

If you notice any of the symptoms of gastric torsion, call your veterinarian immediately. Death can result within a matter of hours!

Bobmar Leading Sweet Louise pictured at 10 weeks of age in August, 1983. Bred and owned by Marilyn Mayfield of Burbank, California.

Chapter 17

Your Dog, Your Veterinarian and You

The purpose of this chapter is to explain why you should never attempt to be your own veterinarian. Quite to the contrary, we urge emphatically that you establish good liaison with a reputable veterinarian who will help you maintain happy, healthy dogs. Our purpose is to bring you up-to-date on the discoveries made in modern canine medicine and to help you work with your veterinarian by applying these new developments to your own animals. If you know a little something about the diseases and how to recognize their symptoms, your chances of catching them in the preliminary stages will help you and your veterinarian effect a cure before a serious condition develops.

Your general knowledge of diseases, their symptoms, and side effects will assist your veterinarian in making a quicker, more accurate diagnosis. He does not expect you to be an expert, but will appreciate your efforts in getting a sick dog to him before it is too late and he cannot save its life.

ACUSCOPING

We are not fully aware of all the remarkable results of acupuncture, but we now hear of a new device called the Acuscope. The Acuscope combines the principles of both acupuncture and biofeedback. This electronically operated tool stimulates an animal's nerves with electricity to reduce stress and pain, and it actually accelerates healing.

A veterinarian in California has been using this device since 1984, based on the pioneering efforts of an upstate New York physician who developed it over a decade ago. It might be a good idea to mention it to your own veterinarian if you find that current methods of treatment are not working to your satisfaction.

CARDIOPULMONARY RESUSCITATION FOR DOGS

There has been a lot of discussion regarding the CPR process of restoring breath to animals. With large dogs, the same procedures can be used as with a human—and I hope all of you know CPR for humans! With small dogs, instead of blows you use "puffs" of air to restore breathing. Briefly, these are the steps: determine unresponsiveness, call for help, open the mouth, look, listen and feel for breathing, check pulse. Breathe for the dog once every three to five seconds. If further aid is required, use 15 chest compressions to every two breaths, or four to six times per minute. If the dog is choking, use four back blows, four abdominal thrusts, or pushes *up under* the rib cage. Check before repeating the cycle of thrusts and blows. Telephone for help and/or transport to the veterinarian immediately. It would be wise to post a diagram of instructions in your kennel room, and to educate all members of your family to this procedure. It could make the difference between life and death.

ASPIRIN USAGE

There is a common joke about doctors telling their patients, when they telephone with a complaint, to take an aspirin, go to bed and let him know how things are in the morning. Unfortunately, that is exactly the way it turns out with a lot of dog owners who think aspirins are cure-alls and give them to their dogs indiscriminately. They finally call the veterinarian when the dog has an unfavorable reaction.

Aspirins are not panaceas for everything—certainly not for every dog. In an experiment, fatalities in cats treated with aspirin in one laboratory alone numbered ten out of 13 within a two-week period. Dogs' tolerance was somewhat better as to actual fatalities, but there was considerable evidence of ulceration on the stomach linings in varying degrees when necropsy was performed.

Aspirin has been held in the past to be almost as effective for dogs as for people when given for many of the everyday aches and pains. The fact remains, however, that medication of any kind should be administered only after veterinary consultation and after a specific dosage suitable to the condition is recommended.

While aspirin is chiefly effective in reducing fever, relieving minor pains, and cutting down on inflammation, the acid has been proven harmful to the stomach when given in strong doses. Only your veterinarian is qualified to determine what the dosage is or whether it should be administered to your particular dog at all.

USING A THERMOMETER

You will notice in reading this chapter dealing with the diseases of dogs that practically everything a dog might contract in the way of sickness has basically the same set of symptoms: loss of appetite, diarrhea, dull eyes, dull coat, warm and/or runny nose and *fever!*

Therefore, it is most advisable to have a thermometer on hand for checking temperature. There are several inexpensive metal, rectal-type thermometers that are accurate and safer than the glass variety that can be broken. Breakage may occur either by dropping it or perhaps by its breaking off in the dog because of improper insertion or an aggravated condition with the dog that makes him violently resist the insertion of the thermometer.

Whatever type you use, it should first be sterilized with alcohol and then lubricated with petroleum jelly to make the insertion as easy as possible.

The normal temperature for a dog is 101.5 ° Fahrenheit, as compared to the human 98.6 °. Excitement as well as illness can cause this to vary a degree or two, but any sudden or extensive rise in body temperature must be considered as cause for alarm. Your first indication will be that your dog feels unduly "warm" and this is the time to take the temperature, *not* when the dog becomes very ill or manifests additional serious symptoms. With a thermometer on hand, you can check temperature quickly and perhaps prevent some illnesses from becoming serious.

COPROPHAGY

Perhaps the most unpleasant of all phases of dog breeding is to come up with a dog that takes to eating stool. This practice, which is referred to politely as coprophagy, is one of the unsolved mysteries in the dog world. There simply is no confirmed explanation as to why some dogs do it.

However, there are several logical theories, all or any of which may be the cause. Some people cite nutritional deficiencies; others say that dogs that are inclined to gulp their food (which passes through them not entirely digested) find it still partially palatable. There is another theory that the preservatives used in some meat are responsible for an appealing odor that remains through the digestive process. Then again, poor quality meat can be so tough and unchewable that dogs swallow it whole and it passes through them in large undigested chunks.

There are others who believe the habit is strictly psychological, the result of a nervous condition or insecurity. Others believe the dog cleans up after itself because it is afraid of being punished as it was when it made a mistake on the carpet as a puppy. Some people claim boredom is the reason, or even spite. Others will tell you a dog does not want its personal odor on the premises for fear of attracting other hostile animals to itself or its home.

The most logical of all explanations and the one veterinarians are inclined to accept is that it is a deficiency of dietary enzymes. Too much dry food can be bad and many veterinarians suggest trying meat tenderizers, monosodium glutamate, or garlic powder, all of which give the stool a bad odor and discourage the dog. Yeast, certain vitamins, or a complete change of diet are even more often suggested. By the time you try each of the above you will probably discover that the dog has outgrown the habit anyway. However, the condition cannot be ignored if you are to enjoy your dog to the fullest.

There is no set length of time that the problem persists, and the only real cure is to walk the dog on leash, morning and night and after every meal. In other words, set up a definite eating and exercising schedule before coprophagy is an established pattern.

MASTURBATION

A source of embarrassment to many dog owners, masturbation can be eliminated with a minimum of training.

The dog that is constantly breeding anything and everything, including the leg of the piano or perhaps the leg of your favorite guest, can be broken of the habit by stopping its cause.

The over-sexed dog, if truly that is what he is, which will never be used for breeding can be castrated. The kennel stud dog can be broken of the habit by removing any furniture from his quarters or keeping him on leash and on verbal command when he is around people or in the house where he might be tempted to breed pillows, people, etc.

Hormonal imbalance may be another cause and your veterinarian may advise injections. Exercise can be of tremendous help. Keeping the dog's mind occupied by physical play when he is around people will also help relieve the situation.

Females might indulge in sexual abnormalities like masturbation during their heat cycle, or, again, because of a hormonal imbalance. But if they behave this way because of a more serious problem, a hysterectomy may be indicated.

A sharp "no" command when you can anticipate the act, or a sharp "no" when caught in the act will deter most dogs if you are consistent in your correction. Hitting or other physical abuse will only confuse a dog.

RABIES

The greatest fear in the dog fancy today is still the great fear it has always been—rabies.

What has always held true about this dreadful disease still holds true today. The only way rabies can be contracted is through the saliva of a rabid dog entering the bloodstream of another animal or person. There is, of course, the Pasteur treatment for rabies which is very effective.

It should be administered immediately if there is any question of exposure. There was of late the incident of a little boy who survived being bitten by a rabid bat. Even more than dogs being found to be rabid, we now know that the biggest carriers are bats, skunks, foxes, rabbits, and other warmblooded animals that pass it from one to another since they do not have the benefit of inoculation. Dogs that run free should be inoculated for protection against these animals.

For many years, Great Britain (because it is an island and because of the country's strictly enforced six-month quarantine) was entirely free of rabies. But in 1969 a British officer brought back his dog from foreign duty and the dog was found to have the disease soon after being released from quarantine. There was a great uproar about it, with Britain killing off wild and domestic animals in a great scare campaign, but the quarantine is once again down to six months and things seem to have returned to a normal, sensible attitude.

Health departments in rural towns usually provide rabies inoculations free of charge. If your dog is outdoors a great deal or exposed to other animals that are, you might wish to call the town hall and get information on the program in your area. One cannot be too cautious about this dread disease. While the number of cases diminishes each year, there are still thousands being reported and there is still the constant threat of an outbreak where animals roam free. Never forget that there is no cure.

Rabies is caused by a neurotropic virus which can be found in the saliva, brain, and sometimes the blood of the afflicted warm-blooded animal. The incubation period is from two weeks to six months, which means you can be exposed to it without any visible symptoms. As we have said, while there is still no known cure, it can be controlled.

You can help effect this control by reporting animal bites and by educating the public on the dangers, symptoms, and prevention, so that we may reduce the fatalities.

There are two kinds of rabies; one form is called "furious" and the other is referred to as "dumb." The mad dog goes through several stages of the disease. His disposition and behavior change radically and suddenly; he becomes irritable and vicious. The eating habits alter, and he rejects food for things like stones and sticks; he becomes exhausted and drools saliva out of his mouth constantly. He may hide in corners, look glassy-eyed and suspicious, bite at the air as he races around snarling and attacking with his tongue hanging out. At this point paralysis sets in, starting at the throat so that he can no longer drink water though he desires it desperately; hence, the term hydrophobia is given. He begins to stagger and eventually to convulse, and death is imminent.

In "dumb" rabies, paralysis is swift; the dog seeks dark, sheltered places and is abnormally quiet. Paralysis starts with the jaws, spreads down the body, and death is quick. Contact by humans or other animals with the drool from either of these types of rabies on open skin can produce the fatal disease, so extreme haste and proper diagnosis is essential. In other words, you do not have to be bitten by a rabid dog to have the virus enter your system. An open wound or cut that comes in touch with the saliva is all that is needed.

The incubation and degree of infection can vary. You usually contract the disease faster if the wound is near the head, since the virus travels to the brain through the spinal cord. The deeper the wound, the more saliva is injected into the body, and the more serious the infection. So, if bitten by a dog under any circumstances—or any warmblooded animal for that matter—immediately wash out the wound with soap and water, bleed it profusely, and see your doctor as soon as possible.

Also, be sure to keep track of the animal that bit, if at all possible. When rabies is suspected, the public health officer will need to send the animal's head away to be analyzed. If it is found to be free of rabies, you will not need to undergo treatment. Otherwise, your doctor may advise that you to have the Pasteur treatment, which is extremely painful. It is rather simple, however, to have the veterinarian examine a dog for rabies without having the dog sent away for positive diagnosis of the disease. A ten-day quarantine is usually all that is necessary for everyone's peace of mind.

Rabies does not respect age, sex, or geographical location. It is found all over the world from North Pole to South Pole, and has nothing to do with the old wives' tale of dogs going mad in the hot summer months. True, there is an increase in reported cases during summer, but only because that is the time of the year for animals to roam free in good weather and during the mating season when the battle of the sexes is taking place. Inoculation and a keen eye for symptoms and bites on our dogs and other pets will help control the disease until the cure is found.

VACCINATIONS

If you are to raise a puppy, or a litter of puppies, successfully, you must adhere to a realistic and strict schedule of vaccinations. Many puppyhood diseases can be fatal—all of them are debilitat-

281

ing. According to the latest statistics, 98% of all puppies are being inoculated after 12 weeks of age against the dread distemper, hepatitis, and leptospirosis and manage to escape these horrible infections. Orphaned puppies should be vaccinated every two weeks until the age of 12 weeks. Distemper and hepatitis live-virus vaccines should be used, since orphaned puppies are not protected with the colostrum normally supplied to them through the mother's milk. Puppies weaned at six to seven weeks should also be inoculated repeatedly because they will no longer be receiving mother's milk. While not all will receive protection from the serum at this early age, it should be given and they should be vaccinated once again at both nine and 12 weeks of age.

Leptospirosis vaccination should be given at four months of age with thought given to booster shots if the disease is known in the area, or in the case of show dogs which are exposed on a regular basis to many dogs from far and wide. While animal boosters are in order for distemper and hepatitis, every two or three years is sufficient for leptospirosis, unless there is an outbreak in your immediate area. The one exception should be the pregnant bitch, since there is reason to believe that inoculation might cause damage to the fetus.

Strict observance of such a vaccination schedule will not only keep your dog free of these debilitating diseases, but will prevent an epidemic in your kennel, in your locality, or to the dogs that are competing at the shows.

SNAKEBITE

As field trials, hunts, and the like become more and more popular with dog enthusiasts, the incident of snakebite becomes more of a likelihood. Dogs that are kept outdoors in runs or dogs that work the fields and roam on large estates are also likely victims.

Most veterinarians carry snakebit serum, and snakebite kits are sold to dog owners for just such a purpose. Catching a snakebite in time may mean the difference between life and death, and whether your area is populated with snakes or not, it behooves you to know what to do in case it happens to you or your dog.

Your primary concern should be to get to a doctor or veterinarian immediately. The victim should be kept as quiet as possible (excitement or activity spreads the venom through the body more quickly) and, if possible, the wound should be bled enough to clean it out before applying a tourniquet if the bite is severe. First of all, it must be determined if the bite is from a poisonous or non-poisonous snake. If the bite carries two horseshoe-shaped pinpoints of a double row of teeth, the bite can be assumed to be non-poisonous. If the bite leaves two punctures or holes—the result of the two fangs carrying venom—the bite is very definitely poisonous and time is of the essence.

Recently, physicians have come up with an added help in the case of snakebite. A first aid treatment referred to as "hypothermia," which is the application of ice to the wound which lowers body temperature to a point where the venom spreads less quickly, minimizes swelling, helps prevent infection, and has some influence on numbing the pain. If ice is not readily available, the bite may be soaked in ice-cold water. But even more urgent is the need to get the victim to a hospital or a veterinarian for additional treatment.

EMERGENCIES

No matter how well you run your kennel or keep an eye on an individual dog, there will almost invariably be some emergency at some time that will require quick treatment until you get the animal to the veterinarian. The first and most important thing to remember is to keep calm! You will think more clearly and your animal will need to know he can depend on you to take care of him. However, he will be frightened and you must beware of fear biting. Therefore, do not shower him with kisses and endearments at this time, no matter how sympathetic you feel. Comfort him reassuringly, but keep your wits about you. Before getting him to the veterinarian, try to alleviate the pain and the shock.

If you can take even a minor step in this direction it will be a help toward the final cure. Listed here are a few of the emergencies that might occur and what you can do *after* you have called the vet and told him you are coming.

BURNS

If you have been so foolish as to not turn your pot handles toward the back of the stove—for your children's sake as well as your dog's—and the dog is burned by the contents of a pot that has been knocked off its burner, apply ice or ice-cold water and treat for shock. Electrical or chemical burns are treated the same, but with an acid or alkali burn, use, respectively, a bicarbonate of soda or a vinegar solution. Check the advisability of covering the burn when you call the veterinarian.

DROWNING

Most animals love the water but sometimes get in "over their heads." Should your dog take in too much water, hold him upside down and open his mouth so that water can empty from the lungs, then apply artificial respiration or mouth-to-mouth resuscitation. With a large dog, hang the head over a step or off the end of a table while you hoist the rear end in the air by the back feet. Then treat for shock by covering him with a blanket.

FITS AND CONVULSIONS

Prevent the dog from thrashing about and injuring himself, cover with a blanket, and hold down until you can get him to the veterinarian.

FROSTBITE

There is no excuse for an animal getting frostbite if you are "on your toes" and care for the animal; however, should frostbite set in, thaw out the affected area slowly by massaging with a circular motion and stimulation. Use petroleum jelly to help keep the skin from peeling off and/or drying out.

HEART ATTACK

Be sure the animal keeps breathing by applying artificial respiration. A mild stimulant may be used, and give him plenty of air. Treat for shock as well, and get him to the veterinarian quickly.

SHOCK

Shock is a state of circulatory collapse that can be induced by a severe accident, loss of blood, heart failure, or any injury to the nervous system. Until you can get the dog to the veterinarian, keep him warm by covering him with a blanket. Try to keep the dog quiet until the appropriate medication can be prescribed. Relapse is not uncommon, so the dog must be observed carefully for several days after initial shock.

SUFFOCATION
Administer artificial respiration and treat for shock with plenty of air.

SUN STROKE
Cooling the dog off immediately is essential. Ice packs, submersion in ice water, and plenty of cool air are needed.

WOUNDS
Open wounds or cuts that produce bleeding must be treated with hydrogen peroxide, and tourniquets should be used if bleeding is excessive. Shock treatment must also be given, and the animal must be kept warm.

THE FIRST AID KIT
It would be sheer folly to try to operate a kennel or to keep a dog without providing for certain emergencies that are bound to crop up when there are active dogs around. Just as you would provide a first aid kit for people, you should also provide a first aid kit for the animals on the premises. The first aid kit should contain the following items:
- medicated powder
- petroleum jelly
- cotton swabs
- 1″ gauze bandage
- adhesive tape
- band-aids
- cotton gauze or balls
- boric acid powder

A trip to your veterinarian is always safest, but there are certain preliminaries for cuts and bruises of a minor nature that you can care for yourself.

Cuts, for instance, should be washed out and medicated powder or petroleum jelly applied with a bandage. The lighter the bandage the better so that the most air possible can reach the wound. Cotton swabs can be used for removing debris from the eyes, after which a mild solution of boric acid wash can be applied. As for sores, use dry powder on wet sores, and petroleum jelly on dry sores. Use cotton for washing out and drying wounds.

A particular caution must be given here on bandaging. Make sure that the bandage is not too tight to hamper the dog's circulation. Also, make sure the bandage is applied correctly so that the dog does not bite at it trying to remove it. A great deal of damage can be done to a wound by a dog tearing at a bandage to get it off. If you notice the dog is starting to bite at it, do it over or put something on the bandage that smells and tastes bad to him. Make sure, however, that the solution does not soak through the bandage and enter the wound. Sometimes, if it is a leg wound, a sock or stocking slipped on the dog's leg will cover the bandage edges and will also keep it clean.

HOW NOT TO POISON YOUR DOG

Ever since the appearance of Rachel Carson's book *Silent Spring*, people have been asking, "Just how dangerous are chemicals?" In the animal fancy where disinfectants, room deodorants, parasitic sprays, solutions, and aerosols are so widely used, the question has taken on even more meaning. Veterinarians are beginning to ask, "What kind of disinfectant do you use?" "Have you any fruit trees that have been sprayed recently?" When animals are brought in to their offices in a toxic condition, or for unexplained death, or when entire litters of puppies die mysteriously, there is good reason to ask such questions.

The popular practice of protecting animals against parasites has given way to their being exposed to an alarming number of commercial products, some of which are dangerous to their very lives. Even flea collars can be dangerous, especially if they get wet or somehow touch the genital regions or eyes. While some products are much more poisonous than others, great care must be taken that they be applied in proportion to the size of the dog and the area to be covered. Many a dog has been taken to the vet with an unusual skin problem that was a direct result of having been bathed with a detergent rather than a proper shampoo. Certain products that are safe for dogs can be fatal for cats. Extreme care must be taken to read all ingredients and instructions carefully before using the products on any animal.

The same caution must be given to outdoor chemicals. Dog owners must question the use of fertilizers on their lawns. Lime, for instance, can be harmful to a dog's feet. The unleashed dog that covers the neighborhood on his daily rounds is open to all sorts of tree and lawn sprays and insecticides that may prove harmful to him, if not as a poison, then as a producer of an allergy.

There are numerous products found around the house that can be lethal, such as rat poison, boric acid, hand soap, detergents, car anti-freeze, and insecticides. These are all available in the house or garage and can be tipped over easily and consumed. Many puppy fatalities are reported as a result of puppies eating mothballs. All poisons should be placed on high shelves out of the reach of *both* children and animals.

Perhaps the most readily available of all household poisons are plants. Household plants are almost all poisonous, even if taken in small quantities. Some of the most dangerous are the elephant ear, the narcissus bulb, any kind of ivy leaves, burning bush leaves, the jimson weed, the dumb cane weed, mock orange fruit, castor beans, Scottish broom seeds, the root or seed of the plant called "four o'clock," cyclamen, pimpernel, lily of the valley, the stem of the sweet pea, rhododendrons of any kind, spider lily bulbs, bayonet root, foxglove leaves, tulip bulbs, monkshood roots, azalea, wisteria, poinsettia leaves, mistletoe, hemlock, locoweed, and arrowglove. In all, there are over 500 poisonous plants in the United States. Peach, elderberry, and cherry trees can cause cyanide poisoning if the bark is consumed. Rhubarb leaves, either raw or cooked, can cause death or violent convulsions. Check out your closets, fields, and grounds around your home, and especially the dog runs, to see what should be eliminated to remove the danger to your dogs.

Be on the lookout for vomiting, hard or labored breathing, whimpering, stomach cramps, and trembling as a prelude to convulsions. Any delay in a visit to your veterinarian can mean death. Take along the bottle, package, or a sample of the plant you suspect to be the cause to help the veterinarian determine the correct antidote.

The most common type of poisoning, which accounts for nearly one-fourth of all animal victims, is staphylococci–infected food. Salmonella ranks third. These can be avoided by serving fresh food and not letting it lie around in hot weather.

There are also many insect poisonings caused by animals eating cockroaches, spiders, flies, butterflies, etc. Toads and some frogs give off a fluid that can make a dog foam at the mouth—and even kill him—if he bites just a little too hard!

Some misguided dog owners think it is "cute" to let their dogs enjoy a cocktail with them before dinner. There can be serious effects resulting from encouraging a dog to drink—sneezing fits, injuries as a result of intoxication, and heart stoppage are just a few. Whiskey for medicinal purposes or beer for brood bitches should be administered only on the advice of your veterinarian.

There have been cases of severe damage and death when dogs have emptied ash trays and eaten cigarettes, resulting in nicotine poisoning. Leaving a dog alone all day in a house where there are cigarettes available on a coffee table is asking for trouble. Needless to say, the same applies to marijuana. All the ghastly side effects are as possible for the dog as for the addict, and for a person to submit an animal to this indignity is indeed despicable. Don't think it doesn't happen. Unfortunately, in all our major cities the practice is becoming more and more a problem for the veterinarian.

Be on the alert and remember that in the case of any type of poisoning, the best treatment is prevention.

ALLERGIES IN DOGS

It used to be that you recognized an allergy in your dog when he scratched out his coat and developed a large patch of raw skin or sneezed himself almost to death on certain occasions. A trip to the veterinarian involved endless discussion as to why it might be and an almost equally endless "hit and miss" cure of various salves and lotions with the hope that one of them would work. Many times the condition would correct itself before a definite cure was affected.

However, during the 1970s through preliminary findings at the University of Pennsylvania Veterinary School there evolved a diagnosis for allergie that eliminated the need for skin sensitivity tests. It is called RAST, and is a radioallergosobant test performed with a blood serum sample. It is not even necessary in all cases for the veterinarian to see the dog.

A cellulose disc laced with a suspected allergen is placed in the serum, and if the dog is allergic to that particular allergen the serum will contain a specific antibody that adheres to the allergen on the disc. The disc is placed in a radioactively "labeled" antiserum that is attracted to that particular antibody. The antiserum binds with the antibody and can be detected with a radiation counter.

Furthermore, the scientists at the University of Pennsylvania also found that the RAST test has shown to be a more accurate diagnostic tool than skin testing because it measures the degree, and not merely the presence, of allergic reactions.

DO ALL DOGS CHEW?

The answer to the question about whether all dogs chew is an emphatic *yes*, and the answer if even more emphatic in the case of puppies.

Chewing is the best possible method of cutting teeth and exercising gums. Every puppy goes through this teething process, yet it can be destructive if the puppy uses shoes or table corners or rugs instead of the proper item for the best possible results. All dogs should have a Nylabone available for chewing, not only to teethe on but also for inducing growth of the permanent teeth, to assure normal jaw development, and to settle the permanent teeth solidly in the jaws. Chewing on a Nylabone also has a cleaning effect and serves as a "massage" for the gums, keeping down the formation of the tartar that erodes tooth enamel.

When you see a puppy pick up an object to chew, immediately remove it from his mouth with a sharp "No!" and replace the object with a Nylabone. Puppies take anything and everything into their mouths so they should be provided with several Nylabones to prevent damage to the household. This same Nylabone eliminates the need for the kind of "bone" which may chip your dog's mouth, stomach, or intestinal walls. Cooked bones, soft enough to be powdered and added to the food, are also permissible if you have the patience to prepare them, but Nylabone serves all the purposes of bones for chewing that your dog may require, so why take a chance on meat bones?

Electrical cords and wires of any kind present a special danger that must be eliminated during puppyhood, and glass dishes that can be broken and played with are also hazardous.

Chewing can also be a form of frustration or nervousness. Dogs sometimes chew for spite, if owners leave them alone too long or too often. Bitches will sometimes chew if their puppies are taken away from them too soon; insecure puppies often chew, thinking that they're nursing. Puppies that chew wool, blankets, carpet corners, or certain other types of materials may have a nutritional deficiency or something lacking in their diet. Sometimes a puppy will crave the starch that might be left in material after washing. Perhaps the articles have been near something that tastes good and that have retained the odor of food.

The act of chewing has no connection with particular breeds or ages, any more than there is a logical reason for dogs to dig holes outdoors or dig on wooden floors indoors.

So we repeat, it is up to you to be on guard at all times until the need—or habit—passes.

HIP DYSPLASIA

Hip dysplasia, or HD, is one of the most widely discussed of all animal afflictions, since it has appeared in varying degrees in just about every breed of dog. True, the larger breeds seem most susceptible, but it has hit the small breeds and is beginning to be recognized in cats as well.

While HD in man has been recorded as far back as 370 BC, HD in dogs was more than likely referred to as rheumatism until veterinary research came into the picture. In 1935 Dr. Otto Schales, at Angell Memorial Hospital in Boston, wrote a paper on hip dysplasia and classified the four degrees of dysplasia of the hip joints as follows:

- Grade 1—slight (poor fit between ball socket)
- Grade 2—moderate (moderate but obvious shallowness of the socket)
- Grade 3—severe (socket quite flat)
- Grade 4—very severe (complete displacement of head of femur at early age)

HD is an incurable, hereditary, though not congenital disease of the hip sockets. It is transmitted as a dominant trait with irregular manifestations. Puppies appear normal at birth but the constant wearing away of the socket means the animal moves more and more on muscle, thereby presenting a lameness, a difficulty in getting up, and severe pain in advanced cases.

The degree of severity can be determined around six months of age, but its presence can be noticed from two months of age. The

The large Gumabone® Flying Disc is most appropriate for any dog, especially a large breed like an English Sheepdog. It can provide entertainment and the much needed exercise.

Canadian Champion Bluprint's Country Squire chasing his basketball. Basketball is one of his favorite toys. Owned by Don and Coreen Eaton of Ellisville, Missouri.

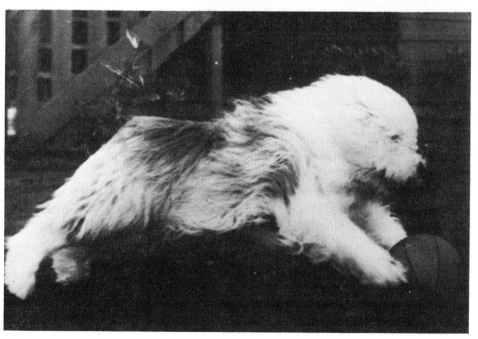

problem is determined by X-ray, and if pain is present it can be relieved temporarily by medication. Exercise should be avoided since motion encourages the wearing away of the bone surfaces.

Dogs with HD should not be shown or bred, if quality in the breed is to be maintained. It is essential to check a pedigree for dogs known to be dysplastic before breeding, since this disease can be dormant for many generations.

The same condition can also affect the elbow joints and is known as elbow dysplasia. This also causes lameness, and dogs so affected should not be used for breeding.

THE UNITED STATES REGISTRY

In the United States we have a central Hip Dysplasia Foundation, known as the OFA (Orthopedic Foundation for Animals). This HD control registry was formed in 1966. X-rays are sent for expert evaluation by qualified radiologists.

All you need do for complete information on getting an X-ray for your dog is to write to the Orthopedic Foundation for Animals at 817 Virginia Ave., Columbia, MO 65201, and request their dysplasia packet. There is no charge for this kit. It contains an envelope large enough to hold your X-ray film (which you will have taken by your own veterinarian), and a drawing showing how to position the dog properly for X-rays. There is also an application card for proper identification of the dog. Then, hopefully, your dog will be certified "normal." You will be given a registry number which you can put on his pedigree, use in your advertising, and rest assured that your breeding program is in good order.

All X-rays should be sent to the address above. Any other information you might wish to have may be requested from Mrs. Robert Bower, OFA, Route 1, Constantine, MO 49042.

We cannot urge strongly enough the importance of doing this. While it involves time and effort, the reward in the long run will more than pay for your trouble. To see the heartbreak of parents and children when their beloved dog has to be put to sleep because of severe hip dysplasia as the result of bad breeding is a sad experience. Don't let this happen to you or to those who will purchase your puppies!

Additionally, we should mention that there is a method of palpation to determine the extent of affliction. This can be painful if the animal is not properly prepared for the examination. There have also been attempts to replace the animal's femur and socket. This is not only expensive, but the percentage of success is small.

For those who refuse to put their dog down, there is a new surgical technique that can relieve pain but in no way constitutes a cure. This technique involves the severing of the pectinius muscle which, for some unknown reason, brings relief from pain over a period of many months—even up to two years. Two veterinary colleges in the United States are performing this operation at the present time. However, the owner must also give permission to "de-sex" the dogs at the time of the muscle severance. This is a safety measure to help stamp out hip dysplasia, since obviously the condition itself remains and can be passed on through generations.

The British Veterinary Association (BVA) has made an attempt to control the spread of HD by appointing a panel of members of their profession, who have made a special study of the disease, to read X-rays. Dogs over one year of age may be X-rayed and certified as free. Forms are completed in triplicate to verify the tests. One copy remains with the panel, one copy is for the owner's veterinarian, and one for the owner. A record is also sent to the British Kennel Club for those wishing to check on a particular dog for breeding purposes.

GERIATRICS

If you originally purchased good healthy stock and cared for your dog throughout his life, there is no reason why you cannot expect your dog to live to a ripe old age. With research and the remarkable foods produced for dogs, especially in this past decade, his chances of longevity have increased considerably. If you have cared for him well, your dog will be a sheer delight in his old age, just as he was while in his prime.

We can assume you have fed him properly if he is not too fat. Have you ever noticed how fat people usually have fat dogs because they indulge their dog's appetite as they do their own? If there has been no great illness, then you will find that very little additional care and attention are needed to keep him well. Exercise is still essential, as are proper food, booster shots, and tender loving care.

Even if a heart condition develops, there is still no reason to believe your dog cannot live to an old age. A diet may be necessary, along with medication and limited exercise, to keep the condition under control. In the case of deafness or partial blindness, additional care must be taken to protect the dog, but neither infirmity will in any way shorten his life. Prolonged exposure to temperature variances; overeating; excessive exercise; lack of sleep; or being housed with younger, more active dogs may take an unnecessary toll on the dog's energies and induce serious trouble. Good judgment, periodic veterinary checkups, and individual attention will keep your dog with you for many added years.

When discussing geriatrics, the question of when a dog becomes old or aged is usually asked. We have all heard the old saying that one year of a dog's life is equal to seven years in a human. This theory is strictly a matter of opinion, and must remain so, since so many outside factors enter into how quickly each individual dog "ages." Recently, a new chart was devised that is more realistically equivalent:

DOG	MAN
6 months	10 years
1 year	15 years
2 years	24 years
3 years	28 years
4 years	32 years
5 years	36 years
6 years	40 years
7 years	44 years
8 years	48 years
9 years	52 years
10 year	56 years
15 years	76 years
21 years	100 years

It must be remembered that such things as serious illnesses, poor food and housing, general neglect, and poor beginnings as puppies will take their toll of a dog's general health and age him more quickly than a dog that has led a normal, healthy life. Let your veterinarian help you determine an age bracket for your dog in his later years.

While good care should prolong your dog's life, there are several "old age" disorders to watch for no matter how well he may be doing. The tendency toward obesity is the most common, but constipation is another. Aging teeth and a slowing down of the digestive processes may hinder digestion and cause constipation, just as any major change in diet can bring on diarrhea. There is also the possibility of loss or impairment of hearing or eyesight which will also tend to make the dog wary and distrustful. Other behavioral changes may result as well, such as crankiness, loss of patience, and lack of interest; these are the most obvious changes. Other ailments may manifest themselves in the form of rheumatism, arthritis, tumors and warts, heart disease, kidney infections, male prostatism, and female disorders. Of course, all these require a veterinarian's checking the degree of seriousness and proper treatment.

THE CURSE OF ALLERGY

The heartbreak of a child being forced to give up a beloved pet because he is suddenly found to be allergic to it is a sad but true story. Many families claim to be unable to have dogs at all; others seem to be able only to enjoy them on a restricted basis. Many children know animals only through occasional visits to a friend's house or the zoo.

While modern veterinary science has produced some brilliant allergists, the field is still working on a solution for those who suffer from exposure to their pets. There is no permanent cure as yet.

Over the last quarter of a century there have been many attempts at a permanent cure, but none have proven successful because the treatment was needed too frequently, or was too expensive to maintain over extended periods of time.

However, we find that most people who are allergic to their animals are also allergic to a variety of other things as well. By eliminating the other irritants, and by taking medication given for the control of allergies in general, many are able to keep pets on a restricted basis. This may necessitate the dog's living outside the house, being groomed at a professional grooming parlor instead of by the owner, or merely being kept out of the bedroom at night. A discussion of this "balance" factor with your medical and veterinary doctors may give new hope to those willing to try.

A paper presented by Mathilde M. Gould, MD, a New York allergist, before the American Academy of Allergists in the 1960s and reported in the September-October 1964 issue of the *National*

Humane Review magazine, offered new hope to those who are allergic by a method referred to as hyposensitization. You may wish to write to the magazine and request the article for discussion of your individual problem with your medical and doctors.

Surely, since the sixties there have been additional advances in the field of allergy since so many people—and animals—are affected in so many ways.

DOG INSURANCE

Much has been said for and against canine insurance, and much more will be said before this kind of protection for a dog becomes universal and/or practical. There has been talk of establishing a Blue Cross-type plan similar to the one now existing for humans. However, the best insurance for your dog is *you!* Nothing compensates for tender, loving care. Like the insurance policies for humans, there will be a lot of fine print in the contracts revealing that the dog is not covered after all. These limited conditions usually make the acquisition of dog insurance expensive and virtually worthless.

Blanket coverage policies for kennels or establishments that board or groom dogs can be an advantage, especially in transporting dogs to and from their premises. For the one-dog owner, however, whose dog is a constant companion, the cost for limited coverage is not necessary.

THE HIGH COST OF BURIAL

Pet cemeteries are mushrooming across the nation. Here, as with humans, the sky can be the limit for those who wish to bury their pets ceremoniously. The costs of plots and satin-lined caskets, grave stones, flowers, etc., run the gamut to match the emotions and means of the owner.

IN THE EVENT OF YOUR DEATH

This is a morbid thought perhaps, but ask yourself the question, "If death were to strike at this moment, what would become of my dogs?"

Perhaps you are fortunate enough to have a relative, child, spouse, or friend who would take over immediately, if only on a temporary basis. Perhaps you have already left instructions in your last will and testament for your pet's housing, as well as a stipend for its care.

Provide definite instructions before a disaster occurs and your dogs are carted off to the pound to be destroyed, or stolen by commercially inclined neighbors with "resale" in mind. It is a simple thing to instruct your lawyer about your wishes in the event of sickness or death. Leave instructions as to feeding, etc., posted on your kennel room or kitchen bulletin board, or wherever your kennel records are kept. Also, tell several people what you are doing and why. If you prefer to keep such instructions private, merely place them in sealed envelopes in a known place with directions that they are to be opened only in the event of your death. Eliminate the danger of your animals suffering in the event of an emergency that prevents your personal care of them.

KEEPING RECORDS

Whether you have one dog or a kennel full of them, it is wise to keep written records. It takes only a few moments to record dates of inoculations, trips to the vet, tests for worms, etc. It can avoid confusion or mistakes or having your dog not covered with immunization if too much time elapses between shots because you have to guess at the date of the last shot.

Make the effort to keep all dates in writing rather than trying to commit them to memory. A rabies injection date can be a problem if you have to recall that "Fido had the shot the day Aunt Mary got back from her trip abroad, and, let's see, I guess that was around the end of June."

In an emergency, these records may prove their value if your veterinarian cannot be reached and you have to call on another, or if you move and have no case history on your dog for the new veterinarian. In emergencies, one does not always think clearly or accurately, and if dates, types of serums used, and other information are a matter of record, the veterinarian can act more quickly and with more confidence.

Australian Champion Flomont Tassybod Debel, U.D., referred to as "The Delux Dog". Tassy has reached the top in obedience training since 1973, when he started at seven months of age. He was first Old English Sheepdog in Victoria to gain a C.D. title. In 1974 it was the C.D.X. and the U.D. in 1976. The title Delux Dog was given when he began doing television commercials, hence the hat, and has been in a TV series entitled Young Ramsay. Owned by Ron and Sue Quayle of Victoria, Australia.

Chapter 18

The Blight of Parasites

FLEAS

Anyone who has ever spent hours peering intently at their dog's warm, pink stomach waiting for a flea to appear will readily understand why I call this chapter the "blight of parasites." It is that dreaded onslaught of the pesky flea that heralds the subsequent arrival of worms.

If you have seen even one flea scoot across that vulnerable expanse of skin, you can be sure there are more lurking on other areas of your dog. They seldom travel alone. So, it is now an established fact that *la puce*, as the French refer to the flea, has set up housekeeping on your dog! It is going to demand a great deal of your time before you manage to evict them—probably just temporarily at that—no matter which species your dog is harboring.

Fleas are not always choosy about their host, but chances are your dog has what is commonly known as *Ctenocephalides canis*, the dog flea. If you are a lover of cats also, your dog might even be playing host to a few *Ctenocephalides felis*, the cat flea, or vice versa. The only thing you can be really sure of is that your dog is supporting an entire community of them, all hungry and sexually oriented, and you are going to have to be persistent in your campaign to get rid of them.

One of the chief reasons fleas are so difficult to catch is that what they lack in beauty and eyesight (they are blind at birth, throughout infancy, and see very poorly if at all during adulthood), they make up for in their fantastic ability to jump and scurry about.

While this remarkable ability to jump—some claim 150 times the length of their bodies—stands them in good stead with circus entrepreneurs and has given them claim to fame as chariot pullers and acrobats in side show attractions, the dog owner can be reduced to tears at the very thought of an onset of fleas.

Modern research has provided a panacea in the form of flea sprays, dips, collars, and tags which can be successful to varying degrees. However, there are those who still swear by the good old-fashioned methods of removing them by hand, which can be a challenge to your sanity as well as your dexterity.

Since the fleas' conformation (they are built like envelopes, long and flat), with their spiny skeletal system on the outside of their bodies, is specifically designed for slithering through forests of hair, they are given a distinct advantage from the start. Two antennae on the head select the best spot for digging and then two mandibles penetrate the skin and hit a blood vessel. It is also at this moment that the flea brings into play his spiny contours to prop himself against surrounding hairs to avoid being scratched off as he puts the bite on your dog. A small projecting tube is then lowered into the hole to draw out blood and another tube pumps saliva into the wound; this prevents the blood from clotting and allows the flea to drink freely. Simultaneously, your dog jumps into the air and gets one of those back legs into action, scratching endlessly and in vain, and ruining some coat at the same time!

If you should be so lucky as to catch an itinerant flea as it mistakenly shortcuts across your dog's stomach, the best hunting grounds in the world are actually in the deep fur all along the dog's back from neck to tail. However, the flea, like every other creature on earth, must have water, so several times during its residency it will make its way to the moister areas of your dog's anatomy such as the corners of the mouth, the eyes, or the genital parts. This is when the flea collars and tags are useful. Their fumes prevent fleas from passing the neck to get to the head of your dog.

Your dog can usually support several generations of fleas, if it doesn't scratch itself to death or go out of its mind with the itching in the interim. The propagation of the flea is insured by the strong mating instinct and the well-judged decision of the female flea as to the best time to deposit her eggs. She has the rare capacity to store semen until the time is right to lay the eggs after some previous brief encounter with a passing member of the opposite sex.

When that time comes for her to lay, she does so without so much as a backward glance and moves on. The dog shakes the eggs off during a normal day's wandering, and they remain on the ground until hatched and the baby fleas are ready to jump back onto another passing dog. If any of the eggs have remained on the original dog, chances are that in scratching an adult flea, he will help the baby fleas emerge from their shells.

Larval fleas are small and resemble slender maggots; they begin their lives eating their own egg shells until the dog comes along and offers them a return to the world of adult fleas, whose excrement provides the predigested blood pellets they must have to thrive. They cannot survive on fresh blood, nor are they capable at this tender age of digging for it themselves.

After a couple of weeks of this freeloading, the baby flea makes his own cocoon and becomes a pupa. This stage lasts long enough for the larval flea to grow legs, mandibles, and sharp spines; and to flatten out and, in general, become identifiable as the commonly known and obnoxious *Ctenocephalides canis*. The process can take several weeks or several months, depending on weather conditions, heat, moisture, et cetera, but generally three weeks is all that is required to enable the flea to start gnawing your dog in its own right.

Thus the life-cycle of the flea is renewed and begun again. If you don't have plans to stem the tide, you will certainly see a population explosion that will make the human being resemble an endangered species. Getting rid of fleas can be accomplished by the aforementioned spraying of the dog, or by flea collars and tags; but air, sunshine and a good shaking out of beds, bedding, carpets, cushions, et al, certainly must be undertaken to get rid of the eggs or larvae lying around the premises.

Should you be lucky enough to get hold of a flea, you must squeeze it to death (which isn't likely) or break it in two with a sharp, strong fingernail (which also isn't likely) or you must release it *under water* in the toilet bowl and flush immediately. This prospect is only slightly more likely.

There are those dog owners, however, who are much more philosophical about the flea, since, like the cockroach, it has been around since the beginning of the world. For instance, that old-time philosopher, David Harum, has been much quoted with his remark, "A reasonable amount of fleas is good for a dog. They keep him from broodin' on bein' a dog." We would rather agree with John Donne who, in his *Devotions*, reveals that, "The flea, though he kill none, he does all the harm he can." This is especially true if your dog is a show dog. If the scratching doesn't ruin the coat, the inevitable infestation of parasites left by the fleas will!

We readily see that dogs can be afflicted by both internal and external parasites. The external parasites are known as the aforementioned fleas, plus ticks and lice; while all of these are bothersome, they can be treated. However, the internal parasites, or worms of various kinds, are usually well-entrenched before discovery and more substantial means of ridding the dog of them completely are required.

INTERNAL PARASITES

The most common worms are the round worms. These, like many other worms, are carried and spread by the flea and go through a cycle within the dog host. They are excreted in egg or larval form and pass on to other dogs in this manner.

Worm medicine should be prescribed by a veterinarian, and dogs should be checked for worms at least twice a year—or every three months if there is a known epidemic in your area—and during the summer months when fleas are plentiful.

Major types of worms are hookworms, whipworms, tapeworms (the only non-round worms in this list), ascarids (the "typical" round worms), heartworms, kidney, and lung worms. Each can be peculiar to a part of the country or may be carried by a dog from one area to another. Kidney and lung worms are fortunately quite rare; the others are not. Some symptoms for worms are intermittent vomiting, eating grass, lack of pep, bloated stomach, rubbing the tail along the ground, loss of weight, dull coat, anemia and pale gums, eye discharge, or unexplained nervousness and irritability. A dog with worms will usually eat twice as much as he normally would.

Never worm a sick dog or a pregnant bitch after the first two weeks she has been bred, and never worm a constipated dog—it will retain the strong medicine within the body for too long a time.

HOW TO TEST FOR WORMS

Worms can kill your dog if the infestation is severe enough. Even light infestations of worms can debilitate a dog to the point where he is more susceptible to other serious diseases that can kill, if the worms themselves do not.

Today's medication for worming is relatively safe and mild, and worming is no longer the traumatic experience for either the dog or owner that it used to be. Great care must be given, however, to the proper administration of the drugs. Correct dosage is a must and clean quarters are essential to rid your kennel of these parasites. It is almost impossible to find an animal that is completely free of parasites, so we must consider worming a necessary evil.

However mild today's medicines may be, it is inadvisable to worm a dog unnecessarily. There are simple tests to determine the presence of worms and this section is designed to help you learn how to administer these tests yourself. Veterinarians charge a nominal fee for this service, if it is not part of their regular office visit examination. It is a simple matter to prepare fecal slides that you can read yourself on a periodic basis. Over the years it will save you much time and money, especially if you have more than one dog or a large kennel.

All that is needed by way of equipment is a microscope with 100X power. These can be purchased in the toy department of a department store or in a regular toy store for a few dollars. The basic, least expensive sets come with the necessary glass slides and attachments.

After the dog has defecated, take an applicator stick, a toothpick with a flat end, or even an old-fashioned wooden matchstick and gouge off a piece of the stool about the size of a small pea. Have one of the glass slides ready with a large drop of water on

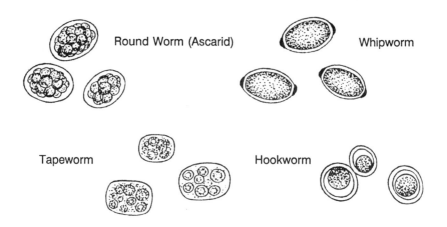

Round Worm (Ascarid)

Whipworm

Tapeworm

Hookworm

Eggs of parasitic worms commonly seen in dogs.

it. Mix the two together until you have a cloudy film over a large area of the slide. This smear should be covered with another slide or a cover slip—though it is possible to obtain readings with just the one open slide. Place your slide under the microscope and prepare to focus in on it. To read the slide you will find that your eye should follow a certain pattern. Start at the top and read from left to right, then right back to the left, and then left over to the right side once again until you have looked at every portion of the slide from the top left to the bottom right side.

Make sure that your smear is not too thick or watery or the reading will be too dark and confused to make proper identification. If you decide you would rather not make your own fecal examinations, but would prefer to have the veterinarian do it, the proper way to present a segment of the stool is as follows:

After the dog has defecated, a portion of the stool, say a square inch from different sections of it, should be placed in a glass jar or plastic container and labeled with the dog's name and address of the owner. If the sample cannot be examined within three or four hours after passage, it should be refrigerated. Your opinion as to what variety of worms you suspect is sometimes helpful to the veterinarian, and may be noted on the label of the jar you submit to him for the examination.

Checking for worms on a regular basis is advisable not only for the welfare of the dog but for the protection of your family, since most worms are transmissible, under certain circumstances, to humans.

Chapter 19

Pursuing a Career in Dogs

Late in 1982, the Pet Food Institute released the findings of an extensive survey they had done on American and their pets. Their figures bore out the fact that Americans owned 49 million dogs, 42 million cats, 25 million birds and 250 million other animals of one kind or another. That adds up to more pets than people in the United States, Great Britain, and Argentina combined!

It is even more amazing when you realize that approximately eight billion dollars a year is spent for care for these pets. Four billion goes for pet food, and nearly two billion to the veterinarians who care them.

1982 was also the year that included the introduction of a soft-drink for dogs and water beds for dogs! We have long known about dog and cat psychiatrists, and we can only imagine how much money is spent for pet sitters, pet cemeteries, and pet advertising. And the years go by, the numbers of pets is bound to increase, as will the amounts of money spent on them.

No, matter how we feel about our indulgences, we do know that we love our pets and that they return to us—a hundredfold—our love and affection, and we know they are worth every cent we spend on them.

One of the biggest joys for those of us who love dogs is to see someone we know or someone in our family grow up in the fancy

American and Canadian Champion Ambelon's Fireworks, bred and owned by Anne M. Baker of Lincoln, Massachusetts. "Rocky" at just 10 months of age earned his championship and had gone Best in Show in Canada. Gilbert photo.

and go on to enjoy the sport of dogs in later life. Many dog lovers, in addition to leaving codicils in their wills, are providing in other ways for veterinary scholarships for deserving youngsters who wish to make their association with dogs their profession. Unfortunately, many children who have this earnest desire are not always able to afford the expense of an education that will take them through veterinary school, and they are not eligible for scholarships.

ANIMAL SCIENCE OPTIONS

In the 1960s, a new program was developed at several colleges. Those not able go all the way to a veterinary degree could earn an Animal Science degree and thus still serve the fancy in a significant way. The Animal Science courses cost less than half of what it would take to become a veterinarian, and those achieving these titles provide tremendous assistance to the veterinarian.

We all have experienced the more and more crowded waiting rooms at the veterinary offices, and are aware of the demands on the doctor's time, not just for office hours but for his research, consultation, surgery, and so forth. The tremendous increase in the number of dogs and cats and other domestic animals, both in cities and the suburbs, has resulted in an almost overwhelming consumption of veterinarians' time.

Until recently, most veterinary assistance was made up of kennel men or women who were restricted to services more properly classified as office maintenance rather than actual veterinary aid. Needless to say, their part in the operation of a veterinary office is both essential and appreciated, as are the endless details and volumes of paperwork capably handled by office secretaries and receptionists.

With exactly this additional service in mind, the two-year programs in animal science for the training of such paraprofessionals were created, thereby opening a new field for animal technologists. The time saved by the assistance of these trained technicians, who now relieve the veterinarians of the more mechanical chores and allow them additional time for diagnosing and general servicing of their clients, has been and will continue to be beneficial to all involved.

"Delhi Tech," the State University Agricultural and Technical College at Delhi, New York, was one of the first to offer the re-

307

quired courses for this degree. Now, many other institutions of learning are offering comparable courses at the college level. Entry requirements are usually that each applicant must be a graduate of an approved high school or have taken the State University admissions examination. In addition, each applicant for the Animal Science Technology program must have some previous credits in mathematics and science, with chemistry an important part of the science background.

The program at Delhi was a new educational venture dedicated to the training of competent technicians for employment in the biochemical field and has been generously supported by a five-year grant, designated as a "Pilot Development Program in Animal Science." This grant provided both personal and scientific equipment with good results when it was done originally pursuant to a contract with the United States Department of Health, Education, and Welfare. Delhi is a unit of the State University of New York and is accredited by the Middle States Association of Colleges and Secondary Schools. The campus provides offices, laboratories, and animal quarters, and is equipped with modern instruments to train technicians in laboratory animal care, physiology, pathology, microbiology, anesthesia, X-ray, and germ-free techniques. Sizable animal colonies are maintained in air-conditioned quarters; animals housed include mice, rats, hamsters, guinea pigs, gerbils, and rabbits, as well as dogs and cats.

First-year students are given such courses as livestock production, dairy food science, general, organic and biological chemistry, mammalian anatomy, histology and physiology, pathogenic microbiology, and quantitative and instrumental analysis, to name a few. Second year students matriculate in general pathology, animal parasitology, animal care and anesthesia, introductory psychology, animal breeding, animal nutrition, hematology and urinalysis, radiology, genetics, food sanitation and meat inspection, histological techniques, animal laboratory practices, and axenic techniques. These, of course, may be supplemented by electives that prepare the student for contact with the public in the administration of these duties. Such recommended electives include public speaking, botany, animal reproduction, and other related subjects.

In addition to Delhi, another to first offer this program was the University of Maine. Part of their program offered some practical

Champion Merriweather's Sweet Baby James, owned and bred by Clare Switzer of Mt. Carmel, Pennsylvania, shown with him here. Whelped in 1981, James was sired by Champion Whisperwood Wild Won X Tamandra Blue Liberty.

Joyce Nielsen and Pippin, winner of the Super Dog contest at the 1982 Greater St. Louis Old English Sheepdog Club show. Her son "Tank" came in 2nd and also won best in match.

training for the students at the Animal Medical Center in New York City. Often after this initial field experience, the students could perform professionally immediately upon entering a veterinarian's employ as personnel to do laboratory tests, X-rays, blood work, fecal examinations, and general animal care. After the courses at college, they were equipped to perform all of the following procedures as paraprofessionals:

- Recording of vital information relative to a case. This would include such information as the client's name, address, telephone number, and other facts pertinent to the visit. The case history would include the breed, age of animal, its sex, temperature, etc.
- Preparation of the animal for surgery.
- Preparation of equipment and medicaments to be used in surgery.
- Preparation of medicaments for dispensing to clients on prescription of the attending veterinarian.
- Administration and application of certain medicines.
- Administration of colonic irrigations.
- Application or changing of wound dressings.
- Cleaning of kennels, exercise runs, and kitchen utensils.
- Preparation of food and the feeding of patients.
- Explanation to clients on the handling and restraint of their pets, including needs for exercise, house training, and elementary obedience training.
- First-aid treatment for hemorrhage, including the proper use of tourniquets.
- Preservation of blood, urine, and pathologic material for the purpose of laboratory examination.
- General care and supervision of the hospital or clinic patients to insure their comfort. Nail trimming and grooming of patients.

Credits are necessary, of course, to qualify for this program. Many courses of study include biology, zoology, anatomy, genetics, and animal diseases, and along with the abovementioned courses, the fields of client and public relations are touched upon as well as a general study of the veterinary medical profession.

By the mid-seventies there were a reported 30,000 veterinarians practicing in the United States. It is estimated that by the end of the 1980s more than twice that number will be needed to take proper care of the domestic animal population in this country. While veterinarians are graduated from 22 accredited veterinary colleges in this country and Canada, recent figures released by the Veterinary Medical Society inform us that only one out of every seven applicants is admitted to these colleges. It becomes more and more obvious that the paraprofessional will be needed to back up the doctor.

Students having the desire and qualifications to become veterinarians, however, may suffer financial restrictions that preclude their education and licensing as full-fledged veterinarians. The Animal Science Technologist with an Associate degree in Applied Science may very well find his niche with a profession in an area close to his actual desire.

Assistance in the pharmaceutical field, where drug concerns deal with laboratory animals, covers another wide area for trained assistants. The career opportunities are varied and reach into job opportunities in medical centers, research institutions, and government health agencies; at present, the demand for graduates far exceeds the current supply of trained personnel.

Beginning yearly salaries are relatively low while estimated costs of basic college expenses are relatively high, but the costs are about half of those involved in becoming a full-fledged veterinarian. High school graduates with a sincere affection and regard for animals and a desire to work with veterinarians and perform such clinical duties as mentioned previously will find they fit in especially well.

Those interested in pursuing a career of this nature may obtain the most current list of accredited colleges and universities offering these programs by consulting the American Veterinary Medical College, 600 S. Michigan Avenue, Chicago, IL 60605.

As the popularity of this profession increased, additional attention was given to the list of services, and the degrees to which one could aspire was expanded. There are para-professionals with Associate of Science degrees, and some colleges and universities have extended the courses to four year's duration which lead to Bachelor of Science degrees.

At the University of Minnesota Technical College, a two-year course offers a degree of Associate in Applied Science after the successful completion of 108 credit hours. This Animal Health

Technology course prepares the students for future careers in the following fields:

- Laboratory Animal Technician (Junior)
- Experimental Animal Technician
- Clinical Laboratory Animal Assistant
- Laboratory Animal Assistant in Radiology
- Laboratory Animal Research Assistant
- Small Animal Technician (General)
- Small Animal Veterinarian's Assistant
- Small Animal Veterinarian's Receptionist
- Animal Hospital Technician
- Zoo Technician
- Large Animal Technician (General)
- Large Animal Veterinarian's Receptionist
- Large Animal Clinic Assistant
- Animal Meat Inspection Technician

CANINE COLLEGE IN JAPAN

The Japanese love dogs. Recent statistics report that there is one dog for every thirteen people, adding up to about eight million dogs on those small islands. Dogs are cherished as pets, guards, and companions, creating a large dog-loving population in the Land of the Rising Sun.

In 1967, Ryouju Yamazaki, a Japanese career counselor, saw the need for a school to train young Japanese women in the art of caring for animals.

Over the years his unique school has had an acknowledged influence on Japanese culture concerning human-animal relationships, and the 400 or more young women engaged in the two-year course are well versed in the grooming, training, and biological research work involved in their career. After graduation these young women will be capable of serving as professional licensed technicians for veterinarians.

The extensive program offered includes canine psychology, veterinary science, public health, judging, ethics, physics, biology, chemistry, business administration, and law. It also touches on specialized training in counseling for the loss of beloved pets, care, therapy, and the like. An especially interesting course is that of health promotion for disturbed children. Forty-five technicians serve on the faculty. Many more highly technical courses are pro-

A 1970 top winner. This one, Ch. Mills Inn Blue Monday being shown by Marilyn Mayfield.

vided in the college curriculum. President Yamazaki is president of the International Dog Education Association, whose health promotion services are comparable to those offered by the University of Pennsylvania and University of Minnesota.

PART TIME KENNEL WORK

Youngsters can get valuable experience and extra money by working part-time after school and on weekends, or full-time during summer vacations, in a veterinarian's office. The exposure to animals and office procedure will be time well spent.

Kennel help is also an area that is wide open for retired men and women. They are able to help out in many areas where they can learn and stay active, and most of the work allows them to set their own pace. The understanding and patience that age and experience brings is also beneficial to the animals they will deal with; for their part, these people find great reward in their contribution to animals and will be keeping active in the business world as well.

PROFESSIONAL HANDLING

For those who wish to participate in the sport of dogs and whose interests or abilities do not center around the clinical aspects of the fancy, there is yet another avenue of involvement.

For those who excel in the show ring, who enjoy being in the limelight and putting their dogs through their paces, a career in professional handling may be the answer. Handling may include a weekend of showing a few dogs for special clients, or it may be a full-time career that can also include boarding, training, conditioning, breeding, and showing dogs for several clients.

Depending on how deep your interest is, the issue can be solved by a lot of preliminary consideration before it becomes necessary to make a decision. The first move would be to have a long, serious talk with a successful professional handler to learn the pros and cons of such a profession. Watching handlers in action from ringside as they perform their duties can be revealing.

Professional handling is not all glamour in the show ring. There is plenty of "dirty work" behind the scenes 24 hours of every day. You must have the necessary ability and patience for this work, as well as the ability and patience to deal with the *clients*, the dog

One of the most famous ladies in the breed for several decades. This Charles Mintzer photograph shows Mona Berkowitz judging our breed at a 1971 Specialty show in Greenwich, Connecticut.

owners who value their animals above almost anything else and would expect a great deal from you in the way of care and handling.

DOG TRAINING

Like the professional handler, the professional dog trainer has a most responsible job. You need not only to be thoroughly familiar with the correct and successful methods of training a dog but must also have the ability to communicate with dogs.

Training schools are quite the vogue nowadays, with all of them claiming success. Careful investigation should be made before enrolling a dog, and even more careful investigation should be made of their methods and of their actual successes before becoming associated with them.

DOG JUDGING

There are also those whose professions, age, or health prevent them from owning, breeding, or showing dogs, and who turn to

315

judging at dog shows after their active years in the show ring are no longer possible. Breeder-judges make a valuable contribution to the fancy by judging in accordance with their years of experience in the fancy, and the assignments are enjoyable. Judging requires experience and a good eye for dogs.

GROOMING PARLORS

If you do not wish the 24-hour a day job that is required by a professional handler or professional trainer, but still love working with and caring for dogs, there is always the very profitable grooming business. Poodles started the ball rolling for the swanky, plush grooming establishments that sprang up all over the major cities, many of which seem to be doing very well. Here again, handling dogs and the public well is necessary for a successful operation, in addition to skill in the actual grooming of dogs of all breeds.

While shops flourish in the cities, some of the suburban areas are now featuring mobile units which, by appointment, will visit a home with a completely equipped shop on wheels and will groom the dog right in one's own driveway.

THE PET SHOP

Part-time or full-time work in a pet shop can help you make up your mind rather quickly as to whether you would like to have a shop of your own. For those who love animals and are concerned with their care and feeding, the pet shop can be a profitable and satisfying association. Supplies that are available for sale in these shops are almost limitless, and a nice living can be garnered from pet supplies if the location and population of the city you choose warrant it.

MISCELLANEOUS

If you find all of the aforementioned too demanding or not within your abilities, there are other aspects of the sport for you to enjoy and participate in at will. Writing (for the various dog magazines, books, or club newsletters), dog photography, portrait painting, club activities, making dog coats, or needlework featuring dogs, typing pedigrees, or even dog walking; all, in their own way, contribute to the sport of dogs and give great satisfaction.

Index

cw Mars.